LONGMANS' MODERN MATHEMATICAL SERIES

General Editors

P. Abbott, B.A., C. S. Jackson, M.A.
F. S. Macaulay, M.A., D.Sc.

THE ELEMENTS OF NON-EUCLIDEAN PLANE GEOMETRY AND TRIGONOMETRY

Longmans' Modern Mathematical Series

THE ELEMENTS OF NON-EUCLIDEAN PLANE GEOMETRY AND TRIGONOMETRY

BY

H. S. CARSLAW

Sc.D. (Camb.), D.Sc. (Glasg.)

PROFESSOR OF MATHEMATICS IN THE UNIVERSITY OF SYDNEY

FORMERLY FELLOW OF EMMANUEL COLLEGE, CAMBRIDGE

WITH DIAGRAMS

LONGMANS, GREEN AND CO.

39 PATERNOSTER ROW, LONDON

FOURTH AVENUE & 30TH STREET, NEW YORK

BOMBAY, CALCUTTA, AND MADRAS

1916

PREFACE

In this little book I have attempted to treat the Elements of Non-Euclidean Plane Geometry and Trigonometry in such a way as to prove useful to teachers of Elementary Geometry in schools and colleges. Recent changes in the teaching of Geometry in England and America have made it more than ever necessary that the teachers should have some knowledge of the hypotheses on which Euclidean Geometry is built, and especially of that hypothesis on which Euclid's Theory of Parallels rests. The historical treatment of the Theory of Parallels leads naturally to a discussion of the Non-Euclidean Geometries; and it is only when the logical possibility of these Non-Euclidean Geometries is properly understood that a teacher is entitled to form an independent opinion upon the teaching of Elementary Geometry.

The first two chapters of this book are devoted to a short discussion of the most important of the attempts to prove Euclid's Parallel Postulate, and to a description of the work of the founders of Non-Euclidean Geometry, Bolyai, Lobatschewsky and Riemann.

In Chapters III.-V. the Non-Euclidean Geometry of Bolyai and Lobatschewsky, now known as the Hyperbolic Geometry, is developed in a systematic manner. The feature of this treatment is that in Chapter III. no use is made of the Principle of Continuity, and that both the Geometry and the Trigonometry of the Hyperbolic Plane are built up without the use of Solid Geometry.

In Chapters VI.-VII. a similar treatment, though in less detail, is given for the Elliptic Geometry.

Chapter VIII. deals with Poincaré's representation of the Non-Euclidean Geometries by the geometry of the families of circles orthogonal or diametral to a fixed circle. From these representations an elementary proof of the impossibility of proving Euclid's Parallel Postulate can be obtained, and they throw fresh light upon the Non-Euclidean Geometries themselves.

This little book could never have been written had it not been for the work of Bonola. It was from him that I first learnt that an elementary treatment of the subject was possible. Both to his historical work, an English translation of which I had the privilege of undertaking, and to his article in Enriques' *Questioni riguardanti la geometria elementare*, especially in its extended form in the German edition of that work, this book owes a very great deal.

The other writers on the same subject to whom I am most indebted are Liebmann and Stäckel. The treatment of Plane Hyperbolic Trigonometry is due to Liebmann; and to the second edition of his well-known *Nichteuklidische Geometrie*, as well as to his original papers, most of which he has sent to me as they appeared, I am much indebted. A similar acknowledgment is due to Stäckel. When he learnt that I was engaged on this work, I received from him, in the most generous way, a set of all his papers on the subject, many of which were inaccessible to me in Australia; and the gift of a copy of his book on *Wolfgang and Johann Bolyai*, immediately on its publication, allowed me to make some use of his final account of the discovery of the Hyperbolic Geometry in reading my proofs.

Other acknowledgments will be found in their proper place in the text. However, I would mention here the frequent use I have made of Halsted's work and of the *Bibliography* of Sommerville; also the assistance which I have received from Dr. F. S. Macaulay, who read all the proofs and made many valuable suggestions and amendments. The work of another of the Editors of this Series, Mr. C. S. Jackson, has made my labour lighter, and one of my colleagues in Sydney, Mr. R. J. Lyons, has also read a great part of the final proofs.

H. S CARSLAW.

SYDNEY, *September*, 1914.

NOTE.

The final proofs of this book had been corrected, and the foregoing preface written and set up in type before the outbreak of the war.

In the course of years the time may come when such co-operation as I have here acknowledged will again be possible.

H. S. C.

SYDNEY, *January*, 1916.

CONTENTS

CHAPTER I.

THE PARALLEL POSTULATE, AND THE WORK OF SACCHERI, LEGENDRE AND GAUSS.

CHAPTER II.

THE WORK OF BOLYAI, LOBATSCHEWSKY, AND RIEMANN, THE FOUNDERS OF THE NON-EUCLIDEAN GEOMETRIES.

CHAPTER III.

THE HYPERBOLIC PLANE GEOMETRY.

CHAPTER IV.

THE HYPERBOLIC PLANE TRIGONOMETRY.

CHAPTER V.

MEASUREMENTS OF LENGTH AND AREA, WITH THE AID OF THE INFINITESIMAL CALCULUS.

CHAPTER VI.

THE ELLIPTIC PLANE GEOMETRY.

CHAPTER VII.

THE ELLIPTIC PLANE TRIGONOMETRY.

CHAPTER VIII.

THE CONSISTENCY OF THE NON-EUCLIDEAN GEOMETRIES AND THE IMPOSSIBILITY OF PROVING THE PARALLEL POSTULATE.

NON-EUCLIDEAN GEOMETRY.

CHAPTER I.

THE PARALLEL POSTULATE, AND THE WORK OF SACCHERI, LEGENDRE AND GAUSS.

§ 1. By the term Non-Euclidean Geometry we understand a system of Geometry built up without the aid of the Euclidean Parallel Hypothesis, while it contains an assumption as to parallels incompatible with that of Euclid.

The discovery that such Non-Euclidean Geometries are logically possible was a result of the attempts to deduce Euclid's Parallel Hypothesis from the other assumptions which form the foundation of his *Elements of Geometry*. It will be remembered that he defines Parallel Lines as follows :

*Parallel straight lines are straight lines which, being in the same plane and being produced indefinitely in both directions, do not meet one another in either direction.**

Then in I. 27 he proves that

If a straight line falling on two straight lines make the alternate angles equal to one another, the straight lines will be parallel to one another.

And in I. 28 that

If a straight line falling on two straight lines make the exterior angle equal to the interior and opposite angle on the same side,

* Here and in other places where the text of Euclid's *Elements* is quoted, the rendering in Heath's Edition (Cambridge, 1908) is adopted. This most important treatise will be cited below as Heath's *Euclid*.

or the interior angles on the same side equal to two right angles, the straight lines will be parallel to one another.

In order to prove the converse of these two propositions, namely (I. 29), that

A straight line falling on parallel straight lines makes the alternate angles equal to one another, the exterior angle equal to the interior and opposite angle, and the interior angles on the same side equal to two right angles,

he found it necessary to introduce the hypothesis as to parallel lines, which he enunciates as follows:

If a straight line falling on two straight lines make the interior angles on the same side less than two right angles, the two straight lines, if produced indefinitely, meet on that side on which are the angles less than the two right angles.

This hypothesis we shall refer to as Euclid's Parallel Postulate. It is true that in some of the MSS. it finds a place among the Axioms. In others it is one of the Postulates, and it seems to belong more properly to that group. No use is made of it in the earlier propositions of the First Book. Accordingly these would find a place in the Non-Euclidean Geometries, which differ only from the Euclidean in substituting for his Parallel Postulate another incompatible with it. Other theorems of the Euclidean Geometry will belong to the Non-Euclidean, if they have been proved, or can be proved, without the aid of the Parallel Postulate, and if these geometries adopt the other assumptions, explicit and implicit, made by Euclid.

§ 2. It is not within the scope of this book to discuss the modern treatment of the assumptions on which the Euclidean and Non-Euclidean Geometries are based. We shall deal simply with the assumption regarding parallels. But it is right to mention that the idea of motion or displacement, which forms part of the method of superposition, itself involves an axiom. The fourth proposition of Euclid's First Book now finds a place among the Axioms of Congruence, and upon this group of axioms the idea of motion is founded. Apparently Euclid recognised that the use of the method of superposition was a blot upon the *Elements*. He adopted it only in I. 4, and refrained from employing it in other places, where it would have shortened the demonstration.

Again, Postulate I., which asserts the possibility of drawing a straight line from any one point to any other, must be held to declare that the straight line so drawn is unique, and that two straight lines cannot enclose a space. And Postulate II., which asserts the possibility of producing a finite straight line continuously in a straight line, must also be held to assert that the produced part in either direction is unique; in other words, that two straight lines cannot have a common segment.

But the following more fundamental and distinct assumptions are made by Euclid, without including them among the axioms or postulates:

(i) *That a straight line is infinite.*

This property of the straight line is required in the proof of I. 16. The theorem that the exterior angle is greater than either of the interior and opposite angles does not hold in the Non-Euclidean Geometry in which the straight line is regarded as endless, returning upon itself, but not infinite.

(ii) *Let* A, B, C *be three points, not lying in a straight line, and let* a *be a straight line lying in the plane* ABC, *and not passing through any of the points* A, B, *or* C. *Then, if* a *passes through a point of the segment* AB, *it must also pass through a point of the segment* BC, *or of the segment* AC (*Pasch's Axiom*).

From this axiom it can be deduced that a ray passing through an angular point, say A, of the triangle ABC, and lying in the region bounded by AB and AC, must cut the segment BC.

(iii) Further, in the very first proposition of the First Book of the *Elements* the vertex of the required equilateral triangle is determined by the intersection of two circles. It is assumed that these circles intersect. A similar assumption is made in I. 22 in the construction of a triangle when the sides are given. The first proposition is used in the fundamental constructions of I. 2 and I. 9-11.

Again, in I. 12, in order to be sure that the circle with a given centre will intersect the given straight line, Euclid makes the circle pass through a point on the side opposite to that in which the centre lies. And in some of the propositions of Book III. assumptions are made with regard to the intersection of the circles employed in the demonstration. Indeed right through the *Elements* constructions are effected by means of straight lines and circles drawn in accordance with Postulates I.-III. Such straight lines and circles determine by their intersection other points in addition to those given; and these points are used to determine new lines, and so on. The existence of these points of intersection must be postulated or proved, in the same way as the existence of the other straight lines and circles in the construction has been postulated or proved.

The *Principle of Continuity*, as it is called, is introduced to fill this gap. It can be stated in different ways, but probably the simplest is that which Dedekind originally adopted in discussing the idea of the irrational number. His treatment of the irrational number depends upon the following geometrical axiom:

*If all the points of a straight line can be separated into two classes, such that every point of the first class is to the left of every point of the other class, then there exists one, and only one, point which brings about this division of all the points into two classes, this section of the line into two parts.**

This statement does not admit of proof. The assumption of this property is nothing less than an axiom by which we assign its continuity to the straight line.

The *Postulate of Dedekind*, stated for the linear segment, can be readily applied to any angle, (the elements in this case being the rays from the vertex), and to a circular arc. By this means demonstrations can be obtained of the theorems as to the intersection of a straight line and a circle, and of a circle with another circle, assumed by Euclid in the propositions above mentioned.† The idea of continuity was adopted by Euclid without remark. What was involved in the assumption and the nature of the irrational number were unknown to the mathematicians of his time.

This Postulate of Dedekind also carries with it the important

---

* Dedekind, *Stetigkeit und irrationale Zahlen*, p. 11 (2nd ed., Braunschweig, 1892); English translation by Beman (Chicago, 1901).

† This question is treated fully in the article by Vitali in Enriques' volume, *Questioni riguardanti la geometria elementare* (Bologna, 1900); German translation under the title, *Fragen der Elementargeometrie*, vol. i. p. 129 (Leipzig, 1911). See also Heath's *Euclid*, vol. i. p. 234.

Postulate of Archimedes, which will be frequently referred to in the following pages :

*If two segments are given, there is always some multiple of the one which is greater than the other.**

§ 3. An interesting discovery, arising out of the recent study of the Foundations of Geometry, is that a great part of Elementary Geometry can be built up without the Principle of Continuity. In place of the construction of Euclid I. 2, the proof of which depends upon this Principle, the following Postulate † is made :

If A, B *are two points on a straight line* a, *and if* A′ *is a point upon the same or another straight line* a′, *then we can always find on the straight line* a′, *on a given ray from* A′, *one and only one point* B′, *such that the segment* AB *is congruent to the segment* A′B′.

In other words, we assume that we can always set off a given length on a given line, from a given point upon it, towards a given side. By the term *ray* is meant the half-line starting from a given point.

With this assumption, for Euclid's constructions for the bisector of a given angle (I. 9), for the middle point of a given straight line (I. 10), for the perpendicular to a given straight line from a point upon it (I. 11), and outside it (I. 12), and, finally, for an angle equal to a given angle (I. 23)—all of which, in the *Elements*, depend upon the Principle of Continuity—we may substitute the following constructions, which are independent, both of that Principle and of the Parallel Postulate.‡

---

* For the proof of the *Postulate of Archimedes* on the assumption of Dedekind's Postulate, see Vitali's article named above, § 3. Another treatment of this question will be found in Hilbert's *Grundlagen der Geometrie*, 3rd ed. § 8. An English translation of the first edition was made by Townsend (Chicago, 1902). The Postulate of Archimedes stated above for linear segments is adopted also for angles, areas, and volumes.

† Cf. Hilbert, *loc. cit.* 3rd ed. § 5, Axioms of Congruence.

‡ The constructions in Problems 1, 2, 3 and 5 are given by Halsted in his book, *Rational Geometry* (2nd ed. 1907). Those for Problems 4 and 6 in the text are independent of the Parallel Postulate, and replace those given by Halsted, in which the Euclidean Hypothesis is assumed.

PROBLEM 1. **To bisect a given angle.**

Construction. On one of the lines bounding the given angle A take any two points B, C.

On the other bounding line take AB′ = AB and AC′ = AC.

Join BC′ and B′C.

Let them intersect at D.

Then AD is the desired bisector.

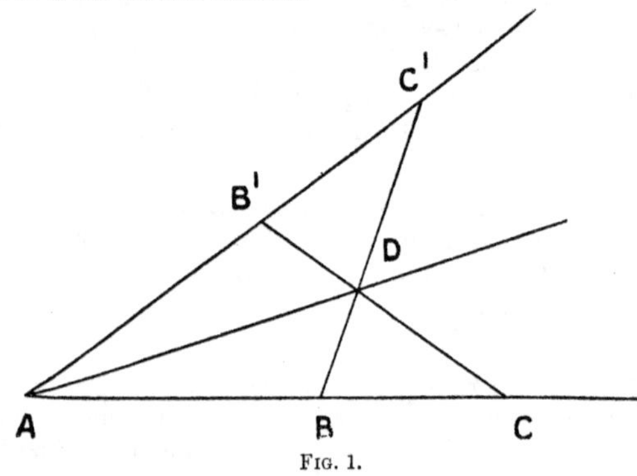

FIG. 1.

Proof. The triangles BAC′ and B′AC are congruent.

Therefore ∠ACB′ = ∠AC′B and ∠DBC = ∠DB′C′.

It follows that the triangles BDC and B′DC′ are congruent, since

BC = B′C′.

Therefore DB′ = DB.

Finally the triangles BAD and B′AD are congruent, and AD bisects the given angle.

PROBLEM 2. **To draw a perpendicular to a given straight line.**

Construction. Let AB be the given straight line.

Take any other straight line AC through A.

Upon AB take AD = AC.

Join CD.

Bisect ∠CAD (by Problem 1), and let the bisector cut CD at G.

On AB take AF = AG, and on the ray AG take AH = AD.

Join FH.

Then FH is perpendicular to AB.

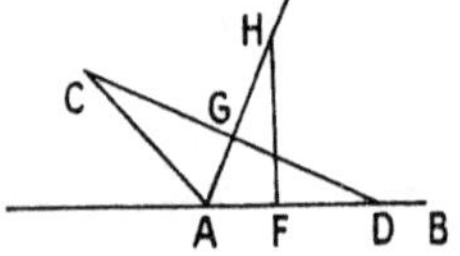

FIG. 2.

Proof. From the triangles ACG and ADG, we have ∠AGD equal to a right angle.

Also the triangles AGD and AFH are congruent.

Therefore ∠AFH = ∠AGD = 1 right angle.

PROBLEM 3. **At a given point on a given straight line to erect the perpendicular.**

Construction. Let A be the given point and BC the given straight line.
Draw the perpendicular ZOY (by Problem 2), meeting BC in O.
Take OY = OZ, and join AY and AZ.
Produce YA through A to X.
Bisect ∠XAZ by AD (by Problem 1).
Then AD is the perpendicular to BC through A.

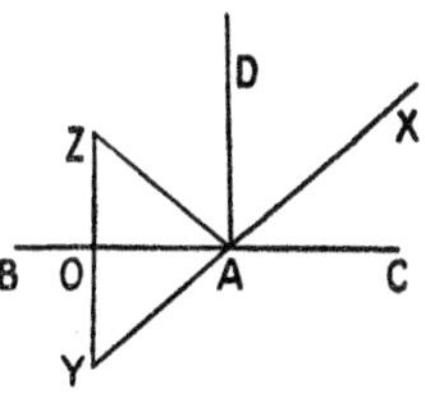

FIG. 3.

Proof. By the construction, the triangles OAZ and OAY are congruent.

Therefore ∠ZAO = ∠YAO

= ∠XAC.

But ∠DAZ = ∠XAD.

Therefore AD is perpendicular to BC.

PROBLEM 4. **From a given point outside a given straight line to draw the perpendicular to the line.**

Construction. Let A, B be two points on the given line, and C the point outside it.
Join AC and BC.
On the segment AB take a point D, and (by Problem 3) draw the perpendicular at D to AB.
By Pasch's Axiom, this line must cut either AC or BC.
Let it cut AC, and let the point of intersection be E.
Produce ED through D to F, so that DE = DF.
Join AF and produce AF to G, such that AG = AC.
Join CG, and let it be cut by AB, or AB produced, at H.
Then CH is the required perpendicular.

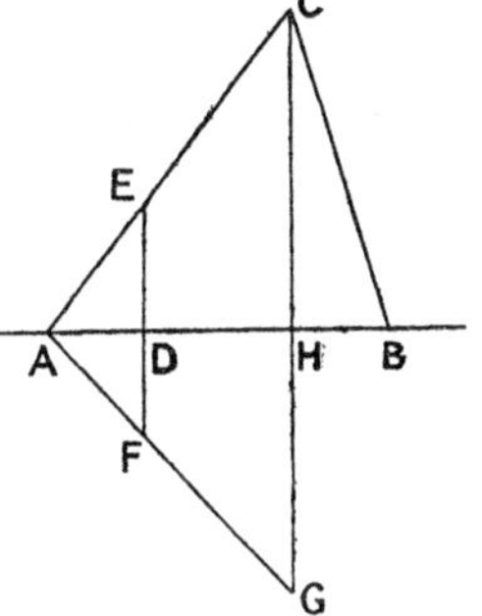

FIG. 4.

Proof. From the construction, the triangles ADE and ADF are congruent, so that AB bisects ∠CAG.
It follows that the triangles ACH and AGH are congruent, and that ∠AHC is a right angle.

PROBLEM 5. **At a given point on a given straight line to make an angle equal to a given angle.**

Construction. Let A be the point on the given line a. (Cf. Fig. 5.)
Let D be the given (acute) angle.
From a point E on one of the lines bounding the angle, draw (by Problem 4) the perpendicular EF to the other bounding line.

On Aa take AC = DF.
At C erect the perpendicular Cc to Aa (by Problem 3).
Make BC = EF, and join AB.

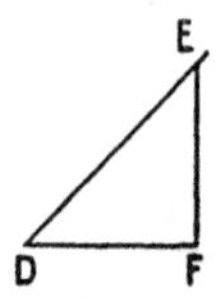

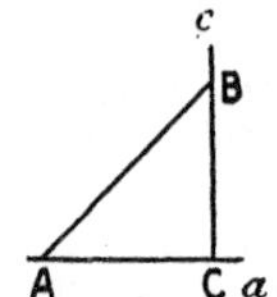

FIG. 5.

Proof. By the construction, the triangles DEF and ABC are congruent.

Therefore $\angle$BAC = $\angle$EDF.

PROBLEM 6. **To bisect a given finite straight line.**

Construction. Let AB be the given segment.

At B draw the perpendicular Bb to AB (by Problem 3).

Upon Bb take any point C and join AC.

At B make $\angle$ABE = $\angle$BAC (by Problem 5).

Let the line BE cut AC at D.

Bisect $\angle$ADB by the line cutting AB at F (by Problem 1).

Then F is the middle point of AB.

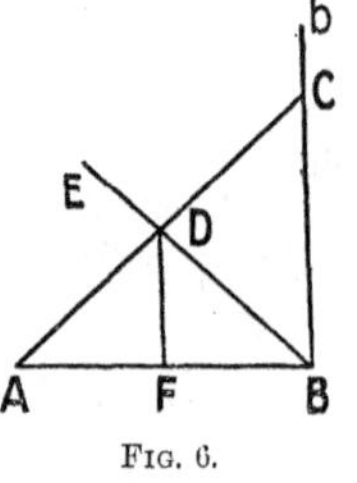

FIG. 6.

Proof. From the construction it follows that the triangles ADF and DBF are congruent.

Thus AF = FB.

Note. This construction has to be slightly modified for the Elliptic Geometry. The point C must lie between B and the pole of AB. [Cf. § 78.]

§ 4. Two Theorems independent of the Parallel Postulate.

1. *The perpendicular to the base of any triangle through its middle point is also perpendicular to the line joining the middle points of the two sides.*

Let ABC be any triangle, and let F and E be the middle points of the sides AB and AC.

Join F and E; and draw AA′, BB′, and CC′ perpendicular to EF from A, B, and C.

Let H be the middle point of BC, and K the middle point of B′C′.

Join HK.

We shall prove that HK is perpendicular to BC and EF.

From the triangles AFA′ and BFB′, which are congruent, we have AA′ = BB′.

Similarly AA′ = CC′.

Therefore BB′ = CC′.

Join BK and KC.

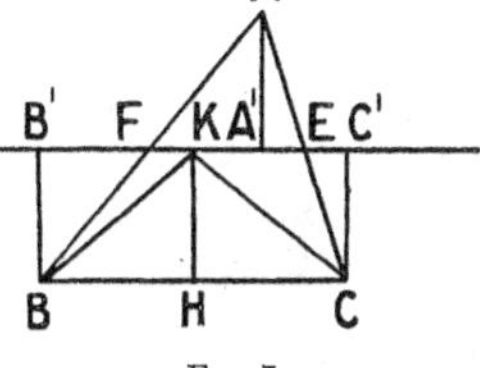

Fig. 7.

In the triangles BB′K and CC′K we have

BB′ = CC′, B′K = C′K,

and the angles at B′ and C′ are equal.

Therefore the triangles are congruent, and BK = CK.

Again, in the triangles BHK and CHK, we have the three sides equal, each to each.

Therefore the triangles are congruent, and

$$\angle BHK = \angle CHK = \text{a right angle}.$$

Also ∠ BKH = ∠ CKH.

But, from the triangles BB′K and CC′K, we have

$$\angle BKB' = \angle CKC'.$$

Therefore ∠ HKB′ = ∠ HKC′ = a right angle.

Thus HK is perpendicular to both BC and EF.

2. *The locus of the middle points of the segments joining a set of points* ABC... *on one straight line and a set* A′B′C′... *on another straight line is a straight line, provided that* AB = A′B′, BC = B′C′, *etc.*

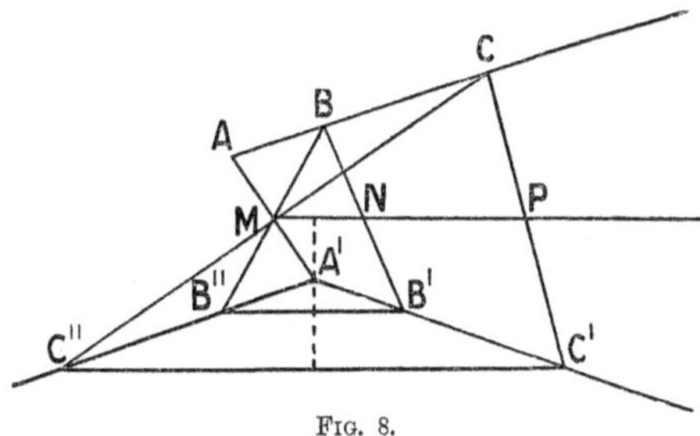

Fig. 8.

Let M, N, and P be the middle points of AA′, BB′, and CC′.

Join BM and produce it to B″, so that BM = MB″.

Join B″A′ and B″B′.

The sides of the triangle $BB'B''$ are bisected at M and N.

Therefore the line bisecting $B'B''$ at right angles is also perpendicular to MN.

But this line bisects $\angle B'A'B''$, since $A'B' = A'B''$.

Now produce $A'B''$ to C'', so that $B''C'' = BC = B'C'$.

Join $C'C''$, MC'' and MC.

The triangles MAC and $MA'C''$ are congruent, and it follows that MC and MC'' are in one straight line.

Since $A'C' = A'C''$, the line bisecting $C'C''$ at right angles coincides with the line bisecting $B'B''$ at right angles.

Therefore MN and MP are perpendicular to the same straight line.

Therefore MNP are collinear.

Proceeding to the points A, B, D, A', B', D' we have a corresponding result, and in this way our theorem is proved.

§ 5. From the *Commentary* of Proclus* it is known that not long after Euclid's own time his Parallel Postulate was the subject of controversy. The questions in dispute remained unsolved till the nineteenth century, though many mathematicians of eminence devoted much time and thought to their investigation. Three separate problems found a place in this discussion:

(i) Can the Parallel Postulate be deduced from the other assumptions on which Euclid's Geometry is based?

(ii) If not, is it an assumption demanded by the facts of experience, so that the system of propositions deduced from the fundamental assumptions will describe the space in which we live?

(iii) And finally, are both it and assumptions incompatible with it consistent with the other assumptions, so that the adoption of the Euclidean Hypothesis can be regarded as an arbitrary specialisation of a more general system, accepted not because it is more true than the others, but because the Geometry founded upon it is simpler and more convenient?

There can be little doubt that Euclid himself was convinced that the first of these questions must be answered in the negative. The place he assigned to the Parallel Postulate and

---

* Cf. Friedlein, *Procli Diadochi in primum Euclidis elementorum librum commentarii* (Leipzig, 1873). Also Heath's *Euclid*, vol. i. Introduction, chapter iv.

his refusal to use it earlier than I. 29 are evidence that with him it had only the value of an hypothesis. It seems at least very probable that he realised the advantage of proving without that postulate such theorems as could be established independently; just as he refrained from using the method of superposition, when other methods were available and sufficient for the demonstration.

But the followers of Euclid were not so clear sighted. Fruitless attempts to prove the Parallel Postulate lasted well into the nineteenth century. Indeed it will be surprising if the use of the vicious *direction*-theory of parallels, advocated at present in some influential quarters in England, does not raise another crop of so-called demonstrations—the work of those who are ignorant of the real foundations on which the Theory of Parallels rests.

The assumption involved in the second question had also an effect on the duration of the controversy. Had it not been for the mistake which identified Geometry—the logical doctrine—with Geometry—the experimental science—the Parallel Postulate would not so long have been regarded as a blemish upon the body of Geometry. However, it is now admitted that Geometry is a subject in which the assertions are that such and such consequences follow from such and such premises. Whether entities such as the premises describe actually exist is another matter. Whenever we think of Geometry as a representation of the properties of the external world in which we live, we are thinking of a branch of Applied Mathematics. That the Euclidean Geometry does describe those properties we know perfectly well. But we also know that it is not the only system of Geometry which will describe them. To this point we shall return in the last pages of this book.

In the answer to the third question the solution of the problem was found. This discovery will always be associated with the names of Lobatschewsky and Bolyai. They were the first to state publicly, and to establish rigorously, that a consistent system of Geometry can be built upon the assumptions, explicit and implicit, of Euclid, when his Parallel Postulate is omitted, and another, incompatible with it, put in its place. The geometrical system constructed upon these foundations is as consistent as that of Euclid. Not only so, by a proper choice of a parameter entering into it, this system can be made to describe and agree with the external relations of things.

This discovery, which was made about 1823-1830, does not detract from the value of Euclid's work. The Euclidean Geometry is not to be replaced by the Non-Euclidean Geometries. The latter have thrown light upon the true nature of Geometry as a science. They have also shown that Euclid's Theory of Parallels, far from being a blot upon his work, is one of his greatest triumphs. In the words of Heath: "When we consider the countless successive attempts made through more than twenty centuries to prove the Postulate, many of them by geometers of ability, we cannot but admire the genius of the man who concluded that such a hypothesis, which he found necessary to the validity of his whole system of geometry, was really indemonstrable." *

§ 6. The Work of Saccheri (1667-1733).

The history of these attempts to prove the Parallel Postulate does not lie within the scope of this work.† But we must refer to one or two of the most important contributions to that discussion from their bearing on the rise and development of the Non-Euclidean Geometries.

Saccheri, a Jesuit and Professor of Mathematics at the University of Pavia, was the first to contemplate the possibility of hypotheses other than that of Euclid, and to work out the consequences of these hypotheses. Indeed it required only one forward step, at the critical stage of his memoir, and the discovery of Lobatschewsky and Bolyai would have been anticipated by one hundred years. Nor was that step taken by his immediate successors. His work seems to have been quickly forgotten. It had fallen completely into oblivion when the attention of the distinguished Italian mathematician Beltrami was called to it towards the end of the nineteenth century. His Note entitled "*un precursore italiano di Legendre e di Lobatschewsky*" ‡ convinced the scientific world of the importance of Saccheri's work, and of the fact that theorems, which had been ascribed to Legendre, Lobatschewsky, and Bolyai, had been discovered by him many years earlier.

---

* Heath's *Euclid*, vol. i. p. 202.

† Cf. Bonola, *La geometria non-euclidea* (Bologna, 1906); English translation (Chicago, 1912). In quoting this work, we shall refer to the English translation.

‡ *Rend. Acc. Lincei* (4), t. v. pp. 441-448 (1889).

Saccheri's little book—*Euclides ab omni nævo vindicatus*—is now easily accessible.* It was published in 1733, the last year of his life. Much of it has been incorporated in the elementary treatment of the Non-Euclidean Geometries. A great deal more would be found therein were it not for the fact that he makes very frequent use of the Principle of Continuity.

It must not be forgotten that Saccheri was convinced of the truth of the Euclidean Hypothesis. He discussed the contradictory assumptions with a definite purpose—not, like Bolyai and Lobatschewsky, to establish their logical possibility—but in order that he might detect the contradiction which he was persuaded must follow from them. In other words, he was employing the *reductio ad absurdum* argument.

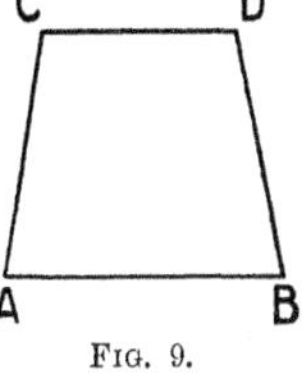

Fig. 9.

The fundamental figure of Saccheri is the two right-angled isosceles quadrilateral ABDC, in which the angles at A and B are right angles, and the sides AC and BD equal. It is easy to show by congruence theorems that the angles at C and D are equal. [Cf. § 28.]

On the Euclidean Hypothesis they are both right angles. Thus, if it is assumed that they are both obtuse, or both acute, the Parallel Postulate is implicitly denied.

Saccheri discussed these three hypotheses under the names :

The Hypothesis of the Right Angle ... $\angle C = \angle D =$ *a right angle.*

The Hypothesis of the Obtuse Angle ... $\angle C = \angle D =$ *an obtuse angle.*

The Hypothesis of the Acute Angle ... $\angle C = \angle D =$ *an acute angle.*

He showed that

According as the Hypothesis of the Right Angle, the Obtuse Angle, or the Acute Angle is found to be true, the sum of the angles of any triangle will be respectively equal to, greater than, or less than two right angles.

Also that

If the sum of the angles of a single triangle is equal to, greater than, or less than two right angles, then this sum will be equal

* Cf. Engel u. Stäckel, *Die Theorie der Parallellinien von Euclid bis auf Gauss*, pp. 31-136 (Leipzig, 1895).

to, greater than, or less than two right angles in every other triangle.

Again, he showed that

The Parallel Postulate follows from the Hypothesis of the Right Angle, and from the Hypothesis of the Obtuse Angle.

He was thus able to rule out the Hypothesis of the Obtuse Angle ; since, if the Parallel Postulate is adopted, the sum of the angles of a triangle is two right angles, and the Hypothesis of the Obtuse Angle is contradicted. It should be remarked that he assumes in this argument that the straight line is infinite. When that assumption is dropped, the Hypothesis of the Obtuse Angle remains possible.

As we have already mentioned, Saccheri's aim was to show that both the Hypothesis of the Acute Angle and that of the Obtuse Angle must be false. He hoped to establish this by deducing from these hypotheses some result, which itself would contradict that from which it was derived, or be inconsistent with a previous proposition. So, having demolished the Hypothesis of the Obtuse Angle, he turned to that of the Acute Angle. In the system built upon this Hypothesis, after a series of propositions, which are really propositions in the Geometry of Lobatschewsky and Bolyai, he believed that he had found one which was inconsistent with those preceding it. He concluded from this that the Hypothesis of the Acute Angle was also impossible ; so that the Hypothesis of the Right Angle alone remained, and the Parallel Postulate must be true.

In his belief that he had discovered a contradiction in the sequence of theorems derived from the Hypothesis of the Acute Angle, Saccheri was wrong. He was led astray by the prejudice of his time in favour of the Euclidean Geometry as the only possible geometrical system. How near he came to the discovery of the Geometry of Lobatschewsky and Bolyai will be clear from the following description of the argument contained in his Theorems 30 to 32 :

He is dealing with the pencil of rays proceeding from a point A on the same side of the perpendicular from A to a given line b, and in the same plane as that perpendicular and the line.

He considers the rays starting from the perpendicular AB and ending with the ray AX at right angles to AB.

In addition to the last ray AX, he shows that, on the hypothesis of the Acute Angle, there are an infinite number of rays which have a common perpendicular with the line b. These rays obviously cannot intersect the line b.

There is no last ray of this set, although the length of the common perpendicular decreases without limit; but there is a lower limit to the set.

Also, proceeding from the line AB, we have a set of rays which intersect the line b. There is no last ray of this set; but there is an upper limit to the set.

The upper limit of the one set and the lower limit of the other, he showed to be one and the same ray.

Thus, there is one ray, the line a_1, which divides the pencil of rays into two parts, such that all the rays on the one side of the line a_1, beginning with AB, intersect the line b; and all the rays on the other side of the line a_1, beginning with the line AX, perpendicular to the line AB, do not intersect b. The line a_1 is the boundary between the two sets of rays, and is asymptotic to b.

The result which Saccheri obtained is made rigorous by the introduction of the Postulate of Dedekind. According to that postulate a division of the two classes such as is described above carries with it the existence of a ray separating the one set of lines from the other.

This ray, which neither intersects b nor has with it a common perpendicular, is the right-handed (or left-handed) parallel of Bolyai and Lobatschewsky to the given line.

§ 7. The Work of Legendre (1752-1833).

The contribution of Legendre must also be noticed. Like Saccheri, he attempted to establish the truth of Euclid's Postulate by examining in turn the Hypothesis of the Obtuse Angle, the Hypothesis of the Right Angle, and the Hypothesis of the Acute Angle. In his work these hypotheses entered as assumptions regarding the sum of the angles of a triangle.

If the sum of the angles of a triangle is equal to two right angles, the Parallel Postulate follows; at any rate, if we assume, as Euclid did, the Postulate of Archimedes.*

Legendre thus turned his attention to the other two cases. He gave more than one rigorous proof that the sum of the angles of a triangle could not be greater than two right angles.

*Cf. Heath's *Euclid*, vol. i. pp. 218-9.

In these proofs the infinity of the line is assumed. One of them is as follows:

Let the sum of the angles of the triangle ABC be $\pi+\alpha$, and let A be the smallest angle.

Bisect BC at D and produce AD to E, making DE = AD.

Join BE.

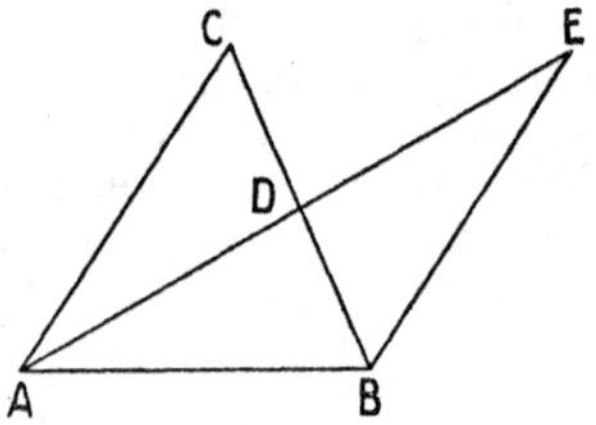

Then from the triangles ADC and BDE, we have

$$\angle CAD = \angle BED,$$
$$\angle ACD = \angle DBE.$$

Thus the sum of the angles of the triangle AEB is also equal to $\pi+\alpha$, and one of the angles BAD or AEB is less than or equal to $\frac{1}{2}\angle CAB$.

Fig. 10.

Apply the same process to the triangle ABE, and we obtain a new triangle in which one of the angles is less than or equal to $\frac{1}{2^2}\angle CAB$, while the sum is again $\pi+\alpha$.

Proceeding in this way after n operations we obtain a triangle, in which the sum of the angles is $\pi+\alpha$, and one of the angles is less than or equal to $\frac{1}{2^n}\angle CAB$.

But we can choose n so large that $2^n\alpha > \angle CAB$, by the Postulate of Archimedes.

It follows that the sum of two of the angles of this triangle is greater than two right angles, which is impossible (when the length of the straight line is infinite).

Thus, we have Legendre's First Theorem that

The sum of the angles of a triangle cannot be greater than two right angles.

Legendre also showed that

If the sum of the angles of a single triangle is equal to two right angles, then the sum of the angles of every triangle is equal to two right angles.

From these theorems it follows that

If the sum of the angles of a single triangle is less than two right angles, then the sum of the angles of every triangle is less than two right angles.

All these results had been obtained many years earlier by Saccheri.

Legendre made various attempts to prove that the sum cannot be less than two right angles, even in a single triangle; but these efforts all failed, as we now know they were bound to do. He published several so-called proofs in the successive editions of his text-book of geometry, the *Éléments de Géométrie*. All contained some assumption equivalent to the hypothesis which they were meant to establish.

For example, in one he assumes that there cannot be an absolute unit of length; * an alternative hypothesis already noted by Lambert (1728-1777).†

In a second he assumes that from any point whatever, taken within an angle, we can always draw a straight line which will cut the two lines bounding the angle.

In a third he shows that the Parallel Postulate would be true, if a circle can always be drawn through any three points not in a straight line.

In another [cf. p. 279, 14th Ed.] he argues somewhat as follows: A straight line divides a plane in which it lies into two congruent parts. Thus two rays from a point enclosing an angle less than two right angles contain an area less than half the plane. If an infinite straight line lies wholly in the region bounded by these two rays, it would follow that the area of half the plane can be enclosed within an area itself less than half the plane.

Bertrand's well-known "proof" (1778) of the Parallel Postulate ‡ and another similar to it to be found in *Crelle's Journal* (1834) fail for the same reason as does Legendre's. They depend upon a comparison of infinite areas. But a process of reasoning which is sound for finite magnitudes need not be valid in the case of infinite magnitudes. If it is to be extended to such a field, the legitimacy of the extension must be proved. Lobatschewsky himself dealt with these proofs, and pointed out the weakness in the argument. First of all, the idea of congruence, as applied to finite areas, is used in dealing with infinite regions, without any exact statement of its meaning in this connection. Further—and here it seems best to quote his

* See below, p. 90. Also Bonola, *loc. cit.* § 20.

† Cf. Engel u. Stäckel, *loc. cit.* p. 200.

‡ Cf. Frankland, *Theories of Parallelism*, p. 26 (Cambridge, 1910).

own words: "when we are dealing with areas extending to infinity, we must in this case, as in all other parts of mathematics, understand by the ratio of two of these infinitely great numbers, the limit to which this tends when the numerator and denominator of the fraction continually increase." *

It is not a little surprising that at the present day mathematicians of distinction have been found quoting Bertrand's argument with approval.†

§ 8. Both Legendre and Saccheri, in their discussion of these hypotheses, make use of the axiom that the length of the straight line is infinite, and they also assume the Postulate of Archimedes. Hilbert ‡ showed that the Euclidean Geometry could be built up without the Postulate of Archimedes. Dehn § investigated what effect the rejection of the Postulate of Archimedes would have on the results obtained by Saccheri and Legendre. He found that the sum of the angles of a triangle can be greater than two right angles in this case. In other words, the Hypothesis of the Obtuse Angle is possible. Again, he showed that without the Postulate of Archimedes we can deduce from the angle-sum in a single triangle being two right angles, that the angle-sum in every triangle is two right angles. But his most important discovery was that, when the Postulate of Archimedes is rejected, the Parallel Postulate does not follow from the sum of the angles of a triangle being equal to two right angles. He proved that there is a Non-Archimedean Geometry in which the angle-sum in every triangle is two right angles, and the Parallel Postulate does not hold.

His discovery has been referred to in this place because it shows that the Euclidean Hypothesis is superior to the others, which have been suggested as equivalent to it. Upon the Euclidean Hypothesis, without the aid of the Postulate of Archimedes, the Euclidean Geometry can be based. If we

* Cf. Lobatschewsky, *New Principles of Geometry with a Complete Theory of Parallels*, Engel's translation, p. 71, in Engel u. Stäckel's *Urkunden zur Geschichte der nichteuklidischen Geometrie*, I. (Leipzig, 1898).

† Cf. Frankland, *The Mathematical Gazette*, vol. vii. p. 136 (1913) and p. 332 (1914); *Nature*, Sept. 7, 1911, and Oct. 5, 1911.

‡ Cf. *loc. cit.* chapter iii.

§ Cf. *Math. Ann.* vol. liii. p. 404 (1900).

substitute for it the assumption that the sum of the angles of a triangle is two right angles—or that the locus of the points equidistant from a straight line is another straight line—different geometries can be created. One of these is the Euclidean Geometry, in which only one parallel can be drawn to a straight line from a point outside it. Another is what Dehn calls the Semi-Euclidean Geometry, in which an infinite number of parallels can be drawn.*

§ 9. The Work of Gauss (1777-1855).

Though Bolyai and Lobatschewsky were the first to publicly announce the discovery of the possibility of a Non-Euclidean Geometry and to explain its content, the great German mathematician Gauss had also independently, and some years earlier, come to the same conclusion. His results had not been published, when he received from Wolfgang Bolyai, early in 1832, a copy of the famous *Appendix,* the work of his son John.

This little book reached Gauss on February 14, 1832. On the same day he wrote to Gerling, with whom he had been frequently in correspondence on mathematical subjects : †

". . . Further, let me add that I have received this day a little book from Hungary on the Non-Euclidean Geometry. In it I find all *my own ideas and* RESULTS, developed with remarkable elegance, although in a form so concise as to offer considerable difficulty to anyone not familiar with the subject. The author is a very young Austrian officer, the son of a friend of my youth, with whom, in 1798, I have often discussed these matters. However at that time my ideas were still only slightly developed and far from the completeness which they have now received, through the independent investigation of this young man. I regard this young geometer v. Bolyai as a genius of the highest order. . . ."

The letter in which Gauss replied to Wolfgang Bolyai three weeks later is better known, but deserves quotation from the light it throws upon his own work : ‡

". . . If I commenced by saying *that I am unable to praise this work* (by John), you would certainly be surprised for a moment. But I cannot say otherwise. To praise it would be to

* Cf. Halsted, *Science,* N.S. vol. xiv. pp. 705-717 (1901).

† Cf. Gauss, *Werke,* vol. viii. p. 220.

‡ Gauss, *Werke,* vol. viii. p. 220.

praise myself. Indeed the whole contents of the work, the path taken by your son, the results to which he is led, coincide almost entirely with my meditations, which have occupied my mind partly for the last thirty or thirty-five years. So I remained quite stupefied. So far as my own work is concerned, of which up till now I have put little on paper, my intention was not to let it be published during my lifetime. Indeed the majority of people have not clear ideas upon the questions of which we are speaking, and I have found very few people who could regard with any special interest what I communicated to them on this subject. To be able to take such an interest one must have felt very keenly what precisely is lacking, and about that most men have very confused ideas. On the other hand, it was my idea to write all this down later, so that at least it should not perish with me. It is therefore a pleasant surprise for me that I am spared this trouble, and I am very glad that it is just the son of my old friend who takes the precedence of me in such a remarkable manner. . . ."

Wolfgang sent a copy of this letter to his son with the remark:

"Gauss's answer with regard to your work is very satisfactory, and redounds to the honour of our country and nation. A good friend says, That's very satisfactory!" *

John Bolyai was the reverse of pleased. That he would be disappointed at the news that Gauss had already reached the same conclusions as himself was natural. But his chagrin led him to doubt whether Gauss had really made these discoveries independently of his work. He conceived the absurd idea that his father must have sent his papers to Gauss some time earlier (they had been in his hands for several years), and that Gauss had made use of them, jealous of being beaten by this young Hungarian. In this he relied upon a remark made by Gauss in 1804, in a letter to his father, when both of them were trying to demonstrate the Parallel Postulate. Wolfgang had sent him what he thought was a rigorous proof, and Gauss replied that his demonstration was invalid, and that he would try as clearly as possible to bring to light the stumbling-

* Cf. Stäckel, "Die Entdeckung der nichteuklidischen Geometrie durch Johann Bolyai," *Math. u. Naturwissenschaftliche Berichte aus Ungarn*, Bd. xvii. p. 17 (1901). Also by the same author in Engel u. Stäckel's *Urkunden zur Geschichte der nichteuklidischen Geometrie, II., Wolfgang u. Johann Bolyai*, vol. i. p. 72 (Leipzig, 1913).

block which he found therein. That this was not unlike the obstacle which so far had baffled his own efforts. "However, I am always hopeful," he added, "that some day, and that in my own lifetime, a way over this obstacle will be revealed." *

Though John Bolyai afterwards saw how groundless his suspicions were, he always held that Gauss had treated him badly in this matter; and it does seem unfortunate that Gauss did not more effectively use his great influence to rescue from ill-merited neglect the notable work of the two comparatively unknown young mathematicians, Bolyai and Lobatschewsky. Not till years after they had passed away did the scientific world realise the immense value of their discoveries.

§ 10. Bolyai's discovery was made in 1823, and first published in 1832. Far away in Kasan, Lobatschewsky—one of the Professors of Mathematics in the local University—not later than 1829, and probably as early as 1826, had also discovered this new Geometry, of which the Euclidean was a special case. Thus it is interesting to trace, so far as we can, Gauss's attitude to the Theory of Parallels at that time. The chief available authorities are some letters of his which still survive, and some notes found among his papers.†

In the early years of the nineteenth century he shared the common belief that a proof of the Euclidean Hypothesis might possibly be found. But in 1817 we find him writing to Olbers as follows:

"Wachter has published a little paper on the 'First Principles of Geometry,' of which you will probably get a copy through Lindenau. Although he has got nearer the root of the matter than his predecessors, his proof is no more rigorous than any of the others. I am becoming more and more convinced that the necessity of our geometry cannot be proved . . ." ‡

In 1819 he learnt from Gerling in Marburg that one of his colleagues, Schweikart—a Professor of Law, but formerly a keen student of Mathematics—had informed him that he was practically certain that Euclid's Postulate could not be proved without some hypothesis or other; and that it seemed to him

---

* Gauss, *Werke*, vol. viii. p. 160.

† See Gauss, *Werke*, vol. viii.

‡ Gauss, *Werke*, vol. viii. p. 177.

not improbable that our geometry was only a special case of a more general one. At the same time Gerling sent him, at Schweikart's request, a Memorandum, which the latter had given him, desiring to know Gauss's opinion upon it.

This Memorandum is as follows: *

"Marburg, December, 1818.

"There are two kinds of geometry—a geometry in the strict sense—the Euclidean; and an astral geometry.

"Triangles in the latter have the property that the sum of their three angles is not equal to two right angles.

"This being assumed, we can prove rigorously:

(*a*) That the sum of the three angles of a triangle is less than two right angles;

(*b*) That the sum becomes always less, the greater the area of the triangle;

(*c*) That the altitude of an isosceles right-angled triangle continually grows, as the sides increase, but it can never become greater than a certain length, which I call the *Constant*.

"Squares have, therefore, the following form (Fig. 11):

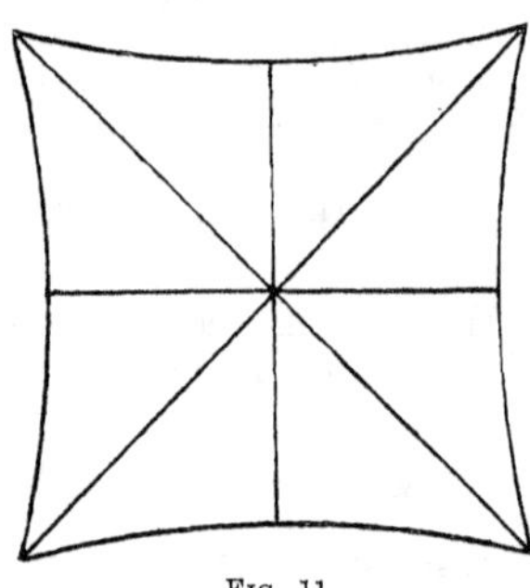

FIG. 11.

"If this Constant were *for us* the radius of the earth (so that every line drawn in the universe from one fixed star to another, distant 90° from the first, would be a tangent to the surface of the earth), it would be infinitely great in comparison with the spaces which occur in daily life.

* Gauss, *Werke*, vol. viii. p. 180.

"The Euclidean geometry holds only on the assumption that the Constant is infinite. Only in this case is it true that the three angles of every triangle are equal to two right angles; and this can easily be proved, as soon as we admit that the Constant is infinite."

This document is of peculiar importance, as it is in all probability the earliest statement of the Non-Euclidean Geometry. From a passage in a letter of Gerling's,* we learn that Schweikart made his discovery when in Charkow. As he left that place for Marburg in 1816, he seems by that date to have advanced further than the stage which Gauss had reached in 1817, according to the letter quoted above.

To Gerling, Gauss replied as follows: †

"... Schweikart's Memorandum has given me the greatest pleasure, and I beg you to convey to him my hearty congratulations upon it. It could almost have been written by myself. (Es ist mir fast alles aus der Seele geschrieben).... I would only further add that I have extended the Astral Geometry so far, that I can fully solve all its problems as soon as the Constant = C is given, *e.g.* not only is the Defect‡ of the angles of a plane triangle greater, the greater the area, but it is exactly proportional to it; so that the area has a limit which it can never reach; and this limit is the area of the triangle formed by three lines asymptotic in pairs...."

From Bolyai's papers it appears that at this date he was attempting to prove the truth of the Parallel Postulate. Also in 1815-17 Lobatschewsky was working on the same traditional lines.

§ 11. The above Memorandum is the only work of Schweikart's on the Astral Geometry that is known. Like Gauss, he seems not to have published any of his researches. However, at his instigation, and encouraged by Gauss, his nephew Taurinus devoted himself to the subject. In 1825 he published a *Theorie der Parallellinien*, containing a treatment of Parallels on Non-Euclidean Lines, the rejection of the Hypothesis of the Obtuse Angle, and some investigations resembling those of Saccheri and Lambert on the Hypothesis of the Acute Angle. For various reasons he decided that the Hypothesis of

* Cf. Gauss, *Werke*, vol. viii. p. 238.

† Gauss, *Werke*, vol. viii. p. 181.

‡ See p. 54.

the Acute Angle must also be rejected, though he recognised the logical possibility of the propositions which followed from it.

Again, it is from a letter which Gauss wrote to Taurinus in 1824, before the publication of his book, that we obtain the fullest information of his views: *

"Your kind letter of the 30th October with the accompanying little theorem I have read not without pleasure, all the more as up till now I have been accustomed to find not even a trace of real geometrical insight in the majority of the people who make new investigations upon the so-called Theory of Parallels. In criticism of your work I have nothing (or not much) more to say than that it is incomplete. It is true that your treatment of the proof that the sum of the angles of a plane triangle cannot be greater than 180° is still slightly lacking in geometrical precision. But there is no difficulty in completing this; and there is no doubt that that impossibility can be established in the strictest possible fashion. The position is quite different with regard to the second part, that the sum of the angles cannot be smaller than 180°. This is the real hitch, the obstacle, where all goes to pieces. I imagine that you have not occupied yourself with this question for long. It has been before me for over thirty years, and I don't believe that anyone can have occupied himself more with this second part than I, even though I have never published anything upon it. The assumption that the sum of the three angles is smaller than 180° leads to a peculiar Geometry, quite distinct from our Euclidean, which is quite consistent. For myself I have developed it quite satisfactorily, so that I can solve every problem in it, with the exception of the determination of a Constant, which there is no means of settling *a priori*. The greater we take this Constant, the nearer does the geometry approach the Euclidean, and when it is given an infinite value the two coincide. The theorems of that Geometry appear almost paradoxical, and to the ignorant, absurd. When considered more carefully and calmly, one finds that they contain nothing in itself impossible. For example, the three angles of a triangle can become as small as we please, if only we may take the sides large enough; however, the area of a triangle cannot exceed a definite limit, no matter how great the sides are taken, nor can it reach that limit. All my attempts to find a

* Cf. Gauss, *Werke*, vol. viii. p. 186. This letter is reproduced in facsimile in Engel u. Stäckel's *Theorie der Parallellinien* (Leipzig, 1895).

contradiction, an inconsistency, in this Non-Euclidean Geometry, have been fruitless. The single thing in it, which is opposed to our reason, is that if it were true, there must exist in space a linear magnitude, *determined in itself* (although unknown to us). But methinks, in spite of the meaningless Word-Wisdom of the Metaphysicians, we know too little or nothing at all about the real meaning of space, to stamp anything appearing unnatural to us as *Absolutely Impossible*. If the Non-Euclidean Geometry were the true one, and that Constant were in some ratio to such magnitudes as we meet in our measurements on the earth or in the heavens, then it might be determined *a posteriori*. Thus I have sometimes in jest expressed the wish, that the Euclidean Geometry were not the true one, because then we would have *a priori* an absolute measure.

"I have no fear that a man who has shown himself to me as possessed of a thinking mathematical head will misunderstand what I have said above. But in every case take it as a private communication, of which in no wise is any public use to be made, or any use which might lead to publicity. Perhaps, if I ever have more leisure than in my present circumstances, I may myself in the future make my investigations known."

§ 12. Finally, in 1831, after Bolyai's *Appendix* was in print, but before a copy had reached him, we find Gauss writing to Schumacher, who thought he had proved that the sum of the angles of a triangle must be two right angles, by a method practically the same as the rotation method of Thibaut, which so unfortunately has lately received official sanction in England and crept into our text-books of Elementary Geometry. He pointed out to him the fallacy upon which that so-called proof rests. Then he added: *

"In the last few weeks I have commenced to put down a few of my own meditations which are already to some extent forty † years old. These I had never put in writing, so that I have been compelled three or four times to think out the whole question afresh. Nevertheless I did not want it to perish with me."

---

* Cf. Gauss, *Werke*, vol. viii. p. 213.

† Forty years before the date of this letter Gauss would be just a little over 14 years old!

The Notes on Parallels,* found among his papers, probably belong to this period. Some use of them will be made below in the formal development of the Geometry of Bolyai and Lobatschewsky.

However his plans were changed when, in February, 1832, Bolyai's work reached his hands. He saw that it was now unnecessary for him to proceed with this work. The enthusiasm with which he read the *Appendix* we have already seen.

I have entered at some length into this story, partly because of its intrinsic interest; partly because of the unfortunate claim made by some mathematicians that to Gauss should be ascribed the discovery of the Non-Euclidean Geometry; partly, also, because it has been suggested that the work of Bolyai and Lobatschewsky had been inspired by the investigations of Gauss.

The claim and the suggestion we now know to be unfounded. The wonderful discovery, which revolutionised the science of Geometry, must always be associated with the names of Bolyai and Lobatschewsky, who, independently and without any knowledge of the work of Gauss, fully developed the new Geometry. While the glory of the discovery is theirs, we must not forget the advance which Gauss, and also Schweikart, had made along the same lines.

* Cf. Gauss, *Werke*, vol. viii. p. 202; also Bonola, *loc. cit.* p. 67.

CHAPTER II.

THE WORK OF BOLYAI, LOBATSCHEWSKY, AND RIEMANN, THE FOUNDERS OF THE NON-EUCLIDEAN GEOMETRIES.

§ 13. John Bolyai (1802-1860).

As we have already seen, John Bolyai, a Hungarian officer in the Austrian army, had in 1823 built up a consistent system of geometry in which the Parallel Postulate of Euclid was replaced by another, contradictory to the former. His discovery was published in 1832 as an Appendix to his father's work: *Tentamen juventutem studiosam in elementa matheseos purae, elementaris ac sublimioris, methodo intuitiva, evidentiaque huic propria, introducendi.* This work is usually referred to as the *Tentamen*. The title of the Appendix contributed by the son, and placed at the end of vol. i. of the *Tentamen*, is: *Appendix. Scientiam spatii absolute veram exhibens: a veritate aut falsitate Axiomatis XI Euclidei (a priori haud unquam decidenda) independentem: adjecta ad casum falsitatis, quadratura circuli geometrica. Auctore Johanne Bolyai de eadem, Geometrarum in Exercitu Caesareo Regio Austriaco Castrensium Capitaneo.*

If we omit the title page, a page explaining the notation, and two pages of errata, the Appendix contains only twenty-four pages.

Bolyai's discovery was made as early as 1823, when he was but 21 years old. At the time, we find him writing to his father as follows: *

"I have resolved to publish a work on the theory of parallels, as soon as I shall have put the material in order, and my cir-

* Stäckel u. Engel, "Gauss die beiden Bolyai und die nichteuklidische Geometrie, *Math. Ann.* vol. xlix. p. 155 (1897). Also Stäckel, *loc. cit.* vol. i. p. 85.

cumstances allow it. At present I have *not yet* completed this work, but the road, which I have followed, has made it almost certain that the goal will be attained, if that is at all possible: the goal is not yet reached, but I have made such wonderful discoveries that I have been almost overwhelmed by them, and it would be the cause of continual regret if they were lost. When you will see them, my dear father, you too will recognise it. In the meantime I can only say this: *I have created a new universe from nothing.* All that I have sent you till now is but a house of cards compared to a tower. I am as fully persuaded that it will bring me honour, as if I had already completed the discovery."

Wolfgang suggested that his son should publish his work, and offered to insert it as an Appendix in the *Tentamen.* He advised him, if he had really succeeded, not to lose time in letting the fact be known, for two reasons: *

"First, because ideas pass easily from one to another, who can anticipate its publication; and, secondly, there is some truth in this, that many things have an epoch, in which they are found at the same time in several places, just as the violets appear on every side in spring. Also every scientific struggle is just a serious war, in which I cannot say when peace will arrive. Thus we ought to conquer when we are able, since the advantage is always to the first comer."

But the publication of the *Tentamen* was delayed for some years. In the meantime the MSS. was placed in his father's hands, and he called some parts of it in question. His doubts were partly removed, and the work was inserted in the first volume, an advance copy of which reached Gauss at Göttingen in February, 1832. The younger Bolyai attached immense importance to the approval of Gauss, at that time the greatest authority in the world of mathematics. The high praise which Gauss gave to his work we have already mentioned.

§ 14. We now give a short description of the Appendix.

(i) It opens with a definition of parallels. *If the ray* AM *is not cut by the ray* BN, *situated in the same plane, but is cut by every ray* BP *comprised in the angle* ABN, *this will be denoted by* BN ||| AM.

* Stäckel, "Die Entdeckung der nichteuklidischen Geometrie durch Johann Bolyai," *Math. u. Naturw. Berichte aus Ungarn,* vol. xvii. p. 14 (1901). Also *loc. cit.* vol. i. p. 86.

In a footnote he adds "pronounced BN *asymptotic* to AM."

Bolyai always used the word *parallel* and the symbol || in the sense of equidistant, while he reserved the word *asymptotic* and this symbol ||| for the new parallels, in the sense in which we shall see Lobatschewsky used the term.

The properties of the new parallels are then established.

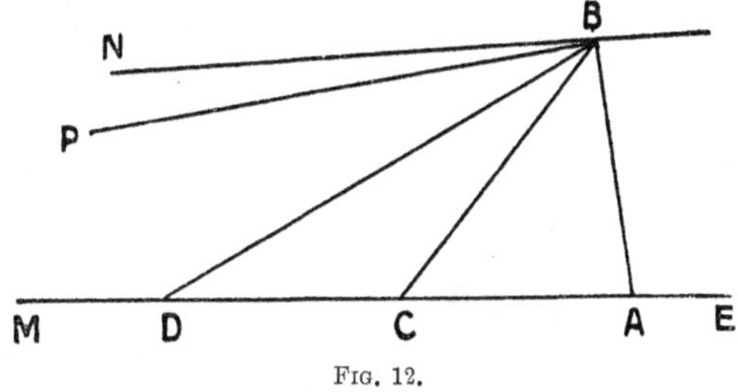

FIG. 12.

(ii) The properties of the circle and sphere of infinite radius are obtained. It is shown that the geometry on the sphere of infinite radius is identical with ordinary plane geometry.

(iii) Spherical Geometry is proved to be independent of the Parallel Postulate.

(iv) The formulae of the Non-Euclidean Plane Trigonometry are obtained with the help of the sphere of infinite radius.

(v) Various geometrical problems are solved for the Non-Euclidean Geometry; *e.g.* the construction of a "square" whose area shall be the same as that of a given circle.*

Bolyai laid particular stress upon the demonstration of the theorems which can be established without any hypothesis as to parallels. He speaks of such results as *absolutely true*, and they form part of Absolute Geometry or the Absolute Science of Space. As the title of the Appendix shows, one of his chief objects was to build up this science.

In the Appendix he says little about the question of the impossibility of proving the truth of the Euclidean Parallel

* Of course the Non-Euclidean "square" is not a quadrilateral with equal sides and all its angles right angles. A rectangle is impossible in the Non-Euclidean plane. The square of Bolyai is simply a regular quadrilateral. The angles are equal, but their size depends on the sides.

Postulate. He refers to the point more than once; but he postpones fuller treatment till a later occasion; an occasion which, so far as the public are concerned, never came. The last sentences of the Appendix (Halsted's translation) are as follows:

"It remains finally, (that the thing may be completed in every respect), to demonstrate the impossibility (apart from any supposition), of deciding *a priori*, whether Σ, or some S (and which one) exists.* This, however, is reserved for a more suitable occasion."

§ 15. Bolyai retired from the army in 1833 and lived till 1860. So far as we know he published nothing further, either in extension of the Appendix or on any other mathematical subject. From several sources, chiefly notes found among his papers, we learn that he occupied himself with some of the problems of the Non-Euclidean Geometry. He carried his work further in the direction of Solid Geometry. He investigated more fully the relation between the Non-Euclidean Geometry and Spherical Trigonometry; and he pondered the question of the possibility or impossibility of proving Euclid's Hypothesis.

An unpublished version of part of the Appendix exists in German,† in which he gives clearer expression to his views upon the last of these topics than is to be found in the corresponding section of the original. In this version, which dates from 1832, the first part of § 33 reads as follows:

"Now I should briefly state the essential result of this theory, and what it is in a position to effect:

"I. Whether Σ or S actually exists, remains here (and, as the author can prove, for ever) undecided.

"II. Now there is a Plane Trigonometry absolutely true (*i.e.* free from every hypothesis), in which, however, (according to I.), the constant i and its very existence remain wholly undetermined. With the exception of this unknown everything is determined. But Spherical Trigonometry was

---

* Bolyai calls Σ the system of Geometry resting upon Euclid's Hypothesis; and S the system founded upon his own definition of parallels.

† Cf. Stäckel, "Untersuchungen aus der absoluten Geometrie aus Johann Bolyai's Nachlass," *Math. u. Naturw. Berichte aus Ungarn*, vol. xviii. p. 280, 1902. Also *loc. cit.* vol. ii. p. 181.

developed absolutely and completely in § 26; so that the ordinary familiar Spherical Trigonometry is not in the least dependent upon Axiom XI. and is unconditionally true.

"III. By means of these two trigonometries and several subsidiary theorems (to be found in the text of § 32) one is able to solve all the problems of Solid Geometry and Mechanics, which the so-called Analysis in its present development has in its power (a statement which requires no further qualification), and this can be done downright without the help of Axiom XI. (on which until now everything rested as chief-foundation-stone), and the whole theory of space can be treated in the above-mentioned sense, from now on, with the analytical methods (rightly praised within suitable limits) of the new (science).

"Taking now into consideration the demonstration of the impossibility of deciding between Σ and S (a proof which the author likewise possesses), the nature of Axiom XI. is at length fully determined; the intricate problem of parallels completely solved; and the total eclipse completely dispelled, which has so unfortunately reigned till the present (for minds thirsting for the truth), an eclipse which has robbed so many of their delight in science, and of their strength and time.

"Also, in the author, there lives the perfectly purified conviction (such as he expects too from every thoughtful reader) that by the elucidation of this subject one of the most important and brilliant contributions has been made to the real victory of knowledge, to the education of the intelligence, and consequently to the uplifting of the fortunes of men."

His proof of the impossibility of proving the Euclidean Hypothesis seems to have rested upon the conviction that the Non-Euclidean Trigonometry would not lead to any contradiction. The following sentences are to be found among his papers:

"We obtain by the analysis of a system of points on a plane obviously quite the same formulae as on the sphere; and since continued analysis on the sphere cannot lead to any contradiction (for Spherical Trigonometry is absolute), it is therefore clear that in the same way no contradiction could ever enter into any treatment of the system of points in a plane." *

* Cf. Stäckel, *loc. cit.* vol. i. p. 121.

And lower down in the same passage:

"But there still remains the question, whether in some way or other the considerations of space would not avail for the establishment of Σ."

Indeed, owing to a mistake in his analysis, he thought for a time that he had actually obtained a proof of the Euclidean Hypothesis on these lines. But he discovered his error later.

From the fact that at one time he was willing to admit that, with the aid of Solid Geometry, evidence against the logical consistency of the Non-Euclidean Geometry might be obtained, we must not imagine that he had failed to grasp the significance of his earlier work. On the contrary, his argument shows that he had seen more deeply into the heart of the matter than Lobatschewsky himself. The latter, as we shall see below, relied simply upon the formulae for the plane. Even when it has been established that the Non-Euclidean Plane Geometry is a perfectly logical and consistent system, the question still remains, whether, somewhere or other, contradictory results might not appear in the theorems of Solid Geometry.

This question, raised for the first time by Bolyai, was settled many years later by Klein,* following upon some investigations of Cayley. We shall give, in the last chapter of this book, an elementary and rigorous demonstration of the logical possibility of the Non-Euclidean Geometry of Bolyai-Lobatschewsky, and shall show how the same argument can be applied to the Non-Euclidean Geometry associated with the name of Riemann.

§ 16. The Work of Lobatschewsky (1793-1856).

Nicolaus Lobatschewsky—Professor of Mathematics in the University of Kasan—was a pupil of Bartels, the friend and fellow-countryman of Gauss. As early as 1815 he was working at the Theory of Parallels, and in notes of his lectures (1815-1817), carefully preserved by one of his students, and now in the Biblioteca Lobatschewskiana of the Kasan Physical-Mathematical Society, no less than three "proofs" of the Parallel Postulate are to be found. From a work on Elementary Geometry, completed in 1823, but never published, the MSS. of which was discovered in 1898 in the archives of the University of Kasan, we know that by that date he had made some

* Cf. "Über die sogenannte Nicht-Euklidische Geometrie," *Math. Ann.* vol. iv. (1871).

advance; for he says regarding the Parallel Postulate, "a rigorous proof of this truth has not hitherto been discovered; those which have been given can only be called explanations, and do not deserve to be considered as mathematical proofs in the full sense." *

Between 1823 and 1826 Lobatschewsky had entered upon the path which finally led him to his great discovery. It is known that in 1826 he read a paper to the Physical-Mathematical Society of Kasan, entitled, *Exposition succincte des principes de la géométrie, avec une démonstration rigoureuse du théorème des parallèles*. The MSS. of this work does not survive, and the last clause in the title is ominous, for it suggests that he had not yet reached his goal. But in 1829-30 he published a memoir in Russian, *On the Principles of Geometry*,† and in a footnote to the first page he explains that the work is an extract from the *Exposition succincte.*

This memoir and many other works of Lobatschewsky have come down to us, for, unlike Bolyai, he was a prolific writer. He published book after book, hoping to gain for the Non-Euclidean Geometry the recognition it deserved—a recognition which in his lifetime it wholly failed to receive. But his first published work contains all that is essential to the treatment of the subject; and fully establishes the truth and value of his discovery. Thus, if the year 1826 cannot, with absolute certainty, be taken as the date at which Lobatschewsky had solved the problem, there is not the least doubt that his discovery of the Non-Euclidean Geometry was an accomplished fact in the year 1829.

§ 17. This memoir consists of nearly seventy pages. The earlier sections, §§ 1 to 7, deal with the ordinary geometrical notions of surface, line, point, distance, etc. In § 8 he introduces his theory of parallels.

This section reads as follows: ‡

---

* I am indebted to Dr. D. M. Y. Sommerville for a rendering of the Appendix I. by Vasiliev to the Russian translation of Bonola's *La geometria non-euclidea*. From this Appendix the sentence in the text is taken.

† When Lobatschewsky's works appeared in Russian. We give the titles in English. This work is available in German in Engel's translation. See Engel u. Stäckel's *Urkunden zur Geschichte der nichteuklidischen Geometrie*, I. (Leipzig, 1898).

‡ Cf. Engel, *loc. cit.* p. 10.

"We have seen that the sum of the angles of a rectilinear triangle cannot be greater than π. There still remains the assumption that it may be equal to π or less than π. Each of these two can be adopted without any contradiction appearing in the deductions made from it; and thus arise two geometries: the one, the *customary*, it is that until now owing to its simplicity, agrees fully with all practical measurements; the other, the *imaginary*, more general and therefore more difficult in its calculations, involves the possibility of a relation between lines and angles.

"If we assume that the sum of the angles in a single rectilinear triangle is equal to π, then it will have the same value in all. On the other hand, if we admit that it is less than π in a single triangle, it is easy to show that as the sides increase, the sum of the angles diminishes.

"In all cases, therefore, two lines can never intersect, when they make with a third, angles whose sum is equal to π. It is also possible that they do not intersect in the case when this sum is less than π, if, in addition, we assume that the sum of the angles of a triangle is smaller than π.

"In relation to a line, all the lines of a plane can therefore be divided into *intersecting* and *not-intersecting* lines. The latter will be called *parallel*, if in the pencil of lines proceeding from a point they form the limit between the two classes; or, in other words, the boundary between the one and the other.

"We imagine the perpendicular a dropped from a point to a given line, and a parallel drawn from the same point to the same line. We denote the angle between a and the parallel by $\mathsf{F}(a)$. It is easy to show that the angle $\mathsf{F}(a)$ is equal to $\frac{\pi}{2}$ for every line, when the sum of the angles of a triangle is equal to π; but, on the other hypothesis, the angle $\mathsf{F}(a)$ alters with a, so that as a increases, it diminishes to zero, and it remains always less than $\frac{\pi}{2}$.

"To extend the meaning of $\mathsf{F}(a)$ to all lines a, on the latter hypothesis, we shall take

$$\mathsf{F}(0)=\frac{\pi}{2}, \quad \mathsf{F}(-a)=\pi-\mathsf{F}(a).$$

In this way we can associate with every acute angle A a positive line a, and with every obtuse angle A, a negative line a, such that

$$A = F(a).$$

Further parallels, in both cases, possess the following properties :

"If two lines are parallel, and two planes passing through them intersect, their intersection is a line parallel to both.

"Two lines parallel to a third are parallel to each other.

"When three planes intersect each other in parallel lines, the sum of the inner plane angles is equal to π."

In § 9 the circle and sphere of infinite radius are introduced ; the *Limiting-Curve* and *Limiting-Surface** of the Non-Euclidean Geometry.

In §§ 11 to 15 he deals with the measurement of triangles and the solution of the problems of parallels.

At the end of § 13 are to be found the fundamental equations (17) connecting the angles and sides of a plane triangle.

§ 16, and those which follow it, are devoted to the determination, in the Non-Euclidean Geometry, of the lengths of curves, the areas of surfaces, and the volumes of solids.

After the most important cases have been examined, he adds a number of pages dealing with definite integrals, which have only an analytical interest.

From the conclusion I make the following extract, as it is related to the question already touched upon in the sections dealing with Bolyai's work—the logical consistency of the new geometry :

"After we obtained the equations (17), which express the relations between the sides and angles of a triangle, we have finally given general expressions for the elements of lines, surfaces, and volumes. After this, all that remains in Geometry becomes Analysis, where the calculations must necessarily agree with one another, and where there is at no place the chance of anything new being revealed which is not contained in these first equations. From them all the relations of the geometrical magnitudes to each other must be obtained. If anyone then asserts that somewhere in the argument a contradiction compels us to give up the fundamental assumption, which we have adopted in this new geometry, this contradiction can only be hidden in equations (17) themselves. But we

* See note on p. 80.

remark that these equations are transformed into the equations (16) of Spherical Trigonometry by substituting *ia*, *ib*, and *ic* for the sides *a*, *b*, and *c*. And in ordinary geometry and Spherical Trigonometry there enter only the relations between lines. It follows that the ordinary geometry, (Spherical) Trigonometry and this new geometry must always be in agreement with one another."*

§ 18. The writings of Lobatschewsky were brought under the notice of Gauss as early as 1841, and we gather from his letters how much impressed he was with them. Indeed it almost appears as if he had thrown himself into the study of Russian that he might be able to read the numerous papers which he hears this "clear-sighted mathematician" had published in that tongue. Through Gauss the elder Bolyai learnt in 1848 of the Russian's work, and in particular of the *Geometrische Untersuchungen zur Theorie der Parallellinien* of 1840. The astonishing news and the volume, which Lobatschewsky had written as a summary of his work, were passed on from the father to his son. How he received the intelligence we learn from the following passage in some unpublished Notes upon *Nicolaus Lobatschewsky's Geometrische Untersuchungen*:†

"Even if in this remarkable work many other methods are adopted, yet the spirit and the result so closely resemble the *Appendix* to the *Tentamen matheseos*, which appeared in Maros-Vásárhely in 1832, that one cannot regard it without astonishment. If Gauss was, as he says, immensely surprised, first by the *Appendix* and soon after by the remarkable agreement of the Hungarian and Russian mathematician, not less so am I.

"The nature of absolute truth can indeed only be the same in Maros-Vásárhely as in Kamschatka and on the Moon, or, in a word, anywhere in the world; and what one reasonable being discovers, that can also quite possibly be discovered by another."

---

*The same point is referred to in Lobatschewsky's other works: cf. (i) *Imaginary Geometry* (Liebmann's translation, p. 8); (ii) *Geometrische Untersuchungen zur Theorie der Parallellinien* (Halsted's translation, p. 163); (iii) *Pangéométrie*, § 8 (quoted by Bonola, *loc. cit.* p. 93).

†Cf. Kürschák u. Stäckel, "Johann Bolyai's Bemerkungen über Nicolaus Lobatschewsky's Geometrische Untersuchungen zur Theorie der Parallellinien," *Math. u. Naturw. Berichte aus Ungarn*, vol. xviii. p. 256 (1902). Also, Stäckel, *loc. cit.* vol. i. p. 140.

Then he goes on to remark that in the world of science discoveries are not unlikely to be made about the same time; but he cannot help wondering whether someone had not brought his own work to Lobatschewsky's notice; after which the latter might have attempted to reach the same goal by another path. And he also makes the absurd suggestion that Lobatschewsky's work might really be due to Gauss himself; that Gauss, unable to endure that anyone should have anticipated him in this matter, and yet powerless to prevent it, might have himself written this work under Lobatschewsky's name. Bolyai was undoubtedly a great genius, but he seems to have been the possessor of an extraordinarily suspicious nature!

The opinion of Gauss on the same work is given in a letter to Schumacher of 1846: *

"... I have lately had occasion again to go through the little book .... by Lobatschewsky. It contains the outlines of that geometry which must exist, and could quite consistently exist, if the Euclidean Geometry is not true. A certain Schweikart called such a geometry the Astral; Lobatschewsky calls it the Imaginary. You are aware that for fifty-four years (since 1792) † I have had the same conviction (with some extension later, of which I shall not say more here). I have found nothing really new to myself in Lobatschewsky's work; but the development is made on other lines than I had followed, and by Lobatschewsky, indeed, in a most masterful fashion and with real geometrical spirit. I feel compelled to bring the book under your notice. It will give you exquisite pleasure. . . ."

Lobatschewsky died in 1856 and Bolyai four years later: one of them, probably, a disappointed man; the other, certainly, an embittered one. Public recognition they had not gained, and in all likelihood the number of mathematicians acquainted with their work was extremely small. Had Gauss only made public reference to their discoveries, instead of confining himself to praise of their work, cordial and enthusiastic though it was, in conversation and correspondence, the world would earlier have granted them the laurels they deserved.

A few years after they had passed away the correspondence of Gauss and Schumacher was published, and the numerous

* Gauss, *Werke*, vol. viii. p. 238.

† Rather an early date, surely, for Gauss was born in 1777.

references to the works of Lobatschewsky and Bolyai showed the mathematicians of that day in what esteem Gauss had held these two still unknown and obscure names. Soon afterwards, thanks chiefly to Lobatschewsky's works, and to the labours of some well-known French, German, and Italian geometers, the Non-Euclidean Geometry, which Bolyai and Lobatschewsky had discovered and developed, began to receive full recognition. To every student of the Foundations of Geometry their names and their work are now equally familiar.

§ 19. The Work of Riemann (1826-1866).

The later development of Non-Euclidean Geometry is due chiefly to Riemann, another Professor of Mathematics at Göttingen. His views are to be found in his celebrated memoir : *Über die Hypothesen welche der Geometrie zu Grunde liegen.* This paper was read by Riemann to the Philosophical Faculty at Göttingen in 1854 as his *Habilitationsschrift,* before an audience not composed solely of mathematicians. For this reason it does not contain much analysis, and the conceptions introduced are mostly of an intuitive character. The paper itself was not published till 1866, after the death of the author ; and the developments of the Non-Euclidean Geometry due to it are mostly the work of later hands.

Riemann regarded the postulate that the straight line is infinite—adopted by all the other mathematicians who had devoted themselves to the study of the Foundations of Geometry—as a postulate which was as fit a subject for discussion as the Parallel Postulate. What he held as beyond dispute was the *unboundedness* of space. The difference between the *infinite* and *unbounded* he puts in the following words :

" In the extension of space construction to the infinitely great, we must distinguish between *unboundedness* and *infinite extent* ; the former belongs to the extent relations ; the latter to the measure relations. That space is an unbounded threefold manifoldness is an assumption which is developed by every conception of the outer world ; according to which every instant the region of real perception is completed, and the possible positions of a sought object are constructed, and which by these applications is for ever confirming itself. The unboundedness of space possesses in this way a greater empirical certainty than any external experience, but its infinite extent by no means follows from this ; on the other hand, if we assume independence of bodies from position, and therefore ascribe to space constant curvature, it must necessarily be finite, provided this curvature has ever so small a positive value." *

§ 20. Riemann, therefore, substituted for the hypothesis that the straight line is *infinite*, the more general one that it is *unbounded*. With this assumption the Hypothesis of the Obtuse Angle need not be rejected. Indeed the argument which led Saccheri, Legendre, and the others to reject that hypothesis depended upon the theorem of the external angle (I. 16). In the proof of this theorem it is assumed that the straight line is infinite.

The Hypothesis of the Obtuse Angle being available, another Non-Euclidean Geometry appeared. The importance of this new Geometry was first brought to light, when the ideas of the Non-Euclidean Geometry were considered in their bearing upon Projective Geometry.

A convenient nomenclature was introduced by Klein.† He called the three geometries *Hyperbolic*, *Elliptic*, or *Parabolic*, according as the two infinitely distant points on a straight line are *real*, *imaginary*, or *coincident*. The first case we meet in the Geometry of Lobatschewsky and Bolyai; the second in the Geometry of Riemann; the third in the Geometry of Euclid. These names are now generally adopted, and the different Non-Euclidean Geometries will be referred to below by these terms.

It is evident that at this stage the development of the Non-Euclidean Geometries passes beyond the confines of Elementary Geometry. For that reason the Elliptic Geometry will not receive the same treatment in this book as the simpler Hyperbolic Geometry. Also it should perhaps be pointed out here—the question will meet us again later—that the Elliptic Geometry really contains two separate cases, and that probably only one of these was in the mind of Riemann. The twofold nature of this Geometry was discovered by Klein.

* This quotation is taken from Clifford's translation of Riemann's memoir (*Nature*, vol. viii. 1873). The surface of a sphere is *unbounded*: it is not infinite. A two-dimensional being moving on the surface of a sphere could walk always on and on without being brought to a stop.

† Cf. Klein, "Über die sogenannte Nicht-Euklidische Geometrie," *Math. Ann.* vol. iv. p. 577 (1871), and a paper in *Math. Ann.* vol. vi. Also Bonola, *loc. cit.* English translation, App. iv.

CHAPTER III.

THE HYPERBOLIC PLANE GEOMETRY.

§21. In this chapter we proceed to the development of the Plane Geometry of Bolyai and Lobatschewsky—the Hyperbolic Geometry. We have already seen that we are led to it by the consideration of the possible values for the sum of the angles of a triangle, at any rate when the Postulate of Archimedes is adopted. This sum cannot be greater than two right angles, assuming the infinity of the straight line. If it is equal to two right angles, the Euclidean Geometry follows. If it is less than two right angles, then two parallels can be drawn through any point to a straight line.

It is instructive to see how Lobatschewsky treats this question in the *Geometrische Untersuchungen*,* one of his later works, written when his ideas on the best presentation of this fundamental point were finally determined.

"All straight lines in a plane which pass through the same point," he says in § 16, "with reference to a given straight line, can be divided into two classes, those *which cut the line*, and those *which do not cut it*. That line which forms the *boundary* between these two classes is said to be *parallel* to the given line.

"From the point A (Fig. 13) draw the perpendicular AD to the line BC, and at A erect the perpendicular AE to the line AD. In the right angle EAD either all the straight lines going out from A will meet the line DC, as, for example, AF; or some of them, as the perpendicular AE, will not meet it.

"In the uncertainty whether the perpendicular AE is the only line which does not meet DC, let us assume that it is

* *Geometrische Untersuchungen zur Theorie der Parallellinien* (Berlin, 1840). English translation by Halsted (Austin, Texas, 1891).

possible that there are other lines, such as AG, which do not cut DC however far they are produced.

"In passing from the lines AF, which cut DC, to the lines AG, which do not cut DC, we must come upon a line AH, parallel to DC, that is to say, a line on one side of which the lines AG do not meet the line DC, while, on the other side, all the lines AF meet DC.

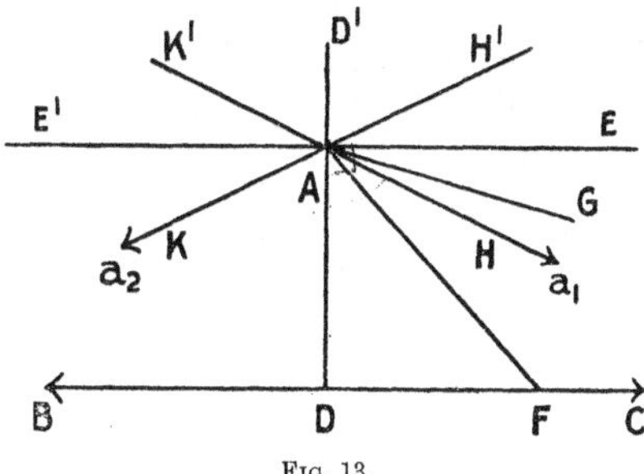

FIG. 13.

"The angle HAD, between the parallel AH and the perpendicular AD, is called *the angle of parallelism,* and we shall denote it by $\Pi(p)$, p standing for the distance AD."

Lobatschewsky then shows that if the *angle of parallelism* were a right angle for the point A and this straight line BC, the sum of the angles in every triangle would have to be two right angles. Euclidean Geometry would follow, and the *angle of parallelism* would be a right angle for any point and any straight line.

On the other hand, if the *angle of parallelism* for the point A and this straight line BC were an acute angle, he shows that the sum of the angles in every triangle would have to be less than two right angles, and the *angle of parallelism* for any point and any straight line would be less than a right angle.

The assumption $\Pi(p)=\frac{\pi}{2}$ serves as the foundation for the ordinary geometry, and the assumption $\Pi(p)<\frac{\pi}{2}$ leads to the new geometry, to which he gave the name *Imaginary Geometry.* In it two parallels can be drawn from any point to any straight line.

In this argument Lobatschewsky relies upon the idea of

continuity without stating the assumptions underlying that term. The same remark applies to the argument of Bolyai. Indeed their argument does not prove the existence of the two parallels. The existence of the two parallels in this geometry is an axiom, just as the existence of only one parallel is an axiom in the Euclidean Geometry.

§ 22. Hilbert's Axiom of Parallels.

Hilbert makes the matter clearer by definitely inserting in his treatment of the Hyperbolic Plane Geometry * the following Axiom of Parallels :

If b *is any straight line and* A *any point outside it, there are always two rays through* A, a_1, and a_2, *which do not form one and the same straight line, and do not intersect the line* b, *while every other ray in the region bounded by* a_1 *and* a_2, *which passes through* A, *does intersect the line* b.

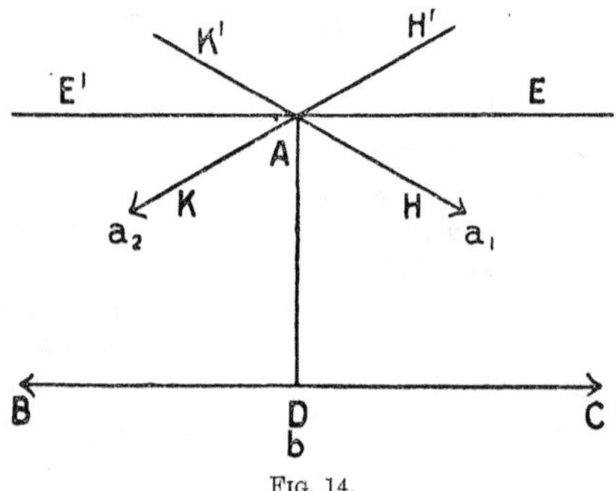

FIG. 14.

Let BC be the line b and AH, AK the rays a_1 and a_2.

From Pasch's Axiom † it follows that no line in the regions H′AH, K′AK cuts BC (Fig. 14).

Hence the rays a_1 (AH) and a_2 (AK) form the boundary between the rays through A which cut BC and the rays through A which do not cut BC.

Through A draw the perpendicular AD to the line b (BC), and also the perpendicular E′AE to the line AD.

Now E′AE cannot intersect BC, for if it cut BC on one side of D, it must cut it at a corresponding point on the other.

* Hilbert, *loc. cit.* p. 160. † Cf. p. 3.

Also it cannot be parallel to BC, because according to the Axiom the two parallels are not to form one and the same straight line.

Therefore the angles between a_1, a_2, and AD must be acute.

We shall now show that they are equal.

If the angles are unequal, one of them must be the greater. Let a_1 make the greater angle with AD, and at A make

$$\angle DAP = \angle DAK.$$

Then AP must cut BC when produced.

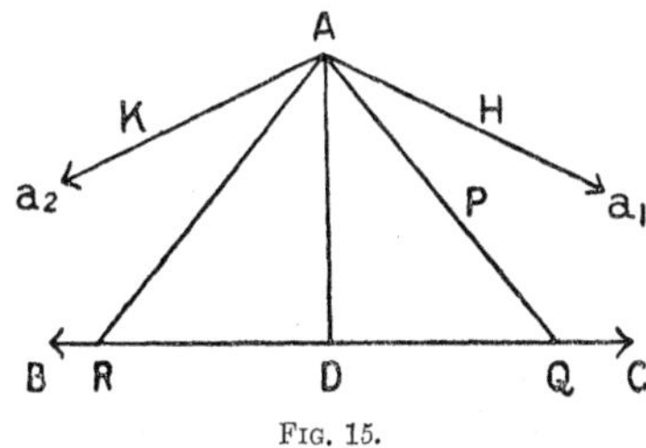

FIG. 15.

Let it cut it at Q.

On the other side of D, from the line b cut off DR = DQ and join AR.

Then the triangles DAQ and DAR are congruent, and AR makes the same angle with AD as a_2, so that AR and a_2 must coincide.

But a_2 does not cut BC; therefore the angles which a_1, a_2 make with AD are not unequal.

Thus we have shown that the perpendicular AD bisects the angle between the parallels a_1 and a_2.

The angle which AD makes with either of these rays is called the *angle of parallelism* for the distance AD, and is denoted, after Lobatschewsky, by $\Pi(p)$, where AD $=p$.

The rays a_1 and a_2 are called the *right-handed* and *left-handed* parallels from A to the line BC.

§ 23. In the above definition of parallels, the starting point A of the ray is material. We shall now show that

A straight line maintains its property of parallelism at all its points.

In other words, *if the ray* AH *is the right-handed (or left-handed) parallel through* A *to the line* BC, *then it is the right-handed (or left-handed) parallel through any point upon the ray* AH, *or* HA *produced, to the given line.*

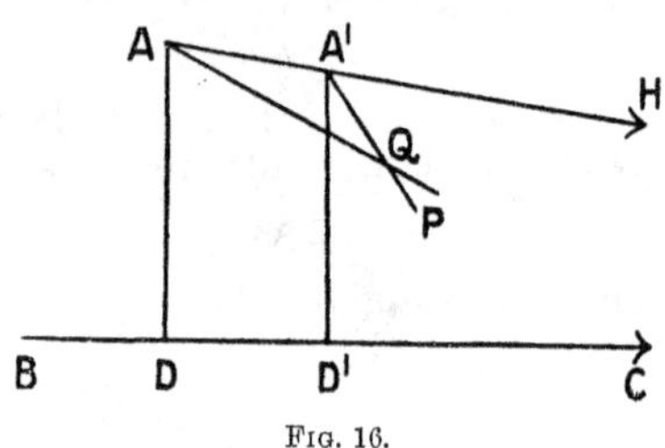

Fig. 16.

Case I. Let A′ be any point upon the ray AH other than A.

Through A′ draw A′D′ perpendicular to BC.

In the region bounded by A′D′ and A′H draw any ray A′P, and take Q any point upon A′P.

Join AQ.

Then AQ produced must cut DC.

It follows from Pasch's Axiom that A′Q must cut D′C.

But A′H does not cut D′C, and A′P is any ray in the region D′A′H.

Therefore A′H is a parallel through A′ to the line BC.

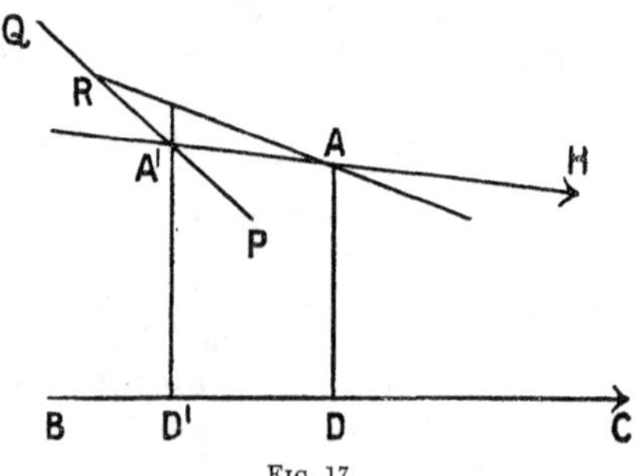

Fig. 17.

Case II. Let A′ be any point upon the ray AH produced backwards through A.

Draw A′D′ perpendicular to BC.

In the region bounded by A′D′ and A′H draw through A′ any ray A′P, and produce PA′ through A′ to Q.

Upon A′Q take any point R and join AR.

Then RA produced must intersect DC.

It follows that A′P must intersect D′C.

Therefore, as above, the ray A′H is a parallel through any point A′, on HA produced, to the line BC.

In both cases the parallels are *in the same sense* or *direction* as the original ray (*i.e.* both right-handed or both left-handed). We are thus entitled to speak of a line AB as a right-handed (or left-handed) parallel to another line CD, without reference to any particular point upon the line AB.

§ **24.** Another property of parallels with which we are familiar in Euclidean Geometry also holds for the Hyperbolic Geometry.

If the line AB *is parallel to the line* CD, *then the line* CD *is parallel to the line* AB.

From A draw AC perpendicular to CD, and from C draw CE perpendicular to AB.

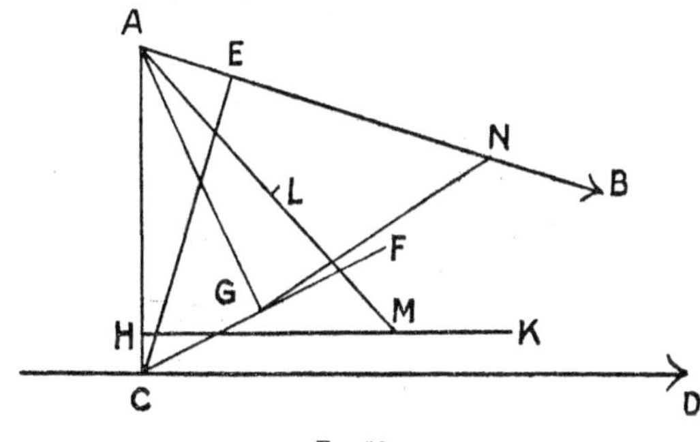

Fig. 18.

In the region DCE draw any ray CF, and from A draw AG perpendicular to CF.

It is easy to show that the point G must lie in the region ECD.

Further, since ∠ ACG is an acute angle and ∠ AGC is a right angle, AC > AG.

From AC cut off AH = AG, and draw HK perpendicular to AH on the same side as CD.

Make $\angle$ HAL = $\angle$ GAB.

Then the ray AL must cut CD, and it follows that HK must cut AL.

Let HK cut AL at M.

From AB cut off AN = AM, and join GN.

Then the triangles HAM and GAN are congruent.

Thus $\angle$ AGN = a right angle.

Therefore GN and GF coincide, and CF produced intersects AB.

But CF was any ray in the region between CE and CD, and CD itself does not cut AB.

Therefore CD is parallel to AB, in the same sense as AB is parallel to CD.*

§ 25. A third important property of parallels must also be proved:

If the line (1) is parallel to the line (2) and to the line (3), the three lines being in the same plane, then the line (2) is also parallel to (3).

Case I. Let the line (1) lie between (2) and (3). (Cf. Fig. 19.)

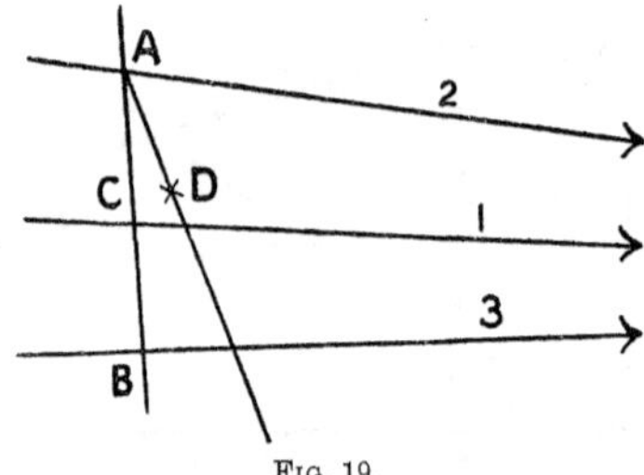

Fig. 19.

Let A and B be two points upon (2) and (3), and let AB cut (1) in C.

Through A let any arbitrary line AD be drawn between AB and (2).

* The proof in the text is adapted from that of Lobatschewsky in *New Principles of Geometry with a Complete Theory of Parallels*, § 96 (Engel's translation, p. 169).

Then it must cut (1), and on being produced must also cut (3).

Since this holds for every line such as AD, (2) is parallel to (3).

Case II. Let the line (1) be outside both (2) and (3), and let (2) lie between (1) and (3). (Fig. 20.)

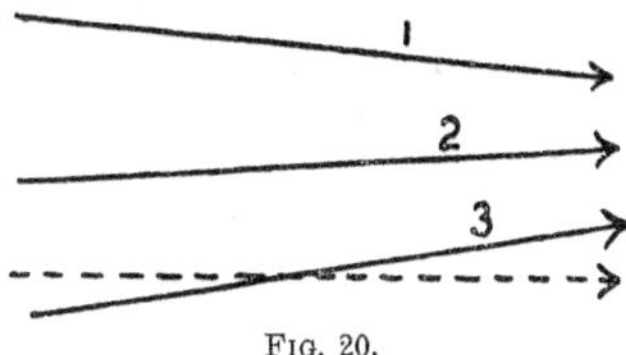

Fig. 20.

If (2) is not parallel to (3), through any point chosen at random upon (3), a line different from (3) can be drawn which is parallel to (2).

This, by Case I., is also parallel to (1), which is absurd.*

§ **26.** We shall now consider the properties of the figure [cf. Fig. 21] formed by two parallel rays through two given points and the segment of which these two points are the ends.

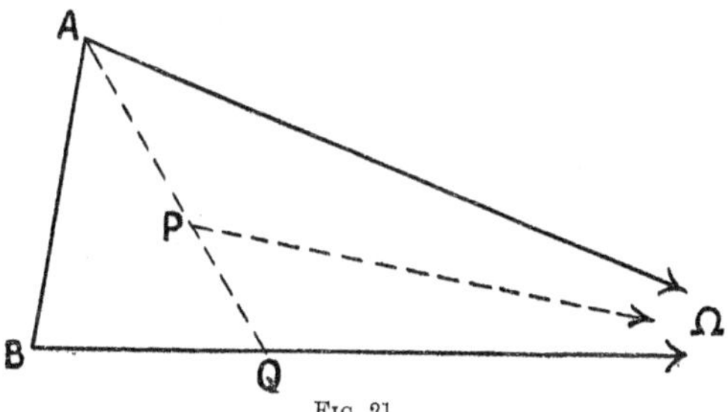

Fig. 21.

It is convenient to speak of two parallel lines as meeting at infinity. In the Hyperbolic Geometry each straight line will have two points at infinity, one for each direction of parallelism. With this notation the parallels through A, B may be said to meet at Ω, the common point at infinity on these lines.

* The proof in the text is due to Gauss, and is taken from Bonola, *loc. cit.* p. 72.

Also, a straight line will be said to pass through this point Ω, when it is parallel to these two lines in the same sense.

1. *If a straight line passes through one of the angular points* A, B, *or* Ω, *and through a point inside this figure, it must cut the opposite side.* (Fig. 21.)

Let P be the point within the figure. Then AP must cut BΩ, by the Axiom of Parallels. Let it cut BΩ at Q. The line PΩ must cut one of the sides AB or BQ of the triangle ABQ, by Pasch's Axiom. It cannot cut BQ, since it is parallel to BΩ. Therefore it must cut AB.

2. *A straight line in the plane* ABΩ, *not passing through an angular point, which cuts one of the sides, also cuts one, and only one, of the remaining sides of this figure.*

Let the straight line pass through a point C on AB. Let CΩ be drawn through C parallel to AΩ and BΩ. If the given line lies in the region bounded by AC and CΩ, it must cut AΩ ; and if it lies in the region bounded by BC and CΩ it must cut BΩ.

Again, if the line passes through a point D on AΩ, and B, D are joined, it is easy to show that it must cut either AB or BΩ.

We shall now prove some further properties of this figure.

3. *The exterior angle at* A *or* B *is greater than the interior and opposite angle.*

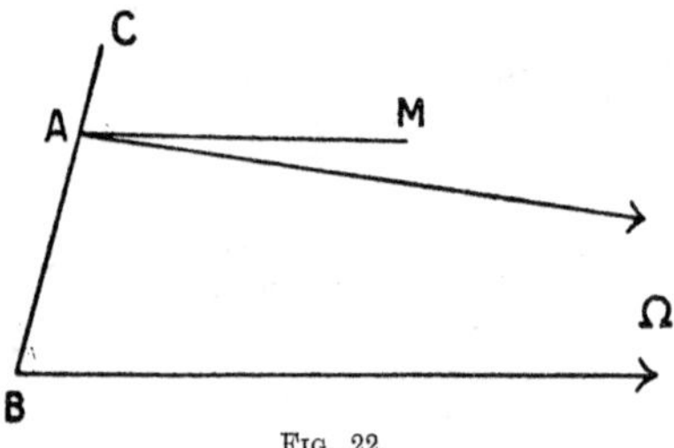

Fig. 22.

Consider the angle at A, and produce the line BA to C. Make ∠CAM = ∠ABΩ. AM cannot intersect BΩ, since the exterior angle of a triangle is greater than the interior and opposite angle. Also it cannot coincide with AΩ, because then the perpendicular to AΩ from the middle point of AB would also be perpendicular to BΩ. The angle of parallelism for this common perpendicular would be a right angle, and this is contrary to Hilbert's Axiom of Parallels.

Therefore $\angle CA\Omega > \angle CAM$, which is equal to $\angle AB\Omega$.

Thus the exterior angle at A is greater than the interior angle at B.

A similar proof applies to the angle at B.

We take now two figures of this nature; each consisting of a segment and two parallels through the ends of the segment.

4. *If the segment* AB = *the segment* A′B′, *and the angle at* A = *the angle at* A′, *then the angles at* B *and* B′ *are equal.*

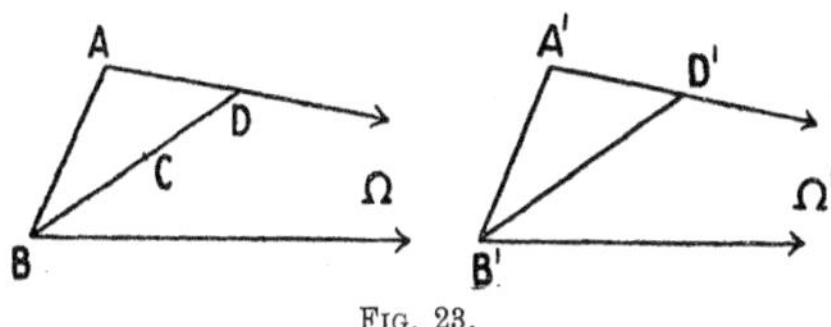

FIG. 23.

If $\angle AB\Omega$ is not equal to $\angle A'B'\Omega'$, one of them must be the greater.

Let $\angle AB\Omega > \angle A'B'\Omega'$.

Make $\angle ABC = \angle A'B'\Omega'$.

Then BC must cut AΩ.

Let it cut it at D; and on A′Ω′ take A′D′ = AD, and join B′, D′.

Then the triangles ABD and A′B′D′ are congruent, so that $\angle A'B'D' = \angle ABD = \angle A'B'\Omega'$, which is absurd.

It follows that $\angle AB\Omega$ is not greater than $\angle A'B'\Omega'$, and that the angles are equal.

5. *If the segment* AB = *the segment* A′B′, *and the angles at* A *and* B *are equal, as also the angles at* A′ *and* B′, *then the four angles at* A, B, A′ *and* B′ *are equal to each other.*

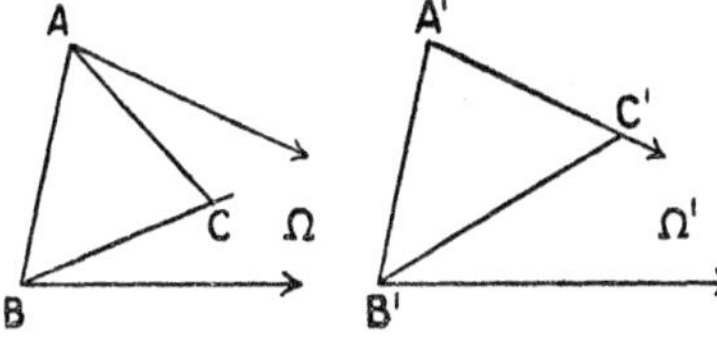

FIG. 24.

If the angle at A is not equal to the angle at A′, one of them must be the greater. Let it be the angle at A.

At A and B draw the rays which make with AB an angle equal to the angle at A′.

These rays must intersect; let them meet at C.

From A′Ω′ cut off A′C′ = AC, and join B′C′.

The triangles ABC and A′B′C′ are congruent, so that

$$\angle A'B'C' = \angle ABC = \angle A'B'\Omega',$$

which is absurd.

Thus the angles at A and A′ must be equal; and it follows that the angles at A, B, A′ and B′ are equal to each other.

6. *If the angles at* A *and* A′ *are equal, and the angles at* B *and* B′ *are also equal, then the segment* AB = *the segment* A′B′.

If AB is not equal to A′B′, one of them must be the greater. Let it be AB.

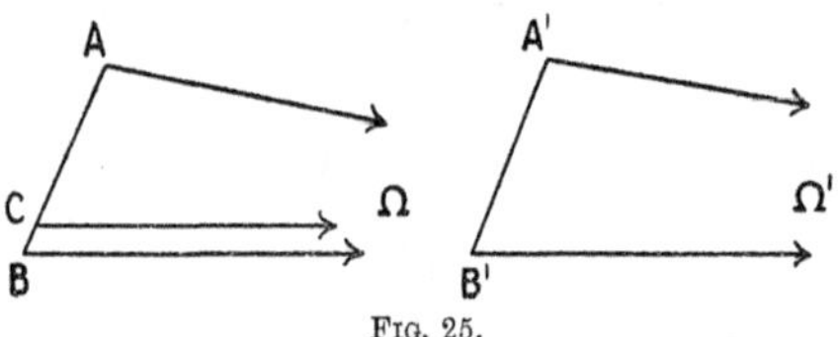

FIG. 25.

From AB cut off AC = A′B′, and draw CΩ parallel to AΩ.

Then, by (4), ∠ ACΩ = ∠ A′B′Ω′ = ∠ ABΩ.

But by (3), ∠ ACΩ > ∠ ABΩ.

Therefore AB cannot be greater than A′B′, and the two segments are equal.

§ 27. The Angle of Parallelism.

From § 26 (4), we can at once deduce that *the angles of parallelism corresponding to equal distances are equal.*

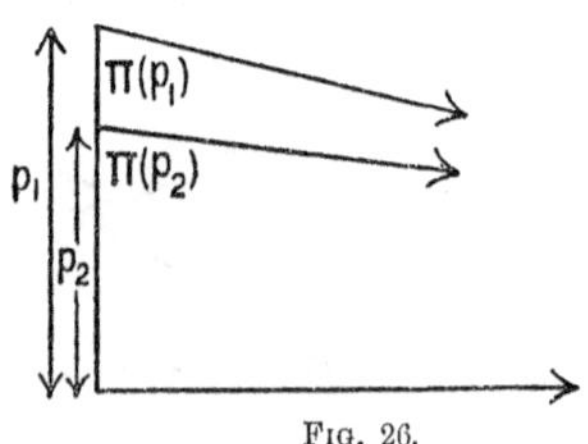

FIG. 26.

Combining this result with § 26 (3), we can assert that

$$\text{If} \quad p_1 > p_2, \quad \text{then} \quad \Pi(p_2) > \Pi(p_1).$$

We shall see later (§ 41) that to any given segment we can find the angle of parallelism, and that to any given acute angle (§ 45) we can find the corresponding distance.

Thus, we can say that

$$\text{If } p_1 = p_2, \text{ then } \Pi(p_1) = \Pi(p_2).$$
$$\text{If } p_1 > p_2, \text{ then } \Pi(p_1) < \Pi(p_2).$$
$$\text{If } p_1 < p_2, \text{ then } \Pi(p_1) > \Pi(p_2).$$

Also
$$\Pi(0) = \frac{\pi}{2},$$
$$\Pi(\infty) = 0.$$

It is convenient to use the notation

$$\alpha = \Pi(a), \quad \beta = \Pi(b), \text{ etc.}$$

Again, if the segment a is given, we can find the angle α [cf. § 41], and thus $\frac{\pi}{2} - \alpha$. And to $\frac{\pi}{2} - \alpha$ there corresponds a distance of parallelism [cf. § 45]. It is convenient to denote this *complementary* segment by a'.

Thus we have
$$\Pi(a') = \frac{\pi}{2} - \Pi(a).$$

Further, in the words of Lobatschewsky,* " we are wholly at liberty to choose what angle we will denote by the symbol $\Pi(p)$, when the line p is expressed by a negative number, so we shall assume
$$\Pi(p) + \Pi(-p) = \pi."$$

§ 28. Saccheri's Quadrilateral.

The quadrilateral in which the angles at A and B are right angles, and the sides AC, BD equal, we shall call Saccheri's Quadrilateral. We have seen that Saccheri made frequent use of it in his discussion of the Theory of Parallels.

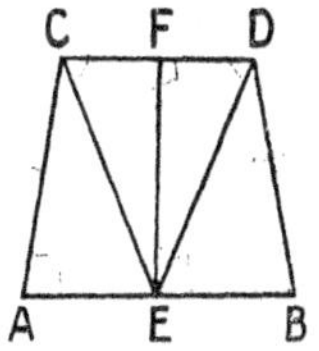

In Saccheri's Quadrilateral, when the right angles are adjacent to the base, the vertical angles are equal acute angles, and the line which bisects the base at right angles also bisects the opposite side at right angles.

FIG. 27.

Let AC and BD be the equal sides, and the angles at A and B right angles.

* *Geometrische Untersuchungen zur Theorie der Parallellinien*, § 23.

Let E, F be the middle points of AB and CD respectively.

Join EF, CE, and DE.

Then the triangles ACE and EDB are congruent, and the congruence of CFE and EFD follows.

Thus the angles at C and D are equal, and EF is perpendicular both to AB and CD.

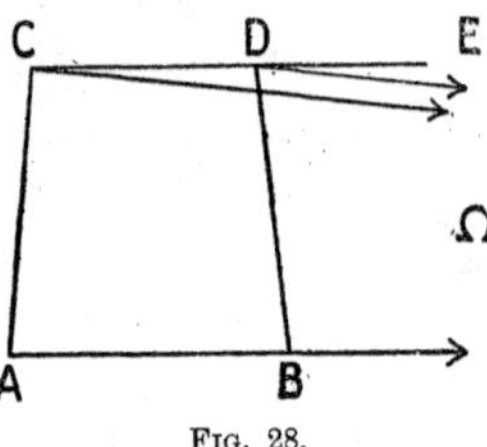

Fig. 28.

Further, the angles at C and D are acute.

To prove this, at C and D draw CΩ and DΩ parallel to AB.

Then, by § 26 (4), ∠ ACΩ = ∠ BDΩ.

Produce CD to E.

By § 26 (3), ∠ EDΩ > ∠ DCΩ.

Therefore, since ∠ ACD = ∠ BDC, it follows that

∠ EDB > ∠ CDB.

Thus ∠ ACD and ∠ BDC are both acute angles.

§ 29. *If in the quadrilateral* ABDC, *the angles at* A *and* B *are right angles, and the side* AC *is greater than* BD, *the angle at* C *is less than the angle at* D.

Since we are given AC > BD, we can cut off from AC the segment AE = BD. When this has been done, join DE.

It follows from § 28 that ∠ AED = ∠ BDE.

But ∠ AED > ∠ ACD and ∠ BDC > ∠ BDE.

Therefore ∠ BDC > ∠ ACD.

Fig. 29.

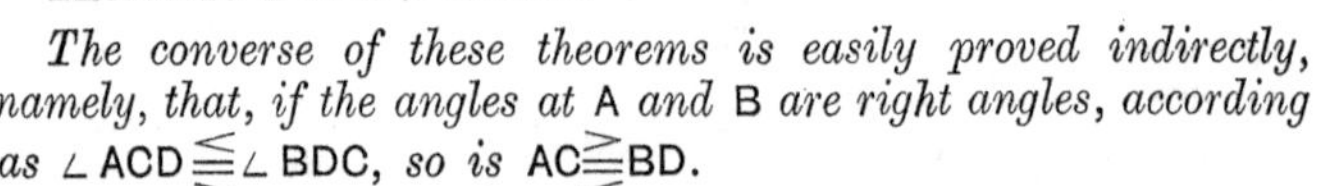
The converse of these theorems is easily proved indirectly, namely, that, if the angles at A *and* B *are right angles, according as* ∠ ACD $\lesseqqgtr$ ∠ BDC, *so is* AC $\gtreqqless$ BD.

§ 30. *If* ABDC *is a quadrilateral in which the angles at* A, B, *and* C *are right angles, then the angle at* D *must be acute.*

Produce BA through A to B′, making AB′ = AB. (Fig. 30.)

Draw B′D′ perpendicular to B′A and equal to BD.

Join CD′, D′A, and DA.

From the congruent triangles D′B′A and DBA, we have

D′A = DA and ∠ D′AB′ = ∠ DAB.

Thus ∠ D′AC = ∠ DAC, and the triangles D′AC and DAC are congruent.

Therefore ∠ D′CA is a right angle, and DC, CD′ form one straight line.

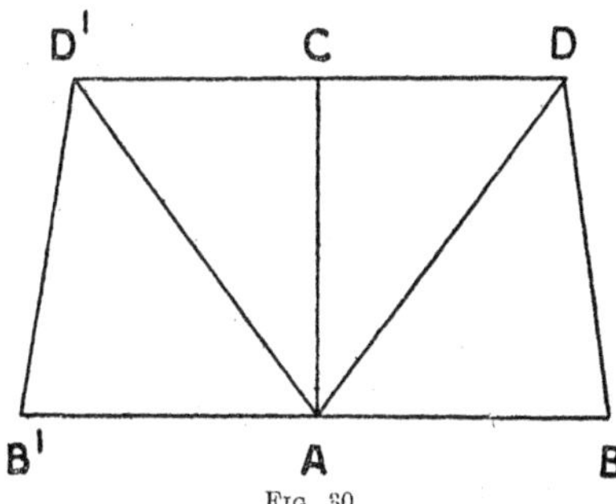

Fig. 30.

Applying the result of § 28 to the quadrilateral D′B′BD, it follows that the angles at D′ and D are equal and acute.

§ 31. The sum of the angles of every triangle is less than two right angles.

Case I. Let the triangle ABC be any right-angled triangle with C = 90°.

At A make ∠ BAD = ∠ ABC.

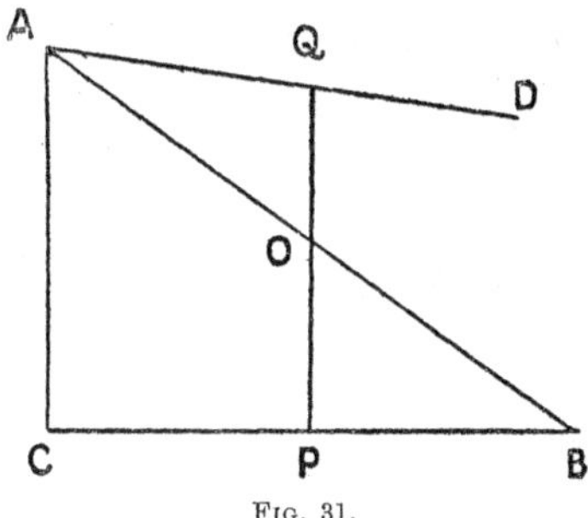

Fig. 31.

From O, the middle point of AB, draw the perpendiculars OP and OQ to CB and AD respectively.

Then the triangles POB and AOQ are congruent, and it follows that OP and OQ are in one and the same straight line.

Thus the quadrilateral ACPQ has the angles at C, P, and Q right angles.

Therefore, by § 30, the angle at A, namely $\angle$ CAD, must be acute.

It follows that the sum of the angles of any right-angled triangle must be less than two right angles.

Case II. Consider now any triangle, not right-angled. Every triangle can be divided into two right-angled triangles by drawing the perpendicular from at least one angular point to the opposite side (Fig. 32).

Let AD be the perpendicular referred to in the triangle ABC, and let the angles α', α'', β, γ be as in the figure.

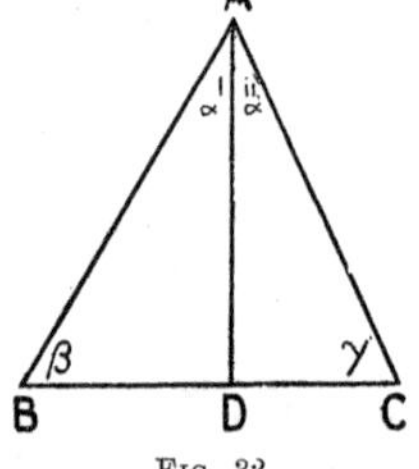

FIG. 32.

Then $A+B+C=(\alpha'+\beta)+(\alpha''+\gamma)$.

But $\alpha'+\beta<1$ right angle

and $\alpha''+\gamma<1$ right angle.

Therefore $A+B+C<2$ right angles.

It should be noticed that no use has been made of the Postulate of Archimedes in proving this result.

The difference between two right angles and the sum of the angles of a triangle will be called the Defect of the Triangle.

COROLLARY. *There cannot be two triangles with their angles equal each to each, which are not congruent.*

It is easy to show that if two such triangles did exist, we could obtain a quadrilateral with the sum of its angles equal to four right angles. We have simply to cut off from one of the triangles a part congruent with the other. But the sum of the angles of a quadrilateral cannot be four right angles, if the sum of the angles of every triangle is less than two right angles.

§ 32. Not-intersecting Lines.

It follows from the Theorem of the External Angle (I. 16) that if two straight lines have a common perpendicular, they cannot intersect each other. And they cannot be parallel, since this would contradict Hilbert's Axiom of Parallels [cf. § 26 (3)].

The converse is also true, namely, that

*If two straight lines neither intersect nor are parallel, they must have a common perpendicular.**

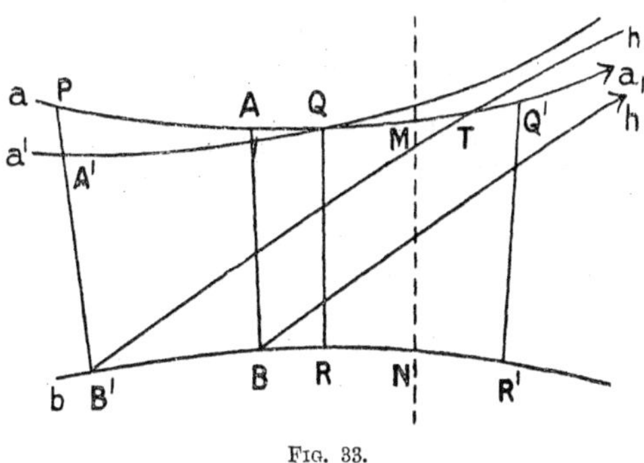

FIG. 33.

Let a and b be the two given lines, which neither intersect nor are parallel.

From any two points A and P on the line a, draw AB and PB′ perpendicular to the line b.

If AB = PB′, the existence of a common perpendicular follows from § 28. Therefore we need only discuss the case when AB is not equal to PB′.

Let PB′ be the greater.

Cut off A′B′ from PB′ so that A′B′ is equal to AB.

At A′ on the line A′B′, and on the same side of the line as AB, draw the ray a' making with A′B′ the same angle as a, or PA produced, makes with AB.

We shall now prove that a' must cut the line a.

Denote the ray PA by a_1, and draw from B the ray h parallel to a_1.

Since a, b are *not-intersecting lines*, the ray h must lie in the region between BA and B′B produced.

Through B′ draw the ray h', on the same side of B′A′ as h is of BA, and making the same angle with the ray B′B as h does with B′B produced.

From § 26 (3), it follows that the parallel from B′ to h and a_1 lies in the region between h' and B′B.

---

* This proof is due to Hilbert ; cf. *loc. cit.* p. 162.

Therefore h' must cut a_1.

Let it cut this line at T.

Since a' is parallel to B'T, it follows that the ray a' must cut PT (Pasch's Axiom).

Let these rays a_1, a' intersect at Q.

From Q draw QR perpendicular to the line b, and from the line b cut off BR' equal to B'R and on the opposite side of B from B'.

In the same way, from the line a cut off AQ' equal to A'Q, and on the opposite side of A from P.

In this way we obtain a quadrilateral ABR'Q' congruent with A'B'RQ.

Thus QRR'Q' is a Saccheri's Quadrilateral, and the line joining the middle points of QQ', RR' is perpendicular to a and b.

§ **33.** *Two parallel lines approach each other continually, and their distance apart eventually becomes less than any assigned quantity.*

Let a and b be two parallel lines.

Upon a take any two points P and Q, PQ being the direction of parallelism for the lines.

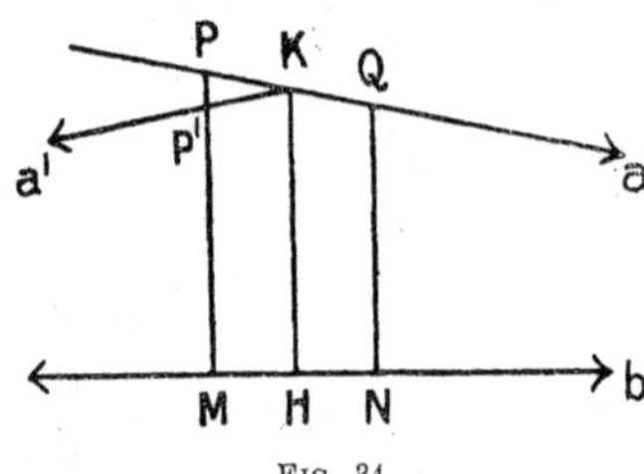

Fig. 34.

From P and Q draw the perpendiculars PM and QN to b.

Bisect MN at H, and draw the perpendicular at H to the line b.

This must intersect the segment PQ; let it do so at K.

At K draw the ray a' parallel to b in the other direction.

This ray must intersect PM, since it enters the triangle PKM at the vertex K.

Let it cut PM at P'.

Since the triangles KHM and KHN are congruent, and $\angle$ HKP′ = $\angle$ HKQ, it easily follows that P′M is equal to QN.

But P′ lies on the segment PM.

Therefore PM is greater than QN, and we have shown that as we pass along the line a, in the direction of parallelism, the distance from b continually diminishes.

We have now to prove the second part of the theorem.

Let a and b be two parallel lines as before, and P any point on the line a.

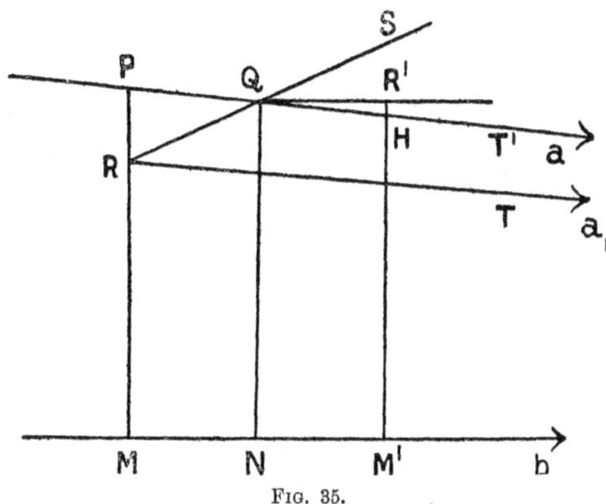

FIG. 35.

Draw PM perpendicular to b, and let ϵ be any assigned length as small as we please.

If PM is not smaller than ϵ, cut off MR $= \epsilon$.

Through R draw the ray a_1 (RT) parallel to a and b in the same sense.

Also draw through R the ray RS perpendicular to MR.

RS must cut the ray a; since $\angle$ PRT is an obtuse angle.

Let it cut a at Q and draw QN perpendicular to b.

Now the lines RQS and the line b have a common perpendicular.

Therefore they are not-intersecting lines.

It follows that $\angle$ NQR is greater than the angle of parallelism for the distance QN.

At Q make $\angle$ NQR′ = $\angle$ NQR.

Then $\angle$ NQR′ > $\angle$ NQT′, T′ being any point upon PQ produced.

From the line b cut off $NM' = NM$, on the other side of N from M, and from QR' cut off $QR' = QR$.

Join $R'M'$.

Then $R'M'$ is perpendicular to b, and is cut by the ray PQ between R' and M'.

Let the point of section be H.

Then $M'H < M'R'$, and $M'R' = MR$.

Therefore we have found a point on the line a whose distance from b is less than the given length ϵ.

§ 34. *The shortest distance between any two not-intersecting lines is their common perpendicular, and as we proceed along either of the lines from the point at which it is cut by the common perpendicular the distance from one to the other continually increases.*

Let the common perpendicular to two not-intersecting lines a and b meet them at A and B.

Let P and Q be two other points on one of the lines on the same side of A, and such that $AP < AQ$.

Draw PM and QN perpendicular to the other line.

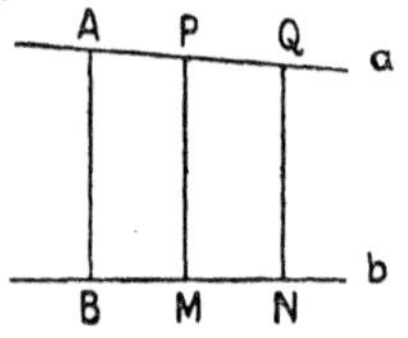

Then in the quadrilateral ABMP, the angle A is a right angle and the angle APM is acute (cf. § 30).

FIG. 36.

Therefore $PM > AB$ (cf. § 29).

Also in the quadrilateral PQMN, the angle MPQ is obtuse and PQN is acute.

Therefore $QN > PM$.

Thus, as we pass along the ray APQ... the distance from the line b continually increases from its value at A.

It can be shown that two parallel lines continually diverge towards the side opposite to the direction of parallelism, and that two intersecting lines continually diverge from the point of intersection. Also, the distance apart, both in the case of intersecting lines, of parallel lines, in the direction opposite to that of parallelism, and of not-intersecting lines will become eventually greater than any assigned length.

The theorems of §§ 33-4 were all proved by Lobatschewsky; cf. *New Principles of Geometry with a Complete Theory of Parallels* (Engel's translation), § 108 *et seq.*

§ 35. The correspondence between a Right-Angled Triangle and a Quadrilateral with Three Right Angles and One Acute Angle.

The sides of a right-angled triangle ABC, in which C is the right angle, are denoted as usual by a, b, and c; the angles A and B by λ and μ; and the distances corresponding to the angles of parallelism λ and μ are denoted by l and m. Between these quantities a, b, c, l, m, λ, and μ certain relations hold.

Similarly the elements of a quadrilateral, in which three angles are right angles, the remaining angle being necessarily acute, are connected by certain relations.

We proceed to find the equations connecting these quantities, and to establish a very important correspondence between the two figures.

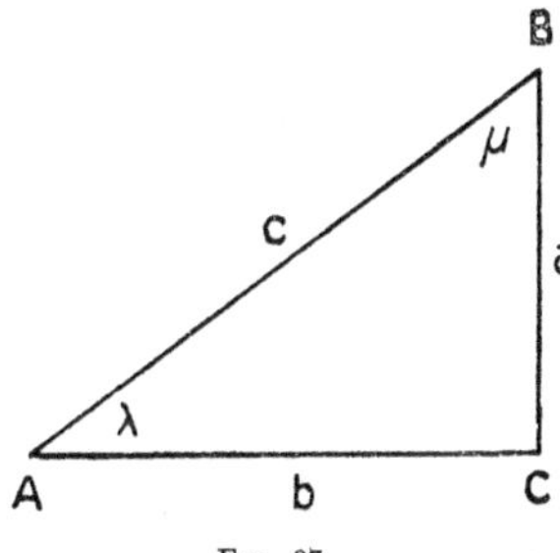

Fig. 37.

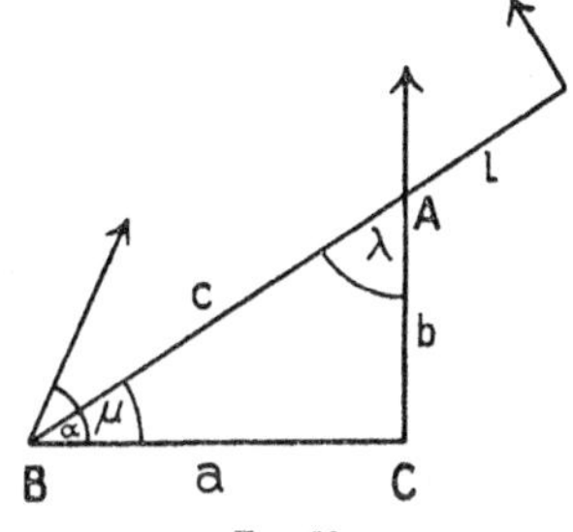

Fig. 38.

I. *The Right-Angled Triangle.*

Let ABC be any right-angled triangle. Produce the hypothenuse through A a distance l, and at the other end of the segment l draw the parallel to the line CA. Also draw through B the parallel to both these lines.

It follows from Fig. 38 that

$$\mu + \Pi(c+l) = \Pi(a) = \alpha, \qquad \text{(1)}$$

and in the same way we have

$$\lambda + \Pi(c+m) = \Pi(b) = \beta. \qquad \text{(1')}$$

Now draw through A the parallel to the line BC (Fig. 39). Also draw the line perpendicular to c, which is parallel to BC in the same sense. This line will cut the hypothenuse, or the hypothenuse produced, according as m is less than or greater than c.

If $m < c$, we have

$$\lambda + \beta = \Pi(c - m). \qquad \text{(2)}$$

If $m > c$, then we would have

$$\pi - \lambda - \beta = \Pi(m - c).$$

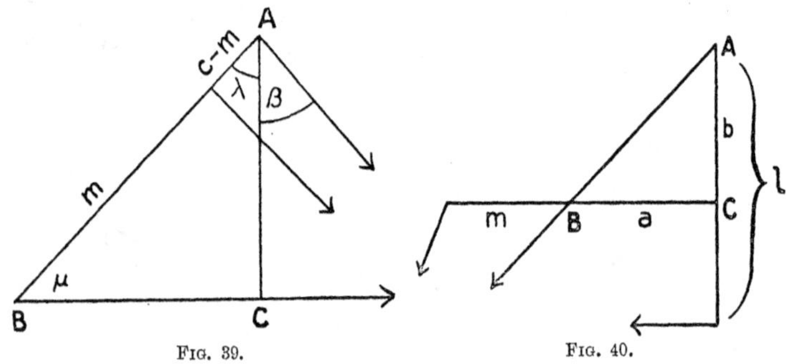

FIG. 39. FIG. 40.

With the usual notation (cf. § 27) this reduces to

$$\lambda + \beta = \Pi(c - m).$$

In the same way we have

$$\mu + \alpha = \Pi(c - l). \qquad \text{(2')}$$

Finally, produce CB through B, and draw the perpendicular to CB produced which is also parallel to AB (Fig. 40). Also produce AC through C, and draw the perpendicular to AC which is parallel to AB.

From Fig. 40, if we suppose a line drawn through C parallel to AB, it is clear that

$$\Pi(l - b) + \Pi(m + a) = \frac{\pi}{2}, \qquad \text{(3)}$$

and similarly

$$\Pi(m - a) + \Pi(l + b) = \frac{\pi}{2}. \qquad \text{(3')}$$

II. *The Quadrilateral with Three Right Angles and an Acute Angle.*

Let PQRS be a quadrilateral in which the angles P, Q, R are right angles. We denote the sides, for reasons that will presently appear, by l_1, a_1, m_1', and c_1; the acute angle by β_1; and l_1, c_1 contain this angle β_1.

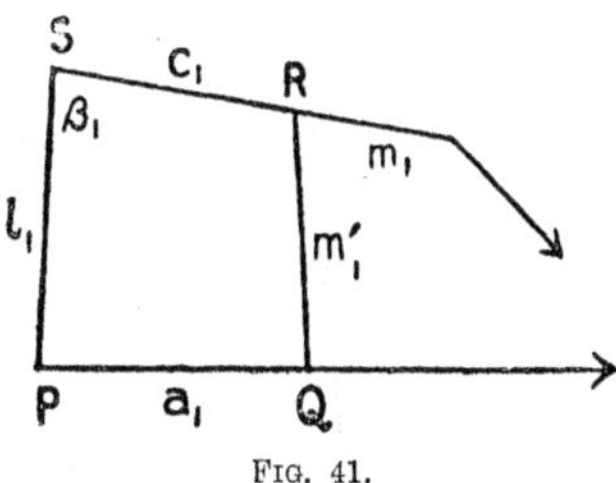

FIG. 41.

Produce c_1 through R a distance m_1, and draw the perpendicular at the end of that segment. Since $\Pi(m_1) + \Pi(m_1') = \frac{\pi}{2}$, if the parallel through R to PQ is supposed drawn, it follows that this perpendicular is parallel to PQ (Fig. 41).

It follows that $\lambda_1 + \Pi(c_1 + m_1) = \beta_1$, ...(I.)

and correspondingly $\gamma_1 + \Pi(l_1 + a'_1) = \beta_1$. ....(I′.)

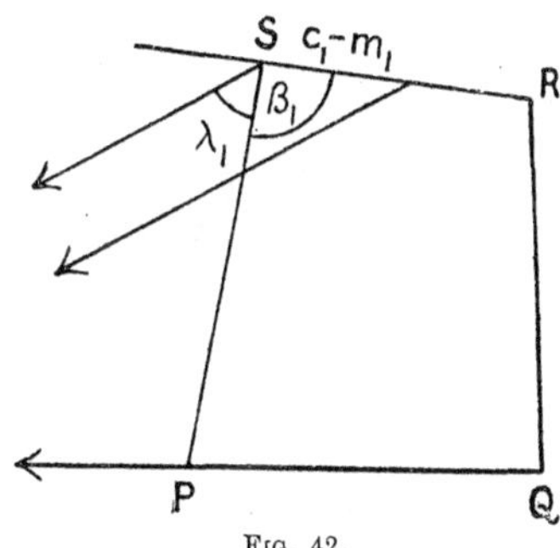

FIG. 42.

From RS cut off the segment m_1; then it is obvious from Fig. 42 that

$\lambda_1 + \beta_1 = \Pi(c_1 - m_1)$, ...(II.)

and correspondingly $\gamma_1 + \beta_1 = \Pi(l_1 - a_1')$. ....(II′.)

Finally, from QP cut off the segment m_1, and from PS produced the segment b_1, and raise the perpendiculars at the ends of these lines (Fig. 43).

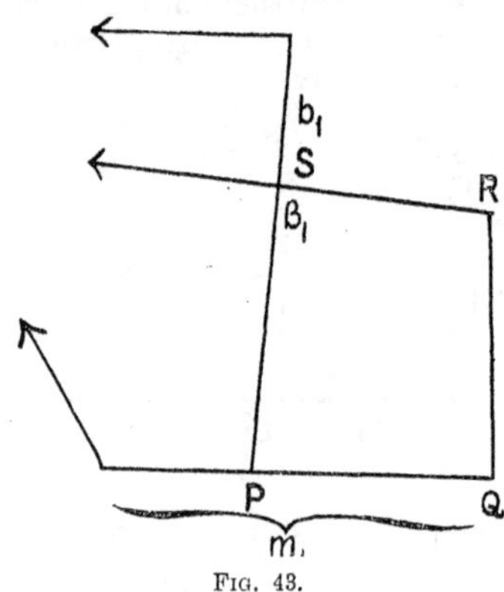

FIG. 43.

It follows that

$$\Pi(l_1 + b_1) + \Pi(m_1 - a_1) = \frac{\pi}{2}, \quad \text{(III.)}$$

and correspondingly

$$\Pi(c_1 + b_1) + \Pi(a_1' - m_1') = \frac{\pi}{2}. \quad \text{(III'.)}$$

III. We are now able to establish the correspondence between the two figures.

A right-angled triangle is fully determined when we know c and μ; a quadrilateral of this nature, when we know c_1 and m_1'.

Let $$c_1 = c \quad \text{and} \quad \Pi(m_1') = \frac{\pi}{2} - \mu,$$

so that $$m_1 = m.$$

Then it follows from (1′) and (2) that

$$\lambda + \beta = \Pi(c - m),$$
$$-\lambda + \beta = \Pi(c + m),$$

and therefore

$$2\lambda = \Pi(c - m) - \Pi(c + m),$$
$$2\beta = \Pi(c - m) + \Pi(c + m).$$

But from (I.) and (II.) we have

$$\lambda_1 + \beta_1 = \Pi(c_1 - m_1) = \Pi(c - m),$$
$$-\lambda_1 + \beta_1 = \Pi(c_1 + m_1) = \Pi(c + m).$$

Therefore $\lambda_1 = \lambda$ and $\beta_1 = \beta$.

From (III′) and (III.), we now obtain

$$\Pi(m - a) = \frac{\pi}{2} - \Pi(l + b),$$

$$\Pi(m_1 - a_1) = \Pi(m - a_1) = \frac{\pi}{2} - \Pi(l_1 + b_1) = \frac{\pi}{2} - \Pi(l + b).$$

Thus $m - a_1 = m - a,$

and $a_1 = a.$

Therefore we have obtained the important result :

If a, b, c, (λ, μ) *are the five elements of a right-angled triangle, then there exists a quadrilateral with three right angles and one acute angle, in which the sides are* c, m′, a, *and* l, *taken in order, and the acute angle* β *lies between* c *and* l.*

The converse of this theorem also holds.

§ 36. The Closed Series of Associated Right-Angled Triangles.

We have seen that to the right-angled triangle $a, b, c, (\lambda, \mu)$ there corresponds a quadrilateral with three right angles and

---

* This result was given by Lobatschewsky in his earliest work, *On the Principles of Geometry* (cf. §§ 11, 16, Engel's translation, pp. 15 and 25), but his demonstration requires the theorems of the Non-Euclidean Solid Geometry. The proof in the text is due to Liebmann (*Math. Ann.* vol. lxi. p. 185 (1905), and *Nichteuklidische Geometrie*, 2nd ed. § 10), who first established the correspondence between the right-angled triangle and the quadrilateral with three right angles and an acute angle by the aid of Plane Geometry alone.

This is an important development, as the Parallel Constructions depend upon this correspondence, and the Non-Euclidean Plane Geometry and Trigonometry is now self-contained.

Further, as we shall see below (§ 45), the existence of a segment corresponding to any given angle of parallelism can be established without the use of the Principle of Continuity, on which Lobatschewsky's demonstration depends. Therefore, though the existence of p, when $\Pi(p)$ is given, is assumed in the above demonstration, the correspondence between the triangle and quadrilateral is independent of that principle.

an acute angle β, the two sides enclosing the acute angle being c and l, and the other two a and m'.

If we interchange c and l, and m' and a, we obtain the same quadrilateral. It follows that, given the right-angled triangle $a, b, c, (\lambda, \mu)$, there exists another right-angled triangle whose elements are $a_1, b_1, c_1, (\lambda_1, \mu_1)$, where

$$a_1 = m', \ b_1 = b, \ c_1 = l, \ \lambda_1 = \gamma, \ \mu_1 = \frac{\pi}{2} - \alpha.$$

Thus, starting with the right-angled triangle

$$a, \ b, \ c, \ (\lambda, \ \mu), \quad \text{.........................(1)}$$

we obtain a second right-angled triangle whose elements are

$$m', \ b, \ l, \ \left(\gamma, \ \frac{\pi}{2} - \alpha\right). \quad \text{.....................(2)}$$

If we now take the sides and opposite angles of this triangle in the reverse order, *i.e.* write it as the triangle

$$b, \ m', \ l, \ \left(\frac{\pi}{2} - \alpha, \ \gamma\right),$$

we obtain another right-angled triangle with the elements

$$c', \ m', \ a', \ \left(\lambda, \ \frac{\pi}{2} - \beta\right). \quad \text{.................(3)}$$

Writing this as

$$m', \ c', \ a', \ \left(\frac{\pi}{2} - \beta, \ \lambda\right),$$

we obtain another with the elements

$$l', \ c', \ b', \ \left(\frac{\pi}{2} - \alpha, \ \mu\right). \quad \text{...................(4)}$$

From this we obtain in its turn

$$l', \ a, \ m, \ \left(\gamma, \ \frac{\pi}{2} - \beta\right). \quad \text{.....................(5)}$$

Again, from this we have

$$b, \ a, \ c, \ (\mu, \ \lambda), \quad \text{.........................(6)}$$

the last being the original triangle.

The relation between the elements of these triangles can be put in the form of the following rule :

Let a, b, c, $(\lambda = \Pi(l)$, $\mu = \Pi(m))$ *be the sides, hypothenuse, and the angles opposite the sides of a right-angled triangle. Write the letters* a′, l, c, m, b′ *in cyclic order on the sides of a pentagon. The six triangles which form the closed series of associated triangles are obtained, if we write the letters* a_r', l_r, c_r, m_r, b_r' *in the same or reverse order on the sides, starting with any one side, and take the elements with the suffices equal to those on the same sides without the suffices.*

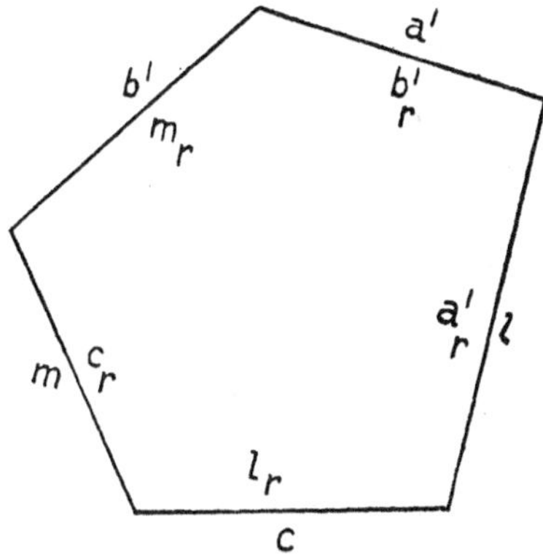

FIG. 44.

E.g. from Fig. 44,

$$a_r' = l, \quad i.e. \quad a_r = l';$$
$$b_r' = a', \quad i.e. \quad b_r = a;$$
$$m_r = b', \quad i.e. \quad \mu_r = \frac{\pi}{2} - \beta;$$
$$c_r = m;$$
$$l_r = c, \quad i.e. \quad \lambda_r = \gamma;$$

giving the triangle (5) above.

These results have an important bearing on certain problems of construction. For example, the problem of constructing a right-angled triangle when the hypothenuse c and a side a are given, with the usual construction involves the assumption as to the intersection of a circle and a straight line ; an assumption which depends upon the Principle of Continuity. But we know that with the triangle $a, b, c, (\lambda, \mu)$ there is associated a triangle $l', a, m, \left(\gamma, \frac{\pi}{2}-\beta\right)$. In this triangle we are given a side a and the adjacent angles $\gamma, \frac{\pi}{2}$; and it can be constructed without that assumption. The associated triangle gives us the second side b of the required triangle. This argument depends upon the theorem proved in §§41-3, that we can always find $\Pi(p)$ when p is given, and that proved in § 45, that given $\Pi(p)$, we can always find p.

§ 37. Proper and Improper Points.

In the Euclidean Plane two lines either intersect or are parallel. If we speak of two parallels as intersecting at "a point at infinity" and assign to every straight line "a point at infinity," so that the plane is completed by the introduction of these *fictitious* or *improper* points, we can assert that any two given straight lines in the plane intersect each other.

On this understanding we have two kinds of pencils of straight lines in the Euclidean Plane : the ordinary pencil whose vertex is a *proper* point, and the set of parallels to any given straight line, a pencil of lines whose vertex is an *improper* point.

Also, in this Non-Euclidean Geometry, there are advantages to be gained by introducing *fictitious* points in the plane. If two coplanar straight lines are given they belong to one of three classes. They may intersect in the ordinary sense ; they may be parallel ; or they may be *not-intersecting lines* with a common perpendicular. Corresponding to the second and third classes we introduce two kinds of *fictitious* or *improper* points. Two parallel lines are said to intersect at *a point at infinity*. And every straight line will have two points at infinity, one corresponding to each direction of parallelism. All the lines parallel to a given line in the same sense will thus have a common point—*a point at infinity* on the line.

Two *not-intersecting* lines have a common perpendicular. The lines are said to intersect in *an ideal point* corresponding to this perpendicular. And all the lines perpendicular to one and the same straight line are said to intersect in *the ideal point* corresponding to this line.

We shall denote an ordinary point—a *proper* point—by the usual capital letter, *e.g.* A. An *improper* point—*a point at infinity*—by the Greek capital letter, *e.g.* Ω; and a point belonging to the other class of improper points—*an ideal point*—by a Greek capital letter with a suffix, to denote the line to which the *ideal point* corresponds, *e.g.* Γ_c.

Thus any two lines in the hyperbolic plane determine a pencil.

(i) If the lines intersect in an ordinary point A, the pencil is the set of lines through the point A in the plane.

(ii) If the lines are parallel and intersect in the improper point Ω, the pencil is the set of lines in the plane parallel to the given lines in the same sense.

(iii) If the two lines are perpendicular to the line c, and thus intersect in the ideal point which we shall denote by Γ_c, the pencil is the set of lines all perpendicular to the line c.

§ **38.** We now enumerate all the cases in which two points in the Hyperbolic Plane fix a straight line and the corresponding constructions:

(1) Two ordinary points A and B. The construction of the line joining any two such points is included in the assumptions of our geometry.

(2) An ordinary point [A] and a point at infinity [Ω]. The line AΩ is constructed by drawing the parallel through A to the line which contains Ω, in the direction corresponding to Ω. This construction is given below in §§ 41-3.

(3) An ordinary point [A] and an ideal point [Γ_c]. This line is constructed by drawing the perpendicular from A to the representative line c of the ideal point.

(4) Two points at infinity [Ω, Ω']. The line $\Omega\Omega'$ is the common parallel to the two given lines on which Ω, Ω' lie. These lines are not parallel to each other or Ω and Ω' would be the same point. The construction of this line is given below in § 44.

(5) An ideal point [Γ_c] and a point at infinity [Ω] not lying on the representative line c of the ideal point. The line $\Gamma_c\Omega$ is the line which is parallel to the direction given by Ω and perpendicular to the representative line c of the ideal point. The construction of this line is given below in § 45.

(6) Two ideal points $[\Gamma_c, \Gamma'_{c'}]$, when the lines c and c' do not intersect and are not parallel. The line $\Gamma_c\Gamma'_{c'}$ is the common perpendicular to the two not-intersecting lines c and c'. The construction of this line was given in § 32.

The pairs of points which do not determine a line are as follows:

(i) An ideal point and a point at infinity lying on the representative line of the ideal point.

(ii) Two ideal points, whose representative lines are parallel or meet in an ordinary point.*

§ 39. With this notation the theorems as to the concurrence of the lines bisecting the sides of a triangle at right angles, the lines bisecting the angles of a triangle, the perpendiculars from the angular points to the opposite sides, which hold in the Euclidean Geometry, will be found also to be true in this Non-Euclidean Geometry. Lines will be said to intersect in the sense of §§ 37, 38. Also, in speaking of triangles, it is not always necessary that they should have ordinary points for their angular points. The figure of § 26 is a triangle with one angular point at an improper point—a point at infinity. It will be seen that a number of the theorems of that section are analogous to familiar theorems for ordinary triangles.

With regard to the concurrence of lines in the triangle we shall only take one case—the perpendiculars through the middle points of the sides.

The perpendiculars to the sides of a triangle at their middle points are concurrent.

Let ABC be the triangle and D, E, F the middle points of the sides opposite A, B and C.

Case (i) If the perpendiculars at the middle points of two of the sides intersect in an ordinary point, the third perpendicular must also pass through this point. The proof depends on the congruence theorems as in the Euclidean case.

---

* In the foundation of Projective Geometry independent of the Parallel Postulate, this difficulty is overcome by the introduction of new entities, called *improper* lines, and *ideal* lines, to distinguish them from the ordinary or *proper* lines. Cf. Bonola, *loc. cit.* English translation, App. IV.

Case (ii) Let the perpendiculars at D and E be not-intersecting lines, and let D′E′ be the line perpendicular to both.

From A, B, and C draw AA′, BB′, and CC′ perpendicular to D′E′.

Then it is not difficult to show from congruent triangles that

$$AA' = CC' \text{ and } BB' = CC'.$$

Thus $AA' = BB'$.

Let F′ be the middle point of A′B′.

From § 28 it follows that FF′ is perpendicular to AB and A′B′.

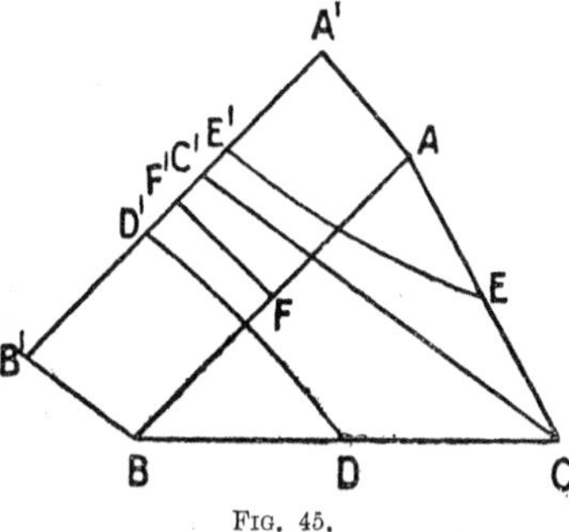

Fig. 45.

Therefore, in this case the three perpendicular bisectors of the sides meet in *an ideal point.*

Case (iii) There remains the case when the lines through D and E perpendicular to the sides are parallel. It follows from Cases (i) and (ii) that the perpendicular to the third side through F cannot intersect the other perpendiculars either in an ordinary point, or in an ideal point. It must therefore be parallel to these two lines in the same sense; or it must be parallel to the first in one sense and to the other in the opposite sense.

The second alternative we shall show to be impossible; so the first necessarily will be true.

When the angular points of a triangle are all at infinity (Ω', Ω'', Ω''') a straight line cannot cut all three sides. For if it cuts two of them at P and Q, say, PQ produced must be one of the rays through Q which does not intersect the other side. (Cf. Fig. 46.)

But if BC is the greatest side of the triangle, the angle at A is the greatest angle.

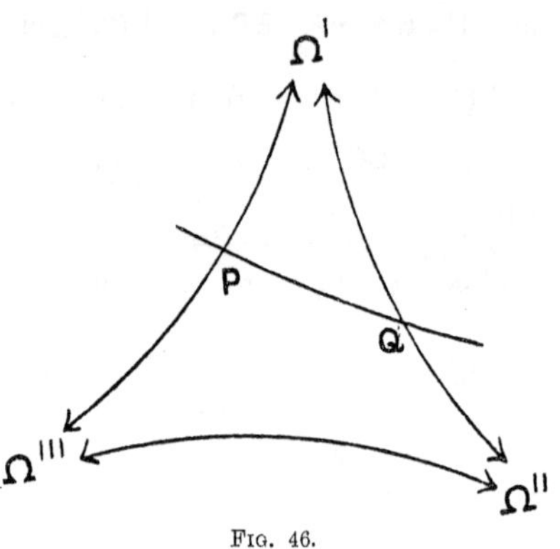

FIG. 46.

If, then, we make ∠CAP = ∠ACB, AP produced must cut BC. (Fig. 47.)

Let it cut it at Q.

Then EQ is perpendicular to AC.

A similar argument applies to the perpendicular through F.

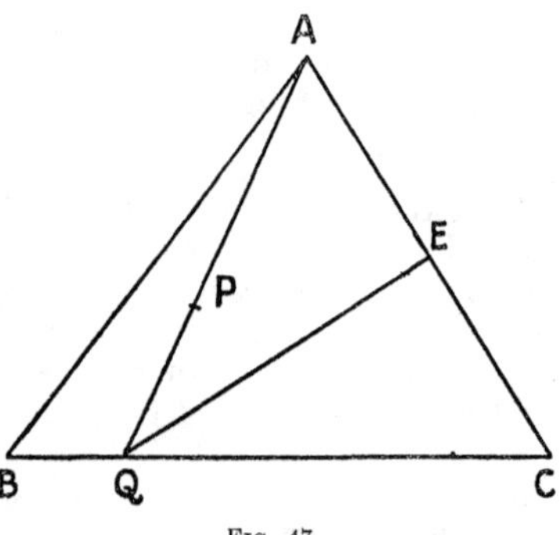

FIG. 47.

Therefore the perpendiculars at E and F both intersect BC.

It follows that the three perpendiculars cannot form a triangle whose angular points are all at infinity.

Therefore they are parallel to one another in the same sense and intersect in an improper point—a point at infinity.

If we take these three cases together, it will be seen that the theorem is established.

§ 40. The Parallel Constructions.

In Hilbert's Parallel Axiom the assumption is made that from any point outside any straight line two parallels can always be drawn to the line. In other words, it is assumed that to any segment p there corresponds an angle of parallelism $\Pi(p)$.

The fundamental problems of construction with regard to parallels are the following:

1. To draw the parallel to a given straight line from a given point towards one end.

2. To draw a straight line which shall be parallel to one given straight line, and perpendicular to another given straight line which intersects the former.

In other words:

1. Given p, to find $\Pi(p)$.

2. Given $\Pi(p)$, to find p.

For both of these problems Bolyai gave solutions; and one was discussed by Lobatschewsky. In both cases the argument, in one form or other, makes use of the Principle of Continuity.

In the treatment followed in this book the Hyperbolic Geometry is being built up independently of the Principle of Continuity. For that reason neither Bolyai's argument (Appendix, §§ 34, 35), nor Lobatschewsky's discussion * of the second problem, will be inserted.

§ 41. To draw the Parallel to a given Line from a Point outside it. Bolyai's Classical Construction (Appendix, § 34).

To draw the parallel to the straight line AN *from a given point* D, Bolyai proceeds as follows:

Draw the perpendiculars DB and EA to AN (Fig. 48), and the perpendicular DE to the line AE.

* Cf. Lobatschewsky, *Geometrische Untersuchungen zur Theorie der Parallelinien*, § 23 (Halsted's translation, p. 135). Also *New Principles of Geometry*, § 102 (Engel's translation).

The angle EDB of the quadrilateral ABDE, in which three angles are right angles, is a right angle, or an acute angle, according as ED is equal to or greater than AB (cf. § 29).

With centre A describe a circle whose radius is equal to ED.

It will intersect DB at a point C, coincident with B, or between B and D.

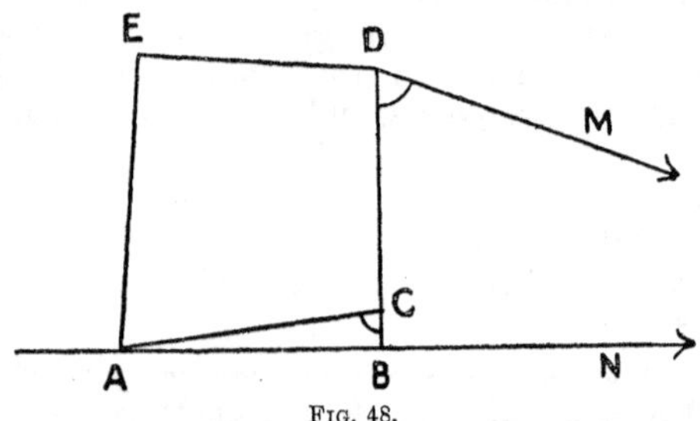

FIG. 48.

The angle which the line AC makes with DB is the angle of parallelism corresponding to the segment BD.

Therefore a parallel to AN can be drawn by making the angle BDM equal to the angle ACB.

Bolyai's proof is omitted for the reasons named above; but it should be remarked that his construction holds both for the Euclidean and Non-Euclidean Geometries; in his language it belongs to the Absolute Science of Space.

§ 42. The correspondence which we have established in § 35 between the right-angled triangle and the quadrilateral with three right angles and one acute angle, leads at once to Bolyai's construction.

We have seen that, *to the right-angled triangle* a, b, c, (λ, μ), *there corresponds a quadrilateral with three right angles and an acute angle* β, *the sides containing the acute angle being* c *and* l, *and the other two,* a *and* m′.

Therefore we can place the right-angled triangle in the quadrilateral, so that the side a of the triangle coincides with the side a of the quadrilateral, and the side b of the triangle lies along the side l of the quadrilateral. Then the hypothenuse of the triangle will be parallel to the side c of the quadrilateral, since it makes an angle $\frac{\pi}{2} - \mu$ with m'.

§ 43. Second Proof of Bolyai's Parallel Construction.

The following proof of the validity of Bolyai's construction is due to Liebmann:* it will be seen that it depends (1) on Theorem (2) of § 4, regarding the locus of the middle points of the segments AA′, BB′, etc., joining a set of points, A, B, C, ..., A′, B′, C′, ..., on two straight lines, such that AB = A′B′, BC = B′C′, etc.; and (2) on the concurrence of the perpendicular bisectors of the sides of a triangle (cf. § 39).

Let A be the given point, and AF the perpendicular from A to the given line.

It is required to draw from A the parallel to the ray FΩ.

Let us suppose the parallel AΩ drawn.

From AΩ and FΩ cut off equal segments AS and FD, and join SD.

Let M and M′ be the middle points of AF and SD.

From § 4 we know that the line MM′ is parallel to AΩ and FΩ.

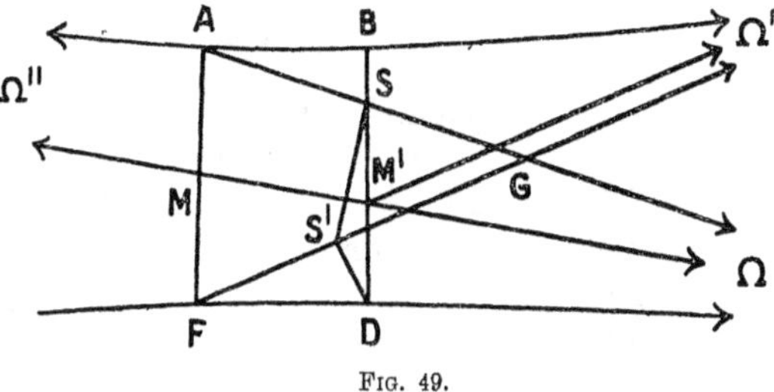

Fig. 49.

Draw the line Ω″AΩ′ through A perpendicular to AF, and produce M′M through the point M.

Then it is clear that the ray M′M is parallel to the line AΩ″.

Draw from F the parallel FΩ′ to AΩ′, and let it intersect AΩ in G.

From FΩ′ cut off FS′ equal to AS. Join SS′ and S′D.

The line GM bisects SS′ at right angles, and is perpendicular to the line ΩΩ′.

Also the perpendicular bisector of DS′ bisects the angle DFS′, and is perpendicular to ΩΩ′.

---

* *Ber. d. k. sächs. Ges. d. Wiss. Math. Phys. Klasse*, vol. lxii. p. 35 (1910); also *Nichteuklidische Geometrie* (2nd ed.), p. 35.

These two bisectors have therefore an ideal point in common, and the perpendicular bisector of SD must pass through the same ideal point (cf. § 39); *i.e.* it must also be perpendicular to $\Omega\Omega'$.

Suppose the parallel $M'\Omega'$ drawn through M' to $A\Omega'$.

The bisector of the angle $\Omega' M' \Omega$ is perpendicular to $\Omega\Omega'$, and therefore to SD.

It follows that $M'S$ bisects the angle $\Omega'' M' \Omega'$.

But $M'\Omega''$ and $M'\Omega'$ are the parallels from M' to $\Omega'' A \Omega'$.

Therefore $M'S$ is perpendicular to $\Omega'' A \Omega'$.

And AS was made equal to FD in our construction.

The result to which we are brought can be put in the following words: Let the perpendicular AF be drawn from the point A to the given line a ($F\Omega$), and let the perpendicular $A\Omega'$ be drawn at A to AF. From any point D on the ray $F\Omega$ drop the perpendicular DB to $A\Omega'$. This line DB cuts off from the parallel $A\Omega$ a length equal to FD.

The parallel construction follows immediately. We need only describe the arc of a circle of radius FD with A as centre. The parallel $A\Omega$ is got by joining A to the point at which this arc cuts DB.

The existence of the parallel, given by Hilbert's Axiom, allows us to state that the arc will cut the line once between B and D, without invoking the Principle of Continuity.*

§ 44. Construction of a Common Parallel to two given Intersecting Straight Lines.†

Let $O\Omega$ and $O\Omega'$ be the two rays a and b meeting at O and containing an angle less than two right angles.

From these rays cut off any two equal segments OA and OB.

From A draw the parallel $A\Omega'$ to the ray $O\Omega'$, and from B the parallel $B\Omega$ to the ray $O\Omega$.

Bisect the angles $\Omega A \Omega'$ and $\Omega B \Omega'$ by the rays a' and b'.

By § 26 (4), we know that

$$\angle OA\Omega' = \angle OB\Omega.$$

* In Euclid's *Elements* the fundamental problems of construction of Book I. can be solved without the use of Postulate 3: "To describe a circle with any centre and distance." To draw the parallel from a given point to a given line can be reduced to one of the problems of § 3. On the other hand, in the Hyperbolic Geometry, the parallel-construction requires this postulate as to the possibility of drawing a circle.

† Cf. Hilbert, *loc. cit.* p. 163.

It follows that $\angle \Omega A \Omega' = \angle \Omega B \Omega'$,

$$\angle \Omega AE = \angle \Omega' BF = \angle \Omega BF.$$

We shall now show that the lines a' and b' neither intersect, nor are parallel.

If possible, let them intersect at M.

The triangle AOB is isosceles, and $\angle OAB = \angle OBA$.

Therefore $\angle BAM = \angle ABM$, and $AM = BM$.

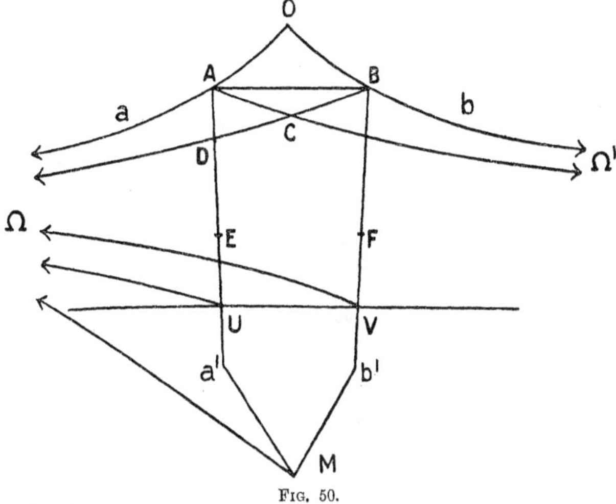

Fig. 50.

Through M draw the parallel $M\Omega$ to $A\Omega$ and $B\Omega$.

Then, since $AM = BM$ and $\angle MA\Omega = \angle MB\Omega$, by § 26 (4), we must have

$$\angle AM\Omega = \angle BM\Omega,$$

which is absurd.

The lines AE and BF therefore do not intersect at an ordinary point, and this proof applies also to the lines produced through A and B.

Next, let us suppose that they are parallel.

Since the ray a' lies in the region $BA\Omega$, it must intersect $B\Omega$.

Let it cut that line at D.

Then we have $\angle \Omega AE = \angle DBF$, and $\angle AD\Omega = \angle BDE$.

Also we are supposing DE and BF parallel, and we have $A\Omega$ and $D\Omega$ parallel.

It follows from § 26 (6) that AD = DB.

Therefore we have ∠ DAB = ∠ DBA.

But ∠ BAC = ∠ ABC.

Therefore we have ∠ DAB = ∠ CAB, which is absurd.

Thus, the rays AE and AF cannot be parallel.

Similarly the rays EA, FB produced through A and B cannot be parallel.

We have now shown that the lines a' and b' neither intersect nor are parallel.

They must, therefore, have a common perpendicular (§ 32).

We shall now show that this common perpendicular is parallel to both OΩ and OΩ'.

Let it cut the lines AE and BF at U and V.

Then AU = BV, by § 29.

If VU is not parallel to AΩ, draw through U the ray UΩ parallel to AΩ, and through V the ray VΩ parallel to AΩ.

Then, by § 26 (4), ∠ AUΩ = ∠ BVΩ.

Also the angles AUV and BVU are right angles, so the exterior angle at U would be equal to the interior and opposite angle ΩVU, which is impossible (§ 26 (3)).

Thus we have shown that the ray VU is parallel to OΩ.

The same argument applies to the ray UV and OΩ'.

Therefore we have proved that there is a common parallel to the two given intersecting rays, and we have shown how to construct it.

COROLLARY. *A common parallel can be drawn to any two given coplanar lines.*

If the given lines intersect when produced, the previous proof applies.

If they do not intersect, take any point A on the line (i) and draw a parallel from A to the line (ii).

We can now draw a common parallel to the two rays through A, and by § 25 this line will also be parallel to the two given lines.

§ 45. Construction of the Straight Line which is perpendicular to one of two Straight Lines containing an Acute Angle, and parallel to the other.

Let a(OA) and b(OB) be the two rays containing an acute angle.

At O make $\angle AOB' = \angle AOB$, and denote the ray OB′ by b'.

The common parallel to the rays b and b' will be perpendicular to OA. (Cf. § 22.)

We have thus solved the second fundamental problem of parallels. *To a given angle of parallelism to find the corresponding segment.* In other words, given $\Pi(p)$ to find p.

Incidentally we have also shown that to any acute angle $\Pi(p)$, however small, or however near a right angle, there corresponds a segment p.

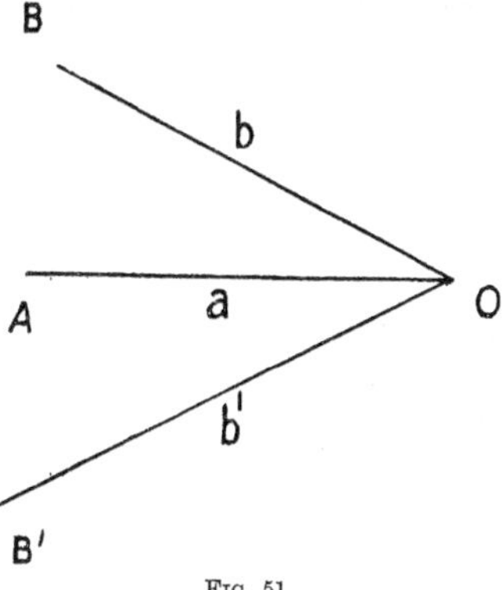

Fig. 51.

Corollary. *If two coplanar lines are not-intersecting lines, we can still draw a line parallel to one and perpendicular to the other.*

We need only take a point on the line (i), and draw from it a ray parallel to the line (ii). The line perpendicular to (i) and parallel to the ray just drawn will be parallel to the line (ii).

§ 46. Corresponding Points on two Straight Lines.

P *and* Q *are said to be corresponding points on two straight lines when the segment* PQ *makes equal angles with the two lines on the same side.*

If the lines intersect at an ordinary point O, and P is any point upon one of them, we need only take OQ = OP, and the point Q on the second line will correspond to P on the first.

Obviously there is only one point on the second ray corresponding to the point P on the first; and if R is the point corresponding to Q on a third ray through O, then P and R are corresponding points.

Also the locus of the points on the rays of a pencil, whose vertex is an ordinary point O, which correspond to a given point P on one of the rays, is the circle with centre O and radius OP.

§ 47. We proceed to the case when the lines are parallel and thus intersect at an improper point (a point at infinity).

1. *If* (i) *and* (ii) *are any two parallel straight lines, there exists one and only one point on* (ii) *which corresponds to a given point on* (i).

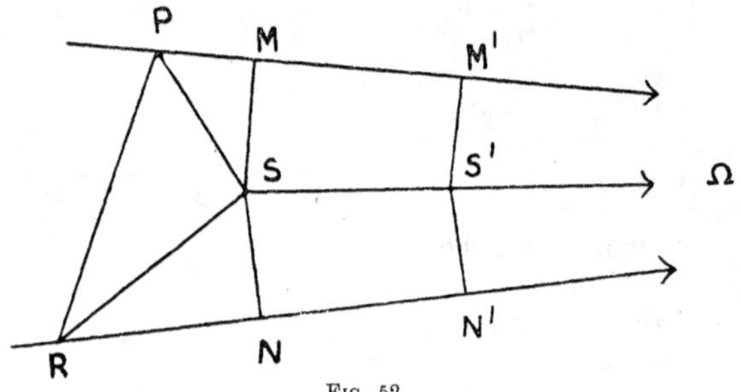

FIG. 52.

Let P be the given point on (i) and take any point R on (ii). Bisect the internal angles at P and R. The bisectors must meet in an ordinary point.

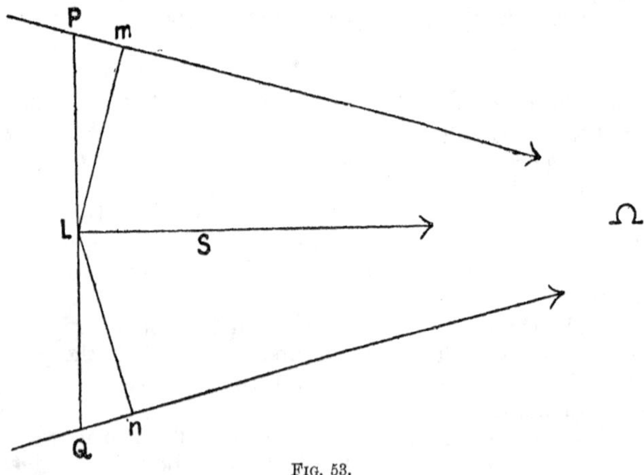

FIG. 53.

Let them meet at S, and from S draw SM and SN perpendicular to (i) and (ii).

Then $SM = SN$.

Through S draw $S\Omega$ parallel to $P\Omega$.

It will also be parallel to $R\Omega$, and it will bisect $\angle MSN$, since there is only one angle of parallelism for a given distance.

Let S' be any point upon the parallel through S to (i) and (ii).

From S' draw $S'M'$ and $S'N'$ perpendicular to these lines.

By congruence theorems, it is easy to show that $S'M' = S'N'$, and that $S'\Omega$ bisects $\angle M'S'N'$.

From P draw PL perpendicular to $S\Omega$, and from L draw Lm and Ln perpendicular to (i) and (ii). (Cf. Fig. 53.)

Cut off $nQ = mP$ on the opposite side of n from Ω, and join LQ.

Then it follows that PLQ is a straight line, and that Q corresponds to P.

It is easy to show that there can only be one point on the second line corresponding to P on the first.

2. *If* P *and* Q *are corresponding points on the lines* (i) *and* (ii), *and* Q *and* R *corresponding points on the lines* (ii) *and* (iii), *the three lines being parallel to each other, then* P, Q, *and* R *cannot be in the same straight line.*

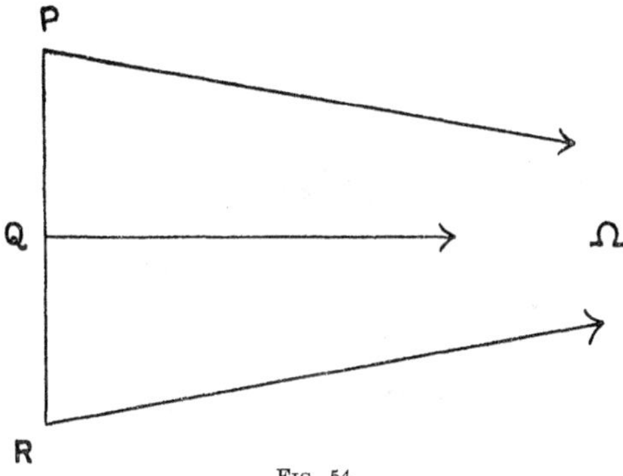

Fig. 54.

If possible, let PQR be a straight line.

By the definition of corresponding points, we have

$$\angle \Omega PQ = \angle \Omega QP,$$

$$\angle \Omega QR = \angle \Omega RQ.$$

Therefore $\angle \Omega PR + \angle \Omega RP =$ two right angles, which is impossible, since PR would make equal alternate angles with $P\Omega$ and $R\Omega$, and these two parallels would have a common perpendicular.

3. *If* P *corresponds to* Q *on the parallels* (i) *and* (ii), *and* Q *to* R *on the parallels* (ii) *and* (iii), *then* P *corresponds to* R *on the parallels* (i) *and* (iii).

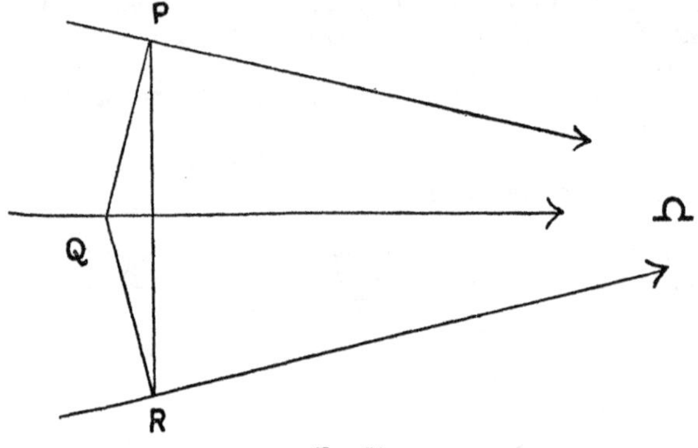

FIG. 55.

This follows from the concurrence of the perpendicular bisectors of the sides of a triangle (§ 39).

The perpendicular bisector of PQ is parallel to the given lines; the same holds of the perpendicular bisector of QR.

It follows that the line bisecting PR at right angles is parallel to the other two bisectors, and to (i) and (iii).

Therefore P and R correspond.

§ 48. The Limiting-Curve or Horocycle.*

We now come to one of the most important curves in the Hyperbolic Geometry.

The locus of the corresponding points on a pencil of parallel lines is a curve called the Limiting-Curve or Horocycle.

It is clear that this is the circle of infinite radius, and from § 47 (2) it follows that it is not a straight line.

* Lobatschewsky uses the terms *grenzkreis*, *courbe-limite*, and *horicycle*; Bolyai speaks of the *linea*-L.

Let P *and* P′ *be any two different points upon the same ray of a pencil of parallel lines; the Limiting-Curve through* P *is congruent with the Limiting-Curve through* P′.

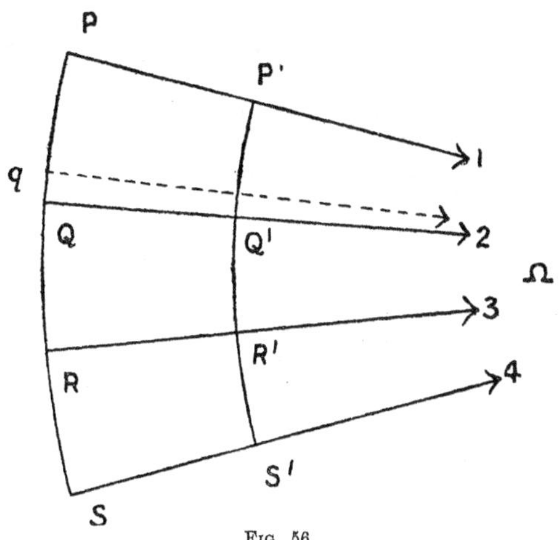

FIG. 56.

We must first explain what we mean by two Limiting-Curves being congruent.

We suppose a set of points obtained on the Limiting-Curve which starts at P′; *e.g.* P′, Q′, R′, S′, etc., on any set of lines 1, 2, 3, 4, ..., of the pencil.

We shall show that a set of points P, q, r, s, etc., exists on the Limiting-Curve through P, such that the segments Pq, P′Q′ are equal, the segments qr, Q′R′ are equal, etc., and these related linear segments make equal angles with the lines of the pencil which they respectively intersect.

To prove this, take the segment P′Q′.

At P make $\angle \Omega \text{P}p = \angle \Omega \text{P}'\text{Q}'$, and take $\text{P}q = \text{P}'\text{Q}'$.

From q draw the ray parallel to PΩ.

Then, by § 26 (4), we know that $\angle \text{P}q\Omega = \angle \text{P}'\text{Q}'\Omega$.

But P′ and Q′ are corresponding points.

Therefore P and q are corresponding points.

Proceeding now from Q′ and q respectively, we find a point r on the Limiting-Curve through P, such that the segments qr and Q′R′ are equal, while qr makes the same angles with the rays passing through its ends, as Q′R′ does with the rays through its ends.

We have thus shown that between the two Limiting-Curves there is a one-one correspondence of the nature stated, and in this case we say that the two curves are congruent.

Further, it is clear that it is immaterial at which line of the pencil we begin our Limiting-Curve.

It is convenient to speak of the point at infinity, through which all the parallel lines of the pencil pass, as the *centre* of the Limiting-Curve; also to call the lines of the pencil the *axes* of the curve. *Concentric* Limiting-Curves will be Limiting-Curves with the same centre.

We can now state the following properties of these curves:

(*a*) The Limiting-Curve in the Hyperbolic Geometry corresponds to the circle with infinite radius in the Euclidean Geometry.

(*b*) Any two Limiting-Curves are congruent with each other.

(*c*) In one and the same Limiting-Curve, or in any two Limiting-Curves, equal chords subtend equal arcs, and equal arcs subtend equal chords.

(*d*) The Limiting-Curve cuts all its axes at right angles, and its curvature is the same at all its points.

§ 49. The Equidistant-Curve.

There remains the pencil of lines through an ideal point: the set of lines all perpendicular to the same line.

1. *If two given lines have a common perpendicular, to any point* P *on the one corresponds one and only one point* Q *on the other.*

Let MN be the common perpendicular to the given lines, and P any point on one of them.

From the other line cut off NQ = MP, Q being on the same side of the common perpendicular as P.

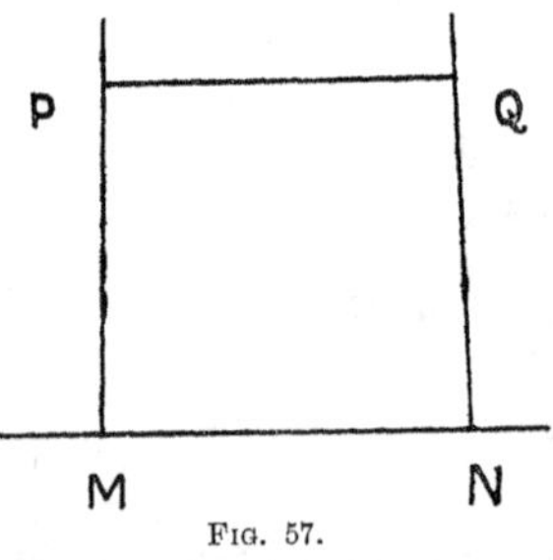

Fig. 57.

Then PMNQ is one of Saccheri's Quadrilaterals, and the angles at P and Q are equal.

Thus Q corresponds to P, and as before there can only be one point on the second line corresponding to a given point on the first.

2. *If the lines* (i), (ii), *and* (iii) *are all perpendicular to the same straight line, then if the point* Q *on* (ii) *corresponds to the point* P *on* (i), *and the point* R *on* (iii) *to the point* Q *on* (ii), *the points* P *and* R *correspond.*

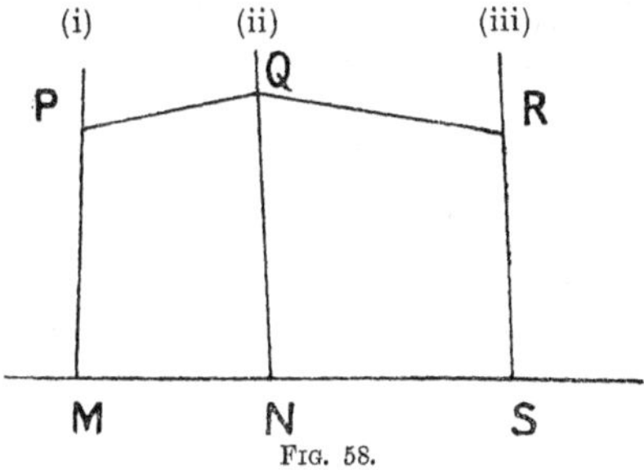

FIG. 58.

Let the common perpendicular meet the lines in M, N, and S.
Then PM = QN and QN = RS.
Therefore PM = RS, and P and R correspond.

3. *The locus of corresponding points upon a pencil of lines whose vertex is an ideal point is called an Equidistant-Curve, from the fact that the points upon the locus are all at the same distance from the line to which all the lines of the pencil are perpendicular. This line is called the base-line of the curve.*

On the Euclidean Plane the Equidistant-Curve is a straight line. On the Hyperbolic Plane *the locus is concave to the common perpendicular.*

This follows at once from the properties of Saccheri's Quadrilateral (cf. § 29). Indeed Saccheri used this curve in his supposed refutation of the Hypothesis of the Acute Angle.

We have thus been led to three curves in this Non-Euclidean Plane Geometry, which may all be regarded as "circles."

(*a*) The locus of corresponding points upon a pencil of lines, whose vertex is an ordinary point, is an ordinary circle, with the vertex as centre and the segment from the vertex to one of the points as radius.

(*b*) The locus of the corresponding points upon a pencil of lines, whose vertex is an improper point—a point at infinity—

is a Limiting-Curve, or Circle of Infinite Radius, with its centre at the vertex of the pencil.

(c) The locus of corresponding points upon a pencil of lines, whose vertex is an improper point—an ideal point—is an Equidistant-Curve, whose base-line is the representative line of the ideal point.

According as the perpendiculars to the sides of a triangle ABC at their middle points meet in an ordinary point, a point at infinity, or an ideal point, the points ABC determine an ordinary circle, a limiting-curve, or an equidistant-curve. (Cf. § 39.)

THE MEASUREMENT OF AREA.

§ 50. Equivalent Polygons.

Two polygons are said to be equivalent when they can be broken up into a finite number of triangles congruent in pairs.

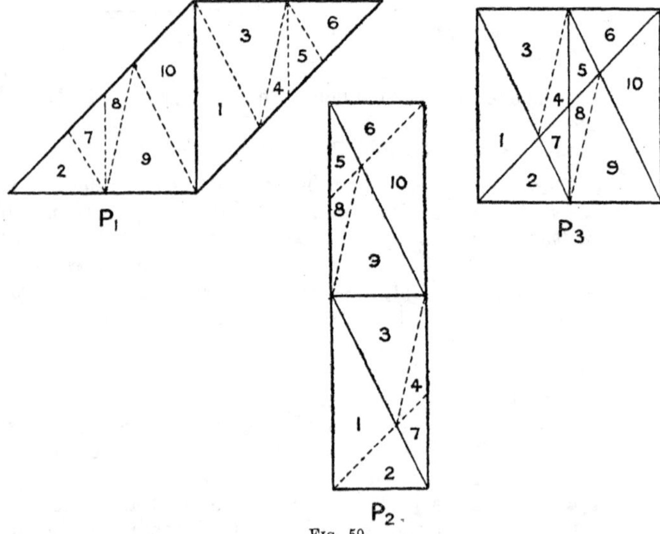

FIG. 59.

With this definition of equivalence, we shall now prove the following theorem :

If two polygons P_1 *and* P_2 *are each equivalent to a third polygon* P_3, *then* P_1 *and* P_2 *are equivalent to each other.*

We are given both for P_1 and P_2 a partition into triangles such that to these two partitions correspond two partitions of P_3, the triangles in the partitions of P_3 being congruent in pairs to the triangles in the partitions of P_1 and P_2.

Consider the two partitions of P_3 simultaneously; in general, every triangle of the one partition will be cut into polygons by the sides of the triangles of the second partition.

We now introduce (cf. Fig. 59) a sufficient number of linear segments, so that each of these polygons shall be cut into triangles.

By this means the two partitions of P_3 are further reduced to the same set of triangles, and this can be associated with a set of triangles in P_1 and P_2 respectively.

Therefore the polygons P_1 and P_2 can be broken up into a finite number of triangles congruent in pairs, and they are equivalent to each other.

§ 51. Equivalent Triangles.

A necessary and sufficient condition that two triangles are equivalent is that they have the same defect. (Cf. § 31.)

The theorem stated above will now be proved. It has to be taken in several steps.

1. *Two triangles with a side of the one equal to a side of the other, and the same defect, are equivalent.*

Consider the triangle ABC, in which E, F are the middle points of the sides CA and AB.

Let the perpendiculars from A, B, and C on EF meet that line at A′, B′, and C′.

Then AA′ = BB′ = CC′, and the quadrilateral BCC′B′ is one of Saccheri's Quadrilaterals, the angles at B′, C′ being right angles, and the sides BB′ and CC′ being equal.

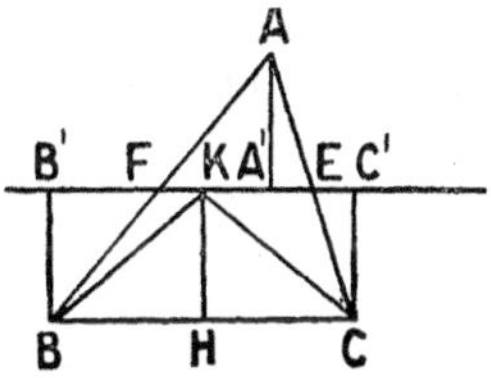

FIG. 60.

Further, the acute angles at B and C in that quadrilateral are each equal to half the sum of the angles of the triangle ABC.

Now, the quadrilateral is made up of the triangles BB′F, CC′E, and the figure BCEF.

Also the triangles BB′F and CC′E are congruent, respectively, with AA′F and AA′E.

Therefore the quadrilateral BB′C′C and the triangle ABC are equivalent.

Next, let $A_1B_1C_1$ be another triangle with its side B_1C_1 equal to BC, and the same defect as the triangle ABC.

For this triangle we get in the same way one of Saccheri's Quadrilaterals, the acute angles at B_1 and C_1 being equal to the acute angles at B and C, while the side B_1C_1 = the side BC.

It is easy to see that these quadrilaterals must be congruent, for if they were not, we should obtain a quadrilateral, in which the sum of the angles would be four right angles, by a process which amounts to placing the one quadrilateral upon the other, so that the common sides coincide.

It follows that the triangles ABC and $A_1B_1C_1$ are equivalent. Thus we have shown that triangles with a side of the one equal to a side of the other, and the same defect, are equivalent.

COROLLARY. The locus of the vertices of triangles on the same base, with equal defects, is an Equidistant-Curve.

2. *Any two triangles with the same defect and a side of the one greater than a side of the other are equivalent.*

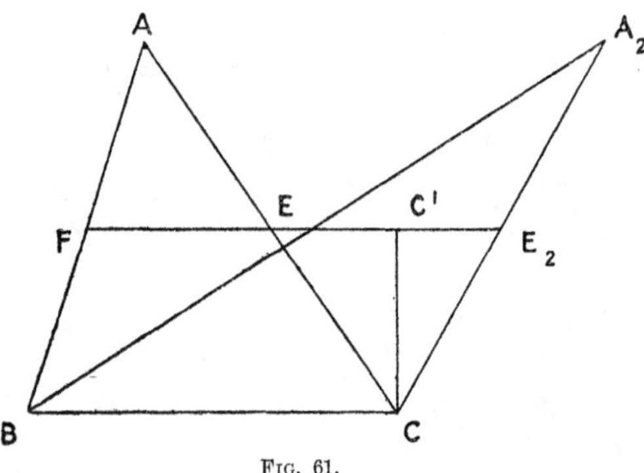

FIG. 61.

Let ABC be the one triangle and $A_1B_1C_1$ the other, and let the side $A_1C_1(b_1)$ be greater than the side AC(b).

Let E, F be the middle points of AC and AB.

From C draw CC′ perpendicular to EF; CC′ cannot be greater than $\frac{1}{2}b$.

Construct the right-angled triangle with a side equal to CC′ and $\frac{1}{2}b_1$ for the hypothenuse.*

Cut off $C'E_2$ equal to the other side of this triangle.

Join CE_2, and produce it to A_2 making $CE_2 = E_2A_2$.

Join A_2B.

Then the triangle A_2BC has a side equal to b_1, and the same defect as the two given triangles.

Also the triangles ABC and A_2BC are equivalent; and the triangles A_2BC and $A_1B_1C_1$, by (1).

Therefore the triangles ABC and $A_1B_1C_1$ are equivalent (§ 50).

3. *Any two triangles, with the same defect, are equivalent.*

For a side of one must be greater than, equal to, or less than, a side of the other.

When it is a case of equality, the triangles are equivalent by (1).

In the other two cases, the same result follows from (2).

4. The converse of this theorem also holds:

Any two equivalent triangles have the same defect.

From the definition of equivalence, the two triangles can be broken up into a finite number of triangles congruent in pairs. But if a triangle is broken up by transversals† into a set of sub-triangles, it is easy to show that the defect of the triangle is equal to the sum of the defects of the triangles in this partition. Further, following Hilbert,‡ it can be shown that any given partition of a triangle into triangles can be obtained by successive division by transversals. It follows that the sum of the defects of the triangles is equal to the defect of the original triangle.

Now the two equivalent triangles can be broken up into a finite number of triangles congruent in pairs. And the defects of congruent triangles are equal.

---

* The construction of the right-angled triangle from a side and the hypothenuse does not involve the Principle of Continuity. The results of § 36 show that this problem can be reduced to that of constructing a right-angled triangle out of a side and the adjacent angle.

† A triangle is said to be broken up by *transversals*, when the partition into triangles is obtained by lines from the angular points to the opposite sides, either in the original triangle or in the additional triangles which have been obtained from the first by division by transversals.

‡ Cf. Hilbert, *loc. cit.* § 20, or Halsted, *Rational Geometry*, p. 87.

Therefore the defects of any two equivalent triangles are equal.

The theorem enunciated at the head of this section is thus established: a necessary and sufficient condition for equivalence of triangles is equal defect.

5. A triangle is said to be equivalent to the sum of two other triangles, when the three triangles can be broken up into a finite number of triangles, such that the triangles in the partition of the first are congruent in pairs with the sum of the triangles in the partitions of the other two.

Now the defect of each triangle is equal to the sum of the defects of the triangles into which it is divided.

It follows that if a triangle is equivalent to the sum of two other triangles, its defect is equal to the sum of their defects.

§ 52. If we regard *area* as a concept associated with a rectilinear figure, just as *length* is with a straight line, it is obvious that *equivalent* figures have *equal area*.* And if, further, we regard the area of a rectilinear figure as a magnitude to which we can ascribe the relations of sum, equality and inequality, greater and less, we obtain at once from the theorems of § 51 the result that the areas of triangles are proportional to their defects. Indeed if we start with any triangle as the triangle of unit area, a triangle which is n times this triangle will have n times its defect.

But closer examination of the argument shows that in this treatment of the question of area various assumptions are made; and the work of some mathematicians of the present day has put the theory of area on a sounder logical basis.† This more exact treatment of the theory of area in the Hyperbolic Plane is simple, and will now be given:

The *measure of area of a triangle* is defined as k^2 multiplied

---

* Hilbert distinguished between *equivalent* polygons, as defined above, and polygons which are *equivalent by completion*. Two polygons are said to be *equivalent by completion*, when it is possible to annex to them *equivalent* polygons, so that the two completed polygons are *equivalent*. If the Postulate of Archimedes is adopted, polygons, which are *equivalent by completion*, are also *equivalent*. Hilbert was able to establish the theory of area on the doctrine of *equivalence by completion* without the aid of the Postulate of Archimedes. *Loc. cit.* Chapter IV.

† Cf. Art. VI. by Amaldi, in Enriques' volume referred to above. Also Finzel, *Die Lehre vom Flächeninhalt in der allgemeinen Geometrie* (Leipzig, 1912).

by its defect, k being a constant depending on the unit triangle, and the unit of angle is chosen so that a right angle has $\frac{\pi}{2}$ for its measure. The number k^2 is introduced to bring the results into agreement with the analytical work in other parts of this book.

It follows from § 51 that

1. If two triangles have the same *measure of area*, they are *equivalent*, and that if two triangles are *equivalent*, they have the same *measure of area*.

2. If a triangle is broken up into a finite number of triangles, the measure of area of the triangle is equal to the sum of the measures of area of the triangles in the partition.

3. If a triangle is equivalent to the sum of two other triangles, the measure of area of this triangle is equal to the sum of the measures of area of the other two triangles.

The measure of area of a polygon is defined to be the sum of the measures of area of the triangles into which it is divided in any given partition.

This sum is independent of the partition which has been chosen. The sum of the defects of the triangles in any partition is equal to $(n-2)$ times two right angles – the sum of the angles of the polygon. This is sometimes called the *Defect of the Polygon*.

With regard to polygons we can now state the following theorems:

1. If two polygons have the same measure of area, they are equivalent. For they are each equivalent to the triangle whose defect is the sum of the defects of the given partitions.

2. If two polygons are equivalent, they have the same measure of area. For they can be broken up into a finite number of triangles congruent in pairs.

3. If a polygon is broken up into a finite number of sub-polygons, the measure of area of the polygon is the same as the sum of the measures of area of the sub-polygons.

4. If a polygon is equivalent to the sum of two other polygons, its measure of area is equal to the sum of the measures of area of these two polygons.

Rectilinear polygons with the same measure of area will be said to have equal area. Thus equivalent polygons have equal area. The area of a polygon will be said to be greater or less than the area of another polygon according as its measure of area is greater or less than the measure of area of the other.

§ 53. In the Euclidean Plane we say that a rectilinear figure contains so many square inches (or sq. ft., etc.), and by considering a curvilinear figure as the limit of a rectilinear figure we obtain a method of measuring curvilinear figures.

In the Hyperbolic Plane there is no such thing as a square inch, or rectangle with equal sides, or any rectangle. To every rectilinear figure there corresponds an equivalent Saccheri's Quadrilateral. To all equivalent rectilinear figures there corresponds one and the same Saccheri's Quadrilateral with a definite acute angle.

This quadrilateral with a given acute angle can be constructed in this geometry immediately. The construction follows from the correspondence established between right-angled triangles and the quadrilateral with three right angles. If the acute angle is β, we obtain the corresponding segment $b\{\beta=\Pi(b)\}$, by the construction of § 45. We draw any right-angled triangle with a side equal to b. The associated quadrilateral has its acute angle equal to β, and the Saccheri's Quadrilateral is obtained by placing alongside it a congruent quadrilateral.

All Saccheri's Quadrilaterals with the same acute angle are equivalent.

Thus it will be seen that there is a fundamental difference between measurement of length and area in the Euclidean and the Hyperbolic Plane.* In the Euclidean, the measures are *relative*. In the Hyperbolic, they are *absolute*. With every linear segment there can be associated a definite angle, namely the angle of parallelism for this segment. With every area, a definite angle can be associated, namely the acute angle of the equivalent Saccheri's Quadrilateral.

---

* Cf. Bonola, *loc. cit.* § 20. Also *supra*, p. 17.

CHAPTER IV.

THE HYPERBOLIC PLANE TRIGONOMETRY.

§ **54.** In this chapter we shall develop the Trigonometry of the Hyperbolic Plane, as in the preceding one we have discussed the Geometry of the Hyperbolic Plane, without introducing the theorems of Solid Geometry into the argument.

The properties of the Limiting-Curve lead to the formulae of Plane Trigonometry, without the use of the Limiting-Surface, as the surface formed by the rotation of a Limiting-Curve about one of its axes is called. The method of Lobatschewsky and Bolyai is founded upon the Geometry upon that Surface.

We begin with some theorems upon Concentric Limiting-Curves.

1. *If* A, B *and* A′, B′ *are the points in which two Concentric Limiting-Curves cut two of their axes, then* AB = A′B′.

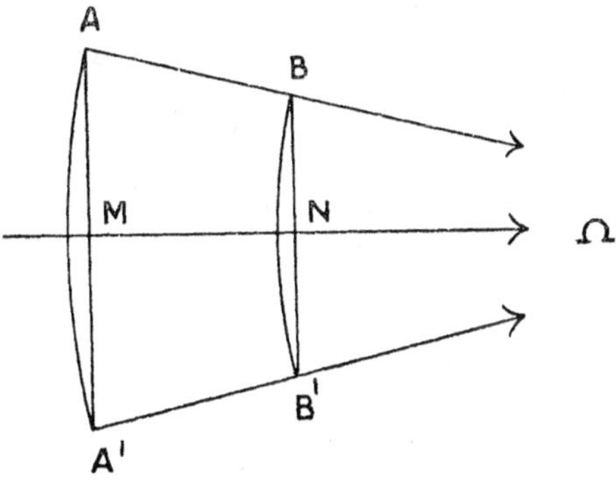

Fig. 62.

Join AA′ and BB′ (Fig. 62).

Through the middle point M of the chord AA′ draw MΩ parallel to the rays of the pencil.

Then $M\Omega$ is perpendicular to the chord BB', and is symmetrical to the two parallels AB and $A'B'$ (cf. § 26 (4) and § 47).

Therefore it passes through the middle point N of BB'.

Then it follows from the quadrilateral $ABB'A'$ that $AB = A'B'$.

2. *If* A, B *and* A', B' *are the points in which two Concentric Limiting-Curves cut two of their axes, and* P, Q *are the middle points of the arcs* AA' *and* BB', *then* PQ *is a line of the pencil.*

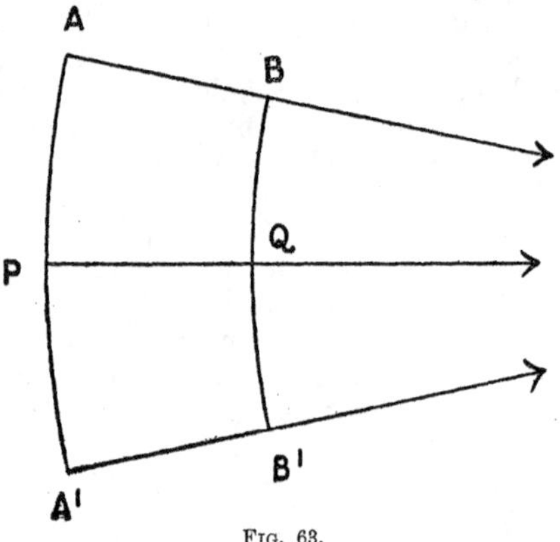

Fig. 63.

Since equal arcs subtend equal chords (cf. § 48), the chords AP and $A'P$ are equal, and the chords BQ and $B'Q$ are equal.

It follows that PQ is the line of symmetry for the two axes AB and $A'B'$, and is parallel to both (cf. § 47).

Corollary. *If the points* $P_1, P_2, P_3, P_4, \ldots$, *divide the arc* AA' *into* n *equal arcs, and the axes through these points are met by the Limiting-Curve* BB' *in* $Q_1, Q_2, Q_3, Q_4, \ldots$, *the points* $Q_1, Q_2, Q_3, Q_4, \ldots$ *divide the arc* BB' *into* n *equal arcs.*

3. *If* A, A', A'', *are three points on a Limiting-Curve, and* B, B', B'', *are the three points in which a Concentric Limiting-Curve is cut by the axes through* A, A', *and* A'', *then*

$$\text{arc } AA' : \text{arc } AA'' = \text{arc } BB' : \text{arc } BB''.$$

First, let the arcs AA' and AA'' be commensurable, and let the one be m times the arc AP and the other n times the arc AP.

Through P draw the line of the pencil. Let it cut the second Limiting-Curve in Q.

Then we know from (2) that the arc BB′ $= m$ times the arc BQ, and that the arc BB″ $= n$ times the arc BQ.

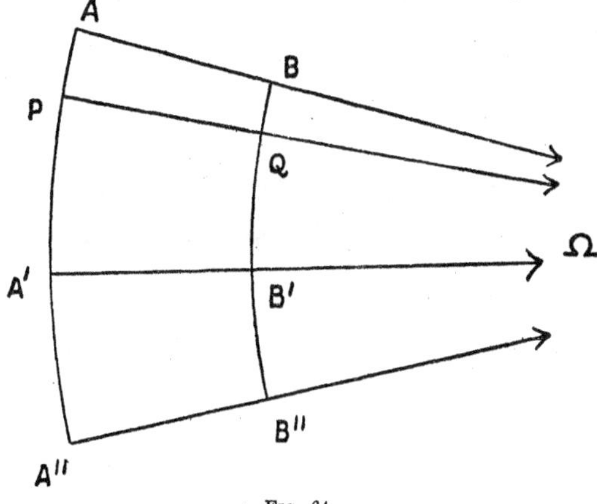

Fig. 64.

Thus the proportion follows.

Secondly, if the arcs are incommensurable, we reach the same conclusion by proceeding to the limit.

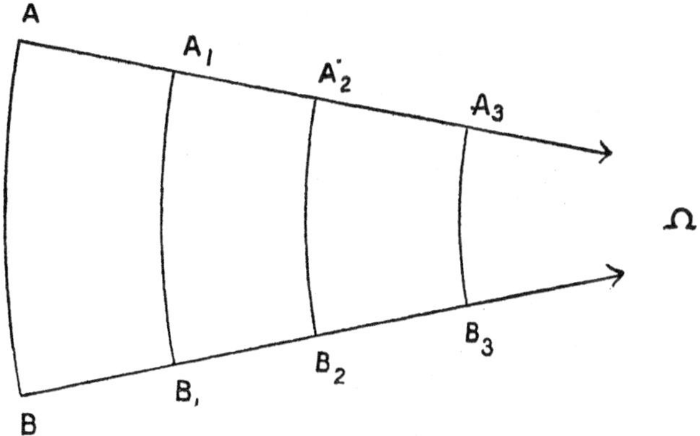

Fig. 65.

§ 55. Let us start with a Limiting-Curve whose centre is Ω, and take any two points A and B upon the curve (Fig. 65).

On the ray $A\Omega$ cut off the equal segments AA_1, A_1A_2, A_2A_3, ... Let the Concentric Limiting-Curves through A_1, A_2, A_3, ..., cut the ray $B\Omega$ in B_1, B_2, B_3, ...

Then we have, by § 54 (1),

$$AA_1 = BB_1 = B_1B_2 = B_2B_3 = \text{etc.}$$

Also, from § 48 and § 54 (3),

$$\text{arc } AB : \text{arc } A_1B_1 = \text{arc } A_1B_1 : \text{arc } A_2B_2 = \text{arc } A_2B_2 : \text{arc } A_3B_3 = \text{etc.}$$

This ratio is greater than unity, and depends only on the length of AA_1.

We may choose the unit segment so that the ratio is equal to e, when $AA_1 = A_1A_2 = A_2A_3 = \ldots =$ the unit segment.

Let the arcs AB, A_1B_1, A_2B_2, etc., be denoted by s, s_1, s_2, etc., when the segment AA_1 is the unit of length.

Then we have

$$s : s_1 = s_1 : s_2 = s_2 : s_3 = \ldots = e.$$

Thus $s_n = se^{-n}$, when n is a positive integer.

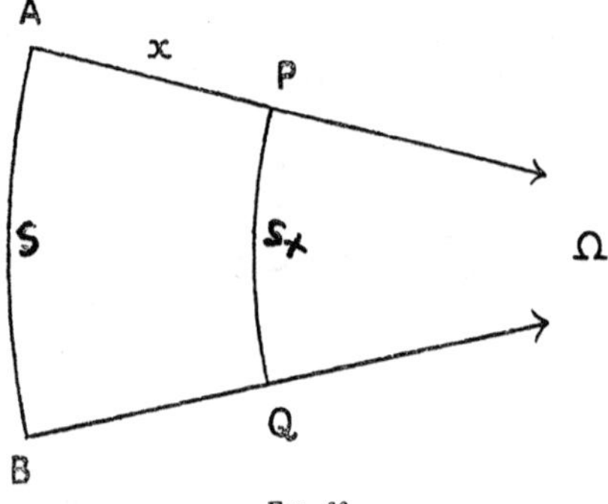

FIG. 66.

It is easy to deduce from this that when the segment AP (Fig. 66) is x units, x being any rational number, and the arc PQ is denoted by s_x, then we have

$$s_x = se^{-x}.$$

We obtain the same result for an irrational number x by proceeding to the limit.

Therefore, with this unit of length we have the following theorem :

If ABDC (Fig. 67) *is a figure bounded by two Concentric Limiting-Curves* AC *and* BD, *and two straight lines* AB *and* CD, *the straight lines being axes of the curves, the lengths* s *and* s_x *of the arcs* AC *and* BD *are connected by the equation*

$$s_x = se^{-x},$$

when the segments AB *and* CD *are* x *units of length, and* AC *is the external curve,* BD *the internal.*

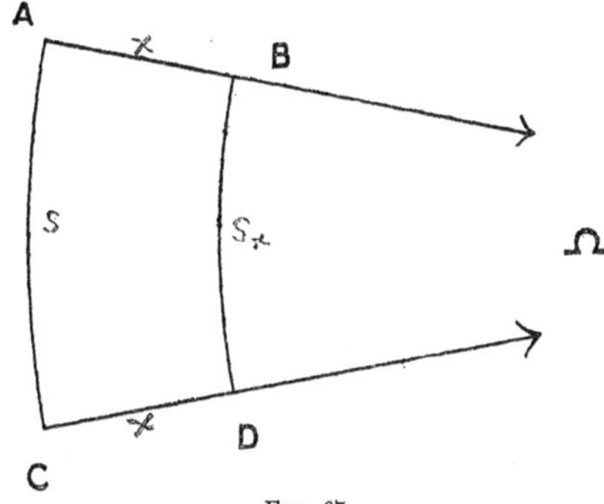

Fig. 67.

If another unit of length had been chosen, so that the ratio of the arc AB (Fig. 65) to the arc A_1B_1 had been $a\ (a > 1)$, when $AA_1 = BB_1 =$ the unit of length, the equation connecting s and s_x would have been

$$s_x = sa^{-x}.$$

Putting $$a = e^{\frac{1}{k}},$$

we have $$s_x = se^{-\frac{x}{k}}.$$

The number k is the parameter of the Hyperbolic Geometry depending upon the unit of length chosen.

§ 56. Since we can find p to satisfy the equation

$$\Pi(p) = \frac{\pi}{4},$$

there is a point Q on the Limiting-Curve through P, such that the tangent at Q is parallel to the axis through P, in the opposite sense to that in which the axis is drawn (Fig. 68).

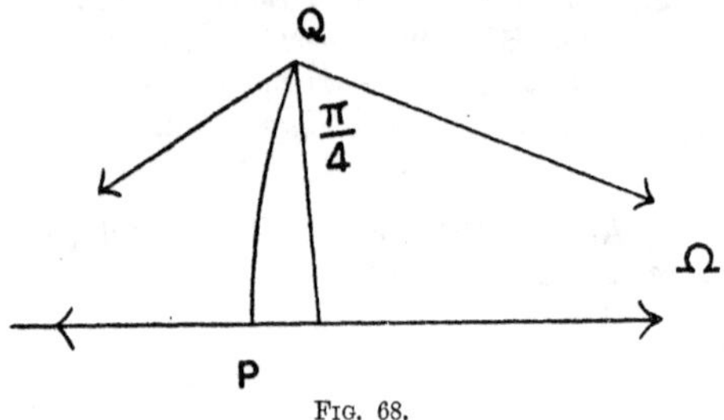

FIG. 68.

We shall for the present denote the length of this arc by S.*

Let B be a point on the Limiting-Curve through A, such that the arc AB is less than S (Fig. 69).

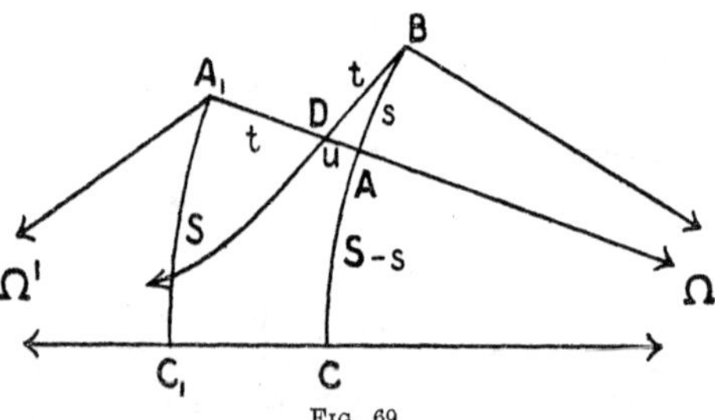

FIG. 69.

It follows that the tangent at B must intersect the axis through A.

Let it cut ΩA in D, and let the segments AD and BD be u and t. It is easy to show that $u < t$.

Produce the arc BA to the point C, such that the arc BC = S.

On ΩD produced take the point A_1, such that $DA_1 = DB = t$.

Then the perpendicular through A_1 to the axis is parallel to BD, and therefore to CΩ′.

Let the Limiting-Curve through A_1 meet CΩ′ in C_1.

Since the tangent at A_1 is parallel to CΩ′, the arc $A_1C_1 = S$.

---

* Cf. p. 119.

It follows from § 55 that

$$\text{arc } A_1C_1 : \text{arc } AC = e^{u+t}.$$

Therefore $$S - s = Se^{-(u+t)}. \qquad (1)$$

Next, produce the arc AB through B to the point P, such that the arc $BP = S$ (Fig. 70).

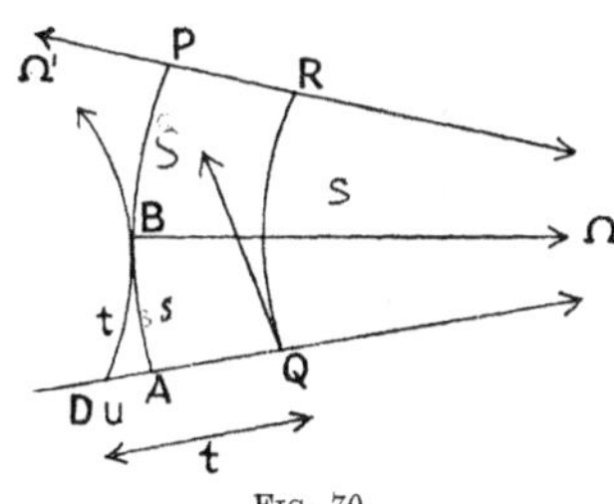

FIG. 70.

Let the tangent at B as before cut the axis through A at D, and let $AD = u$ and $BD = t$.

On AΩ, on the opposite side of A from D, take the point Q, such that $DQ = t$.

Then the perpendicular through Q to the axis is parallel to DB, and, therefore, to PΩ'.

Let the Limiting-Curve through Q cut the axis PΩ in R.

Since the tangent at Q is parallel to the axis through R, arc $QR = S$.

But $AQ = t - u$.

Therefore $$S + s = Se^{t-u}. \qquad (2)$$

From (1) and (2), we have

$$e^u = \cosh t, \qquad (3)$$

and $$s = S \tanh t. \qquad (4)$$

§ 57. The Equation of the Limiting-Curve.

Let Ox and Oy be two lines at right angles, and let P be the point (x, y) on the Limiting-Curve through O, with Ox for axis (Fig. 71).

Draw PM perpendicular to the axis Ox, and let the Concentric Limiting-Curve through M cut the axis through P in N.

Then $OM = PN = x$, $MP = y$.

Let arc $OP = s$, and arc $MN = s'$.

From the construction it follows that $s' < S$.

Now the coordinates of P, x(OM), and y(MP) are, respectively, the u and t of the previous section with reference to the arc s'.

Therefore we have, from § 56 (3),

$$e^x = \cosh y. \quad \text{.........(1)}$$

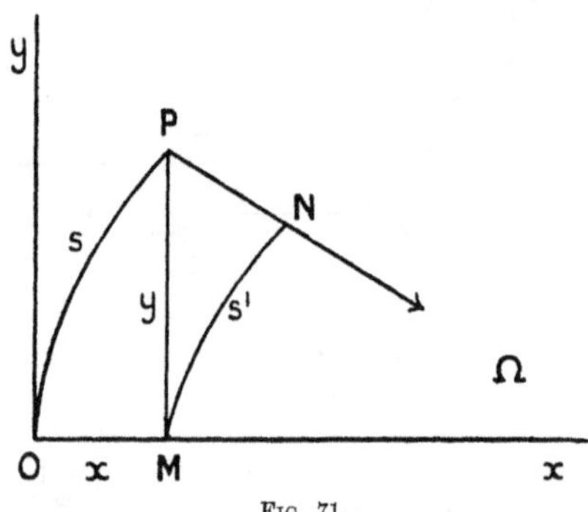

Fig. 71.

This is the equation of the Limiting-Curve through O with its axis coinciding with the axis of x.

Also, we have

$$\begin{aligned} s &= s'e^x \\ &= \mathrm{S}e^x \tanh y, \text{ from § 56 (4)}, \\ &= \mathrm{S} \sinh y. \quad \text{.........(2)} \end{aligned}$$

§ 58. The Hyperbolic Functions of Complementary Segments.

Let Ox and Oy be two lines at right angles, and let the Limiting-Curve through O with axis Ox have the arc OP = S (Fig. 72).

Let A be a point upon Ox, such that OA = x, and let the Limiting-Curve through A be cut by the axis through P in B.

Let arc AB = s.

At A draw the perpendicular to the axis of x. Since it must cut PB, let it intersect it at C.

Produce AC through C to the point D, such that AC = CD.

At D draw DQ perpendicular to CD.

The line DQ must be parallel to CP, since ∠ DCP = ∠ ACB, and CB is parallel to AΩ.

Therefore Oy, CP, and DQ are parallel.

It follows that the segments OA and AD are complementary,

i.e. $$\Pi(\mathsf{OA})+\Pi(\mathsf{AD})=\frac{\pi}{2}.$$

With the usual notation (cf. § 27) we take x' as the complementary segment to x.

Therefore, if $\mathsf{OA}=x, \quad \mathsf{AC}=\dfrac{x'}{2}.$

It follows that $\mathsf{S}e^{-x}=s=\mathsf{S}\tanh\dfrac{x'}{2}.$ (§ 56 (4).)

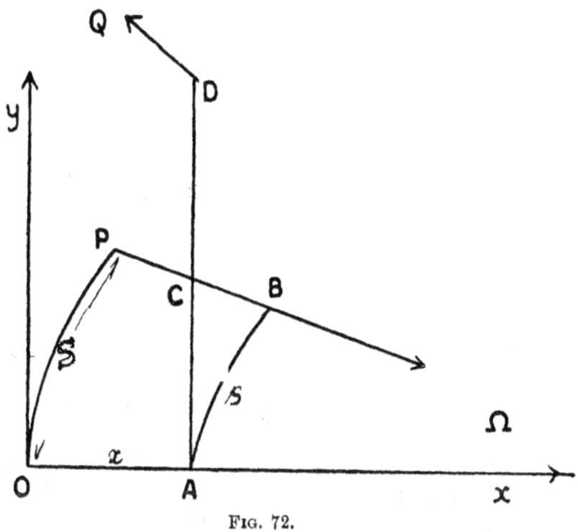

FIG. 72.

Therefore for complementary segments we have

$$e^{-x}=\tanh\frac{x'}{2}.$$

But $\sinh x=\dfrac{e^{x}-e^{-x}}{2}.$

$$\therefore \quad \sinh x=\frac{1}{2}\left(\coth\frac{x'}{2}-\tanh\frac{x'}{2}\right)=\frac{1}{\sinh x'}=\operatorname{cosech} x'.$$

$$\therefore \quad \cosh x=\sqrt{1+\sinh^2 x}=\coth x'.$$

$$\therefore \quad \tanh x=\operatorname{sech} x' \text{ and } \coth x=\cosh x'.$$

Also $\operatorname{sech} x=\tanh x'$ and $\operatorname{cosech} x=\sinh x'$.

§ 59. The Equations connecting the Sides and Angles of a Right-Angled Triangle.

Let ABC be any right-angled triangle, C being the right angle.

Produce the side AC through C, and draw the parallel BΩ through B to AC.

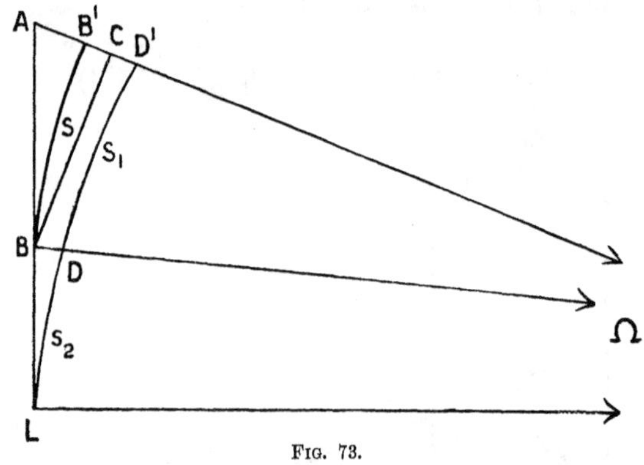

FIG. 73.

Also produce AB through B to L, where AL is the segment l, such that $\lambda = \Pi(l)$. [$\lambda = \angle$ BAC (cf. Fig. 37).]

Through L draw LΩ parallel to BΩ and AC.

Let the Limiting-Curves through B and L, with centre at Ω, meet the axes at B′, D, and D′ (Fig. 73).

Let the arcs BB′, DD′, LD be denoted by s, s_1, s_2, and let the segment BD $= u$.

Then we have

$$\mathrm{S} \sinh a = s = s_1 e^u, \quad [\S\ 57\ (2).]$$

$$s_1 + s_2 = \mathrm{S} \tanh l, \quad [\S\ 56\ (4).]$$

$$s_2 = \mathrm{S} \tanh \mathrm{BL} = \mathrm{S} \tanh (l - c),$$

$$e^u = \cosh \mathrm{BL} = \cosh (l - c). \quad [\S\ 56\ (3).]$$

It follows that

$$\begin{aligned} \sinh a &= \cosh (l - c)\{\tanh l - \tanh (l - c)\} \\ &= \frac{\sinh l \cosh (l - c) - \cosh l \sinh (l - c)}{\cosh l} \\ &= \sinh c / \cosh l. \end{aligned}$$

Thus $$\mathbf{\sinh c = \sinh a \cosh l.} \qquad \text{I.}$$

(Hypothenuse, side, and opposite angle.)

From this formula, connecting the hypothenuse, a side, and the opposite angle of any right-angled triangle, we can obtain the relations between all the other elements, by using the associated triangles of § 36.

We know that, starting with a right-angled triangle in which the elements are

$$a,\ b,\ c,\ (\lambda,\ \mu), \qquad (1)$$

we obtain successively triangles with the elements

$$m',\ b,\ l,\ \left(\gamma,\ \frac{\pi}{2}-\alpha\right), \qquad (2)$$

$$c',\ m',\ a',\ \left(\lambda,\ \frac{\pi}{2}-\beta\right), \qquad (3)$$

$$l',\ c',\ b',\ \left(\frac{\pi}{2}-\alpha,\ \mu\right), \qquad (4)$$

$$l',\ a,\ m,\ \left(\gamma,\ \frac{\pi}{2}-\beta\right) \qquad (5)$$

From the second triangle

$$m',\ b,\ l,\ \left(\gamma,\ \frac{\pi}{2}-\alpha\right),$$

we have
$$\sinh l = \sinh m' \cosh c$$
$$= \frac{1}{\sinh m} \cosh c, \text{ by § 58.}$$

Therefore $$\mathbf{\cosh c = \sinh l \sinh m.} \qquad \text{II.}$$

(Hypothenuse and two angles.)

Also, from the same triangle (by I.),

$$\sinh l = \sinh b \cosh a'$$
$$= \sinh b \coth a.$$

Therefore $$\mathbf{\tanh a = \frac{\sinh b}{\sinh l}.} \qquad \text{III)}$$

(Two sides and an angle.)

Now, since $$\cosh c = \sinh l \sinh m,$$

we have $$\cosh c = \frac{\sinh b}{\tanh a} \times \frac{\sinh a}{\tanh b}.$$

Therefore $\mathbf{\cosh c = \cosh a \cosh b}$. ....IV.

(Hypothenuse and two sides.)

Further, $\cosh a = \sinh l \dfrac{\sinh a}{\sinh b}$ (by III.)

$= \sinh l \dfrac{\cosh m}{\cosh l}$ (by I.).

Therefore $\mathbf{\cosh a = \tanh l \cosh m}$. ....V.

(Side and two angles.)

Applying (IV.) to the triangle

$$c', \; m', \; a', \; \left(\lambda, \; \frac{\pi}{2} - \beta\right),$$

we have $\cosh a' = \cosh c' \cosh m'$,

and this gives $\mathbf{\tanh a = \tanh m \tanh c}$. .. ..VI.

(Hypothenuse, a side, and included angle.)

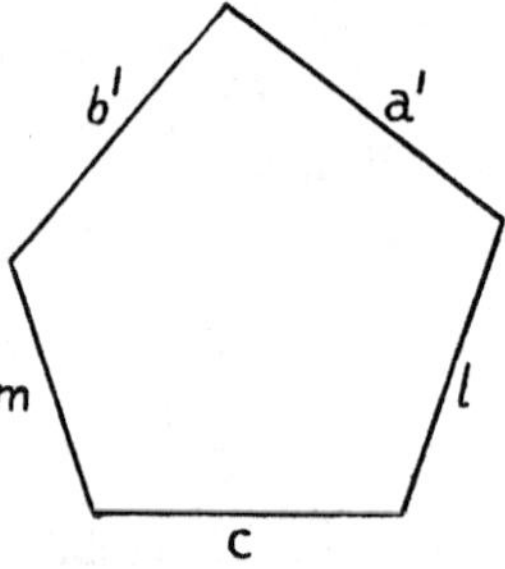

FIG. 74.

These six formulae are all given by a rule similar to Napier's Rules in Spherical Trigonometry:

(i) *Let the letters* a′, l, c, m, b′ *be written one at each of the sides of a pentagon taken in order. Then*

cosh of the middle part = the product of the hyperbolic sines of the adjacent parts

and

cosh of the middle part = the product of the hyperbolic cotangents of the opposite parts.

§ 60. The Equations for an Oblique-Angled Triangle.

In the case of the Oblique-Angled Triangle ABC, the sides opposite the angular points A, B, and C will be denoted by a, b, and c, as usual; but the angles at A, B, and C will be denoted by λ, μ, and ν.

With this notation the distance of parallelism for the angle at A will be l.

We proceed to prove that

I. $\quad \mathbf{\sinh a : \sinh b : \sinh c = sech\, l : sech\, m : sech\, n.}$

This corresponds to the Sine Rule of ordinary Trigonometry.

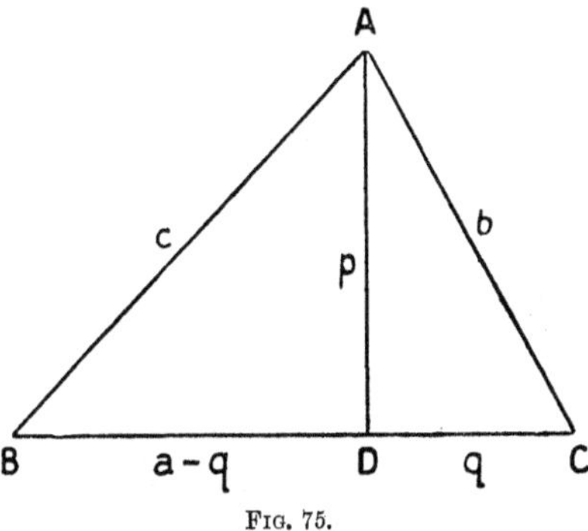

Fig. 75.

Let ABC be all acute angles.

From an angular point, say A, draw the perpendicular AD to the opposite side. We then obtain two right-angled triangles ABD and ACD, as in Fig. 75.

Writing AD $= p$, we have (by § 59, I.)

$$\sinh p = \frac{\sinh c}{\cosh m}, \text{ from the triangle ABD,}$$

and
$$\sinh p = \frac{\sinh b}{\cosh n}, \text{ from the triangle ACD.}$$

Thus we have

$$\sinh b : \sinh c = \operatorname{sech} m : \operatorname{sech} n.$$

Taking another angular point—say B—and proceeding in the same way, we would have

$$\sinh a : \sinh c = \operatorname{sech} l : \operatorname{sech} n.$$

Therefore

$$\sinh a : \sinh b : \sinh c = \operatorname{sech} l : \operatorname{sech} m : \operatorname{sech} n.$$

If one of the angles is obtuse, we obtain the same result, using the notation $\Pi(-x) = \pi - \Pi(x)$.

For the right-angled triangle, the result follows from § 59, I.

II. We shall now prove the theorem corresponding to the Cosine Rule of ordinary Trigonometry.

We take in the first place the case when B and C are acute angles.

From A draw the perpendicular AD to BC.

Let AD $= p$, CD $= q$, and BD $= a - q$ (Fig. 75).

Then, from the triangle ABD we have

$$\cosh c = \cosh(a-q)\cosh p \quad (\S\ 59,\ \text{IV.}),$$

and from the triangle ACD we have

$$\cosh b = \cosh p \cosh q.$$

Also, we have

$$\tanh(a-q) = \tanh c \tanh m \quad (\S\ 59,\ \text{VI.}).$$

Therefore
$$\cosh b = \frac{\cosh c \cosh q}{\cosh(a-q)}$$

$$= \frac{\cosh c(\cosh a \cosh(a-q) - \sinh a \sinh(a-q))}{\cosh(a-q)}$$

$$= \cosh a \cosh c - \sinh a \cosh c \tanh(a-q)$$

$$= \cosh a \cosh c - \sinh a \sinh c \tanh m.$$

If the angle B is obtuse, so that D falls on CB produced, the same result follows, provided account is taken of the notation
$$\Pi(-x) = \pi - \Pi(x).$$

If the angle B is a right angle, the result follows from § 59, IV.

We are thus brought to the Cosine Formula, which may be put in the form:

$$\mathbf{\cosh a = \cosh b \cosh c - \sinh b \sinh c \tanh l.}$$

§ 61. The Measurement of Angles.

Up till this stage, except in §§ 51-2, there has been no need to introduce a unit of angle into our work. The equation $\alpha = \Pi(a)$, connecting the segment and the corresponding angle of parallelism, has had only a geometrical significance. In it α has stood for a certain definite acute angle, which has the property that the perpendicular to one of its bounding lines, at a distance a from the angular point, is parallel to the other bounding line.

When it comes to assigning numerical values to angles, the choice of one number is sufficient, if, in addition, the angle zero is denoted by O. In the Non-Euclidean Trigonometry we shall assign the number $\frac{\pi}{2}$ to the right angle. All other angles will have the numerical values proper to them on this scale.

In the rest of this work, when we use the equation $\alpha = \Pi(a)$, both α and a will be numbers, the one the measure of the angle on this scale, the other the measure of the segment on one of the scales agreed upon below (§ 55), in which the unit segment is the distance apart of two concentric Limiting-Curves, when the ratio of the arcs cut off by two of their axes is e or $e^{\frac{1}{k}}$.

It should perhaps be remarked that in dealing with the trigonometrical formulae in the previous sections the measure of the segment, and not the segment itself, is what we have meant to denote by the letters in the different equations.

§ 62. The Trigonometrical Functions of the Angle.

The Trigonometrical Functions

$$\sin\alpha, \quad \cos\alpha, \quad \tan\alpha, \quad \text{etc.},$$

are defined by the equations:

$$\sin\alpha = \frac{e^{i\alpha} - e^{-i\alpha}}{2i}, \qquad \cos\alpha = \frac{e^{i\alpha} + e^{-i\alpha}}{2},$$

$$\tan\alpha = \frac{\sin\alpha}{\cos\alpha}, \qquad \cot\alpha = \frac{1}{\tan\alpha},$$

$$\sec\alpha = \frac{1}{\cos\alpha}, \qquad \operatorname{cosec}\alpha = \frac{1}{\sin\alpha}.$$

The fundamental equation of the Hyperbolic Trigonometry is

$$\tanh \mathbf{a} = \cos\alpha,$$

when

$$\alpha = \Pi(\mathbf{a}).$$

We proceed to obtain this relation:

Consider the function $f(\alpha)$ defined by the equation

$$\tanh a = \cos f(\alpha).$$

and let us write $a = \Delta(\alpha)$.

When $\alpha = \frac{\pi}{2}$, $a = 0$, $\tanh a = 0$, $\cos f(\alpha) = 0$; *i.e.* $f\left(\frac{\pi}{2}\right) = \frac{\pi}{2}$.

When $\alpha = 0$, $a = \infty$, $\tanh a = 1$, $\cos f(\alpha) = 1$; *i.e.* $f(0) = 0$.

Further, as a increases from 0 to ∞, $f(\alpha)$ diminishes continuously from $\frac{\pi}{2}$ to 0.

Next consider a triangle ABC—not right-angled—and let the perpendicular from B cut the base AC at D. Let the elements of the triangle ABD be denoted by AB $= c$, BD $= a$, DA $= b$, $\angle$ ABD $= \mu$, $\angle$ BAD $= \lambda$. Also let the elements of the triangle BDC be denoted by BC $= c_1$, CD $= b_1$, DB $= a_1$, $\angle$ BCD $= \lambda_1$, $\angle$ DBC $= \mu_1$.

As the side BD is common, $a = a_1$.

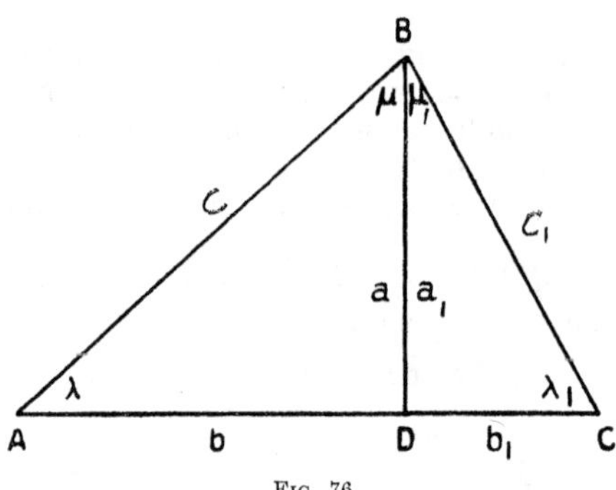

Fig. 76.

Then, from the Cosine Formula, § 60, we have

$$\tanh m = \frac{\cosh c \cosh c_1 - \cosh (b + b_1)}{\sinh c \sinh c_1}.$$

* The method of this and the preceding sections is due to Liebmann, "Elementare Ableitung der nichteuklidischen Trigonometrie," *Ber. d. k. sächs. Ges. d. Wiss. Math. Phys. Klasse*, vol. lix. p. 187 (1907), and *Nichteuklidische Geometrie*, 2nd ed. p. 71. Another method, also independent of the geometry of space, is to be found in Gérard's work, and in the paper by Young referred to below, p. 136.

With the notation of this section, we have

$$\begin{aligned}\cos f(\mu+\mu_1) &= \tanh \Delta(\mu+\mu_1)\\ &= \frac{\cosh c\cosh c_1 - \cosh(b+b_1)}{\sinh c\sinh c_1}\\ &= \coth c\coth c_1 - \frac{\cosh b\cosh b_1}{\sinh c\sinh c_1} - \frac{\sinh b\sinh b_1}{\sinh c\sinh c_1}.\end{aligned}$$

But we know that

$$\tanh a = \tanh c\tanh m, \quad [\S\ 59, \text{VI.}]$$

i.e.

$$\tanh a = \tanh c\cos f(\mu).$$

Similarly

$$\tanh a_1 = \tanh c_1 \cos f(\mu_1).$$

Therefore

$$\coth c\coth c_1 = \coth^2 a\cos f(\mu)\cos f(\mu_1).$$

Further, from § 59, I., we obtain

$$\frac{\sinh b}{\sinh c} = \frac{1}{\cosh m} = \sin f(\mu),$$

$$\frac{\sinh b_1}{\sinh c_1} = \frac{1}{\cosh m_1} = \sin f(\mu_1).$$

Therefore

$$\frac{\sinh b\sinh b_1}{\sinh c\sinh c_1} = \sin f(\mu)\sin f(\mu_1).$$

We are left with the term

$$\frac{\cosh b\cosh b_1}{\sinh c\sinh c_1}.$$

But, from § 59, VI. and IV., we have

$$\frac{\tanh m}{\sinh a} = \frac{\cosh c}{\sinh c\cosh a} = \frac{\cosh b}{\sinh c}.$$

Therefore

$$\frac{\cosh b\cosh b_1}{\sinh c\sinh c_1} = \frac{\cos f(\mu)\cos f(\mu_1)}{\sinh^2 a}.$$

Thus we obtain

$$\begin{aligned}\cos f(\mu+\mu_1) &= \coth^2 a\cos f(\mu)\cos f(\mu_1)\\ &\qquad - \operatorname{cosech}^2 a\cos f(\mu)\cos f(\mu_1) - \sin f(\mu)\sin f(\mu_1)\\ &= \cos f(\mu)\cos f(\mu_1) - \sin f(\mu)\sin f(\mu_1)\\ &= \cos[f(\mu)+f(\mu_1)].\end{aligned}$$

But when $$\mu = \mu_1 = \mu + \mu_1 = 0,$$
$$f(\mu) = f(\mu_1) = f(\mu + \mu_1) = 0.$$

Therefore we have
$$f(\mu + \mu_1) = f(\mu) + f(\mu_1).$$

This is a functional equation from which the continuous function $f(\mu)$ is to be derived.

It may be written $f(x+y) = f(x) + f(y)$,

with $$f(0) = 0, \quad f\left(\frac{\pi}{2}\right) = \frac{\pi}{2}.$$

Thus we have
$$\frac{f(x+h) - f(x)}{h} = \frac{f(y+h) - f(y)}{h}.$$

Proceeding to the limit
$$f'(x) = f'(y).$$

Thus $$f'(x) = \text{constant}.$$

Therefore $$f(x) = \mathsf{A}x + \mathsf{B}.$$

The values of $f(0)$ and $f\left(\frac{\pi}{2}\right)$ determine A and B, so that we have finally
$$f(x) = x.$$

Thus we are led to the desired equation
$$\tanh \mathbf{a} = \cos \alpha.$$

§ 63. From the result proved in last section,
$$\tanh a = \cos \alpha,$$
it follows immediately that
$$\sinh a = \cot \alpha,$$
$$\cosh a = \operatorname{cosec} \alpha,$$
$$\coth a = \sec \alpha,$$
$$\operatorname{sech} a = \sin \alpha,$$
$$\operatorname{cosech} a = \tan \alpha.$$

If we insert these values in the Trigonometrical Formulae of § 59, we obtain:

$$\begin{array}{llll}
\sinh a = \sinh c \sin \lambda & \text{from} & \sinh c = \sinh a \cosh l. \\
\sinh b = \tanh a \cot \lambda & ,, & \sinh b = \tanh a \sinh l. \\
\cosh c = \cot \lambda \cot \mu & ,, & \cosh c = \sinh l \sinh m. \\
\cosh c = \cosh a \cosh b & ,, & \cosh c = \cosh a \cosh b. \\
\cos \lambda = \cosh a \sin \mu & ,, & \cosh a = \tanh l \cosh m. \\
\tanh a = \tanh c \cos \mu & ,, & \tanh a = \tanh m \tanh c.
\end{array}$$

And the formulae of § 60 for the Oblique-Angled Triangle become

$$\sinh a : \sinh b : \sinh c = \sin \lambda : \sin \mu : \sin \nu,$$

$$\cosh a = \cosh b \cosh c - \sinh b \sinh c \cos \lambda.$$

All these results agree with the corresponding formulae in Spherical Trigonometry, when λ, μ, ν *take the place of* A, B, C, *and the Hyperbolic Functions of* a, b, *and* c *take the place of the Circular Functions of* a, b, *and* c.

§ 64. The Angle of Parallelism.

Since $$\tanh a = \cos \alpha,$$

we have $$\frac{1 - \cos \alpha}{1 + \cos \alpha} = \frac{1 - \tanh a}{1 + \tanh a}.$$

Therefore $$\tan^2 \frac{\alpha}{2} = e^{-2a},$$

and $$\tan \frac{\alpha}{2} = e^{-a}.$$

The angle α is acute, so the positive sign has to be taken in extracting the square root.

This may be written

$$\tan \tfrac{1}{2}\Pi(p) = e^{-p}.*$$

§ 65. The formulae of §§ 56-64 have been deduced on the understanding that the unit of length employed is the distance between concentric Limiting-Curves when the ratio of the arcs cut off by two of their axes is e.

---

* This result is given by Bolyai, *Appendix*, § 29, and by Lobatschewsky in his various books, *e.g. Geometrische Untersuchungen zur Theorie der Parallellinien*, § 36.

If a different unit is adopted, so that the ratio of the arc AB to the arc A_1B_1 is a, any number greater than unity, we have the equation

$$s_x = sa^{-x} \text{ instead of } s_x = se^{-x}.$$

Putting $\qquad a = e^{\frac{1}{k}},$

this gives $\qquad s_x = se^{-\frac{x}{k}}.$

This parameter k will enter into all the equations of the preceding sections, so that $\sinh\frac{a}{k}$, $\cosh\frac{a}{k}$, etc., will replace $\sinh a$, $\cosh a$, etc.

And the equation for the Angle of Parallelism will be

$$\tan\tfrac{1}{2}\Pi(p) = e^{-\frac{p}{k}}.$$

The Euclidean Geometry now appears as a special case of the Hyperbolic Geometry, for if we let $k \to \infty$, the formulae of this Non-Euclidean Geometry reduce to those of the Euclidean.

In the first place, since

$$\tan\tfrac{1}{2}\Pi(p) = e^{-\frac{p}{k}},$$

the angle of parallelism becomes $\frac{\pi}{2}$ when $k \to \infty$.

Further, the equations connecting the sides and angles of a right-angled triangle, viz.

$$\sinh\frac{a}{k} = \sinh\frac{c}{k}\sin\lambda,$$

$$\sinh\frac{b}{k} = \tanh\frac{a}{k}\cot\lambda,$$

$$\cosh\frac{c}{k} = \cot\lambda\cot\mu,$$

$$\cosh\frac{c}{k} = \cosh\frac{a}{k}\cosh\frac{b}{k},$$

$$\cos\lambda = \cosh\frac{a}{k}\sin\mu,$$

$$\tanh\frac{a}{k} = \tanh\frac{c}{k}\cos\mu,$$

become
$$\sin \mathsf{A} = \frac{a}{c},$$
$$\cot \mathsf{A} = \frac{b}{a},$$
$$\cot \mathsf{A} \cot \mathsf{B} = 1,$$
$$a^2 + b^2 = c^2,$$
$$\cos \mathsf{A} = \sin \mathsf{B},$$
$$\cos \mathsf{B} = \frac{a}{c},$$
when we write A, B for λ and μ.

From the Sine and Cosine Formulae for the Oblique-Angled Triangle (§ 63) we get at once,
$$\sin \mathsf{A} : \sin \mathsf{B} : \sin \mathsf{C} = a : b : c,$$
$$a^2 = b^2 + c^2 - 2bc \cos \mathsf{A}.$$

Again, $\frac{a}{k}, \frac{b}{k}$, and $\frac{c}{k}$ can be made infinitesimals by letting a, b, and c tend to zero instead of k to infinity. In this case again the Euclidean relations are obtained.

This result can be stated in other terms :

In the immediate neighbourhood of a point on the Hyperbolic Plane, the formulae of the Euclidean Geometry hold true.

Or, again :

The Euclidean Formulae hold true in Infinitesimal Geometry on the Hyperbolic Plane.

These theorems have an important bearing upon the question as to whether the Hyperbolic Geometry can actually represent the external relations of the space in which we live. The experimental fact that, within the limits of error to which all actual observations are subject, the sum of the angles of a triangle is two right angles does not prove that the geometry of our space is the Euclidean Geometry. It might be a Hyperbolic Geometry in which the parameter k was very great.

The Geometry of Bolyai and Lobatschewsky can be made to fit in with the facts of experience by taking k large enough. The Postulate of Euclid reaches the same end by another means. It is a better means, for it gives a simpler geometry.

CHAPTER V.

MEASUREMENTS OF LENGTH AND AREA, WITH THE AID OF THE INFINITESIMAL CALCULUS.

§ 66. In this Chapter we shall apply the Trigonometrical Formulae found in Chapter IV. to the measurements of Length and Areas of Curves.

The first thing to be done is to obtain the expression for the element of arc of a plane curve.

The Element of Arc in Cartesian Coordinates.

In the Euclidean Plane

$$ds^2 = dx^2 + dy^2.$$

We shall now prove that in the Hyperbolic Plane

$$\mathbf{ds^2 = \cosh^2 \frac{y}{k}\, dx^2 + dy^2.}$$

Let P, Q be the points (x, y), $(x + \delta x,\ y + \delta y)$.

Draw PM and QN perpendicular to the axis of x.

Then OM $= x$, MP $= y$, ON $= x + \delta x$, and NQ $= y + \delta y$.

From P draw PH perpendicular to QN.

Let PQ $= \delta s$, PH $= q$, HQ $= p$, and NH $= z$.

Then, in the right-angled triangle PHQ,

$$\delta s^2 = p^2 + q^2,\text{* to the lowest order.}$$

* This follows from § 65, where we have proved that the Euclidean Formulae hold in Infinitesimal Geometry. If we start with

$$\cosh \frac{\delta s}{k} = \cosh \frac{p}{k} \cosh \frac{q}{k},$$

we obtain the same result when we neglect terms above the lowest order.

Also, in the quadrilateral MNHP, the angles at M, N, and H are right angles, and the sides beginning at M are

$$\delta x, \ z, \ q, \ y.$$

These correspond to $a, \ m', \ c, \ l$

in a right-angled triangle. [Cf. § 35.]

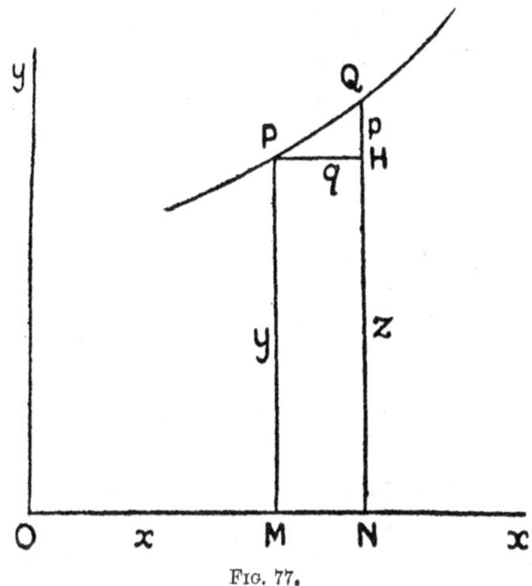

FIG. 77.

Thus we have $$\sinh\frac{\delta x}{k} = \frac{\sinh\frac{q}{k}}{\cosh\frac{y}{k}}. \quad \text{[Cf. § 59, I.]}$$

Therefore $$q = \cosh\frac{y}{k}\,\delta x, \text{ to the lowest order.}$$

Also, we have

$$\cosh\frac{\delta x}{k} = \tanh\frac{y}{k}\coth\frac{z}{k}. \quad \text{[Cf. § 59, V., and § 58.]}$$

Therefore y and z differ by a small quantity when δx is small.

Put $$z = y + \eta.$$

Then we have $\tanh\frac{y+\eta}{k}\cosh\frac{\delta x}{k} = \tanh\frac{y}{k}.$

This gives, to the lowest order,

$$\left(\tanh\frac{y}{k}+\frac{\eta}{k}\right)\left(1+\frac{\delta x^2}{2k^2}\right)=\tanh\frac{y}{k}\left(1+\frac{\eta}{k}\tanh\frac{y}{k}\right),$$

i.e.

$$\eta=-\frac{1}{2k}\sinh\frac{y}{k}\cosh\frac{y}{k}\,\delta x^2.$$

Therefore y and z differ by a quantity of the second order when δx is of the first order.

Now $$p=(y+\delta y)-z.$$

Therefore $$p=\delta y, \text{ to the first order.}$$

It follows from $\delta s^2=p^2+q^2$, that

$$\delta s^2=\cosh^2\frac{y}{k}\,\delta x^2+\delta y^2, \text{ to the lowest order.}$$

Thus we have shown that the element of arc in Cartesian Coordinates is given by

$$\mathbf{ds^2=\cosh^2\frac{y}{k}\,dx^2+dy^2.}$$

§ 67. Element of Arc in Polar Coordinates.

In the Euclidean Plane we have for the element of arc in Polar Coordinates, the equation

$$ds^2=dr^2+r^2d\theta^2.$$

We proceed to find the corresponding formula in the Hyperbolic Plane.

It may be obtained in two ways. It could be deduced from

$$ds^2=\cosh^2\frac{y}{k}\,dx^2+dy^2,$$

by using the relations connecting x, y and r, θ; viz.

$$\left.\begin{aligned}\cosh\frac{r}{k}&=\cosh\frac{x}{k}\cosh\frac{y}{k},\\ \tan\theta&=\frac{\tanh\frac{y}{k}}{\sinh\frac{x}{k}}.\end{aligned}\right\}\text{[Cf. § 63.]}$$

It is simpler and more instructive to obtain the result directly.

Let P, Q be the points (r, θ), $(r+\delta r, \theta+\delta\theta)$.

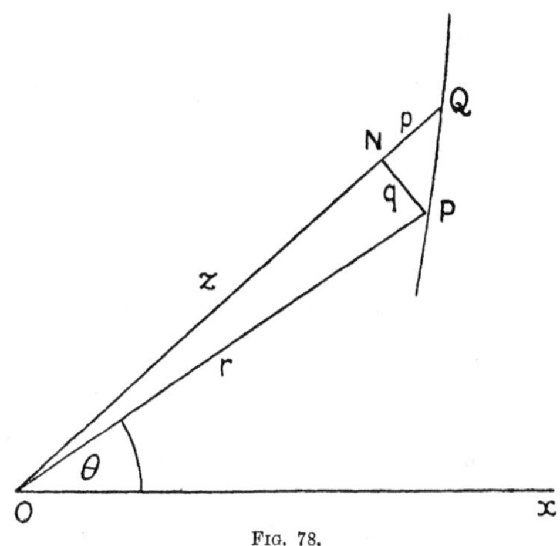

FIG. 78.

Draw PN perpendicular to OQ.

Let PQ $=\delta s$, PN $=q$, NQ $=p$, and ON $=z$.

Then, from the triangle PNQ, we have as before

$$\delta s^2 = p^2 + q^2.$$

Also, from the triangle ONP, we have

$$\sinh\frac{q}{k} = \sinh\frac{r}{k}\sin\delta\theta. \quad [\S\,63.]$$

Therefore $\quad q = k\sinh\frac{r}{k}\,\delta\theta$, to the lowest order.

Also, we have from the same triangle

$$\cosh\frac{r}{k} = \cosh\frac{z}{k}\cosh\frac{q}{k}.$$

Therefore r and z are nearly equal.

Put $$r = z + \xi.$$

Then $\cosh\frac{z}{k}+\frac{\xi}{k}\sinh\frac{z}{k}=\cosh\frac{z}{k}\left(1+\frac{q^2}{2k^2}\right)$,

to the lowest order.

Thus $\xi=\frac{q^2}{2k}\coth\frac{z}{k}$, to the lowest order;

i.e. r and z differ by a small quantity of the second order, when $\delta\theta$ is of the first order.

But $$p=r+\delta r-z.$$

Therefore $$p=\delta r, \text{ to the first order.}$$

It follows that

$$\delta s^2=\delta r^2+k^2\sinh^2\frac{r}{k}\delta\theta^2, \text{ to the lowest order.}$$

Therefore $$\mathbf{ds^2=dr^2+k^2\sinh^2\frac{r}{k}d\theta^2.}$$

§ 68. The Element of Arc in Limiting-Curve Coordinates.

We shall now describe a system of coordinates peculiar to the Hyperbolic Plane. The position of the point P is given by the Limiting-Curve and axis on which it lies, the Limiting-

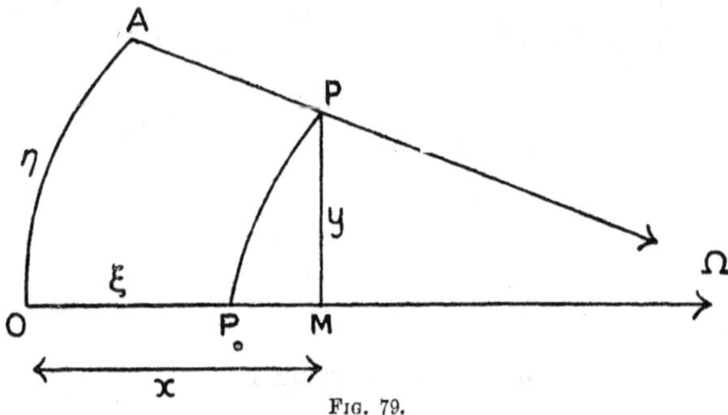

Fig. 79.

Curves being all concentric, their common centre being at infinity on the axis of x.

Let the Limiting-Curve through P cut off a segment of length ξ (OP_0) on the axis of x, and let the axis through P cut off an arc of length η (OA) on the Limiting-Curve through O. (Fig. 79.)

(ξ, η) are called the Limiting-Curve Coordinates of the point P.

Now take another point Q with coordinates

$$(\xi + \delta\xi, \ \eta + \delta\eta).$$

Let the Limiting-Curve through Q cut the axis of x (the axis through O) at Q_0.

Let the Limiting-Curve through P be cut by the axis through Q at S, and the Limiting-Curve through Q by the axis through P in R.

Also, let A and B be the points where the Limiting-Curve through O is cut by the axes through P and Q.

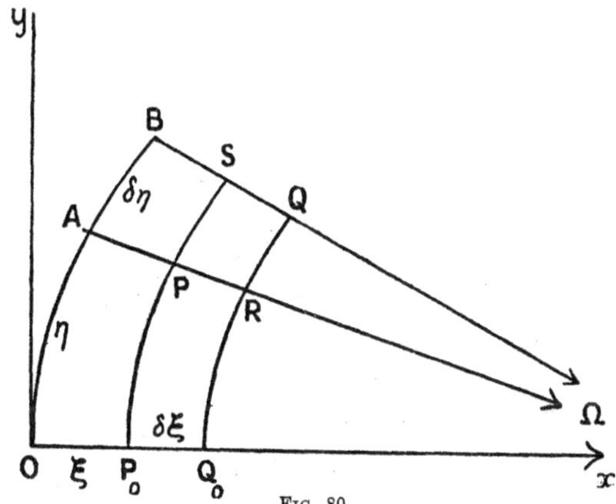

Fig. 80.

Then we have

$$\text{arc OA} = \eta, \quad \text{arc OB} = \eta + \delta\eta,$$
$$OP_0 = \xi, \qquad OQ_0 = \xi + \delta\xi.$$

It follows from the properties of Concentric Limiting-Curves [§ 55], that

$$\text{arc QR} = \delta\eta \, e^{-\frac{\xi + \delta\xi}{k}}$$

$$\therefore \ \text{arc QR} = \delta\eta \, e^{-\frac{\xi}{k}}, \text{ to the first order.}$$

Further, $PR = \delta\xi$, and we write $PQ = \delta s$, as usual.

Now we know that

$$PQ^2 = PR^2 + RQ^2, \text{ to the lowest order.}$$

$$\therefore\ \delta s^2 = \delta\xi^2 + e^{-\frac{2\xi}{k}}\delta\eta^2, \text{ to the lowest order.}$$

Therefore $$\mathbf{ds^2 = d\xi^2 + e^{-\frac{2\xi}{k}}d\eta^2.}$$

This result could also have been deduced from that of § 66 by using the equations connecting (x, y) and (ξ, η). [Cf. § 57 and § 69 (3).]

§ 69. We apply these formulae to find the perimeter of a circle, and the lengths of portions of the Equidistant-Curve and the Limiting-Curve.

1. *The Perimeter of a Circle of Radius* a.

In $$ds^2 = dr^2 + k^2 \sinh^2 \frac{r}{k}\, d\theta^2,$$

we put $$r = a \text{ and } dr = 0.$$

Thus the arc from $\theta = 0$ to $\theta = \theta$ is given by

$$s = k \sinh \frac{a}{k} \times \theta.$$

The Perimeter of the Circle follows by putting $\theta = 2\pi$, and is given by the expression

$$\mathbf{2\pi k \sinh \frac{a}{k}}.$$

2. *The Equidistant-Curve* y = b.

In $$ds^2 = \cosh^2 \frac{y}{k}\, dx^2 + dy^2,$$

we put $$y = b \text{ and } dy = 0.$$

Thus the arc from $x = 0$ to $x = x$ is given by

$$\mathbf{s = x \cosh \frac{b}{k}}.$$

3. *The Limiting-Curve.*

The equation of the Limiting-Curve through the origin, with its centre at infinity on the axis of x, is

$$e^{\frac{x}{k}} = \cosh \frac{y}{k}. \quad \text{[Cf. § 57 (1).]}$$

In $$ds^2 = \cosh^2\frac{y}{k}\,dx^2 + dy^2,$$

we put $$dx = \tanh\frac{y}{k}\,dy.$$

Then $$ds^2 = \left(1 + \sinh^2\frac{y}{k}\right) dy^2.$$

Thus $$ds = \cosh\frac{y}{k}\,dy.$$

It follows that $\mathbf{s = k \sinh \frac{y}{k}}$, when we measure s from the origin.

If we compare this result with § 57 (2), we see that the length of the arc of the Limiting-Curve, such that the tangent at one end is parallel to the axis through the other, is unity, when $k = 1$.

§ 70. The Element of Area.

Let the arc AB be an arc of a Limiting-Curve, centre Ω, such that the tangent at B is parallel to the axis through A.

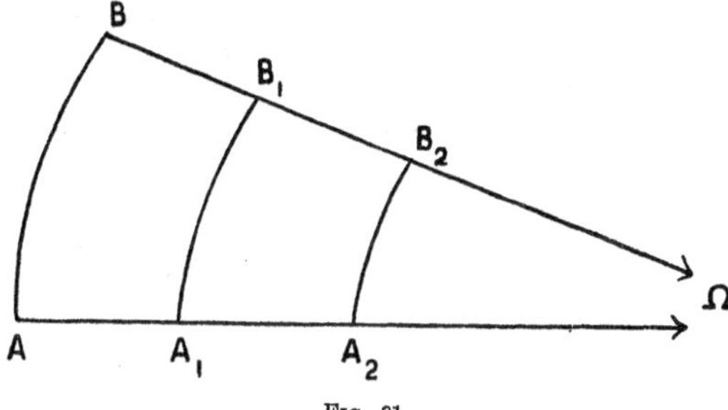

Fig. 81.

Then we know that the length of the arc AB is k. [§ 57 (2) and § 69 (3).]

Also, if $AA_1 = 1$, the length of the arc $A_1B_1 = ke^{-\frac{1}{k}}$;

if $A_1A_2 = 1$, the length of the arc $A_2B_2 = ke^{-\frac{2}{k}}$,

and so on.

Let the area of ABB_1A_1 be denoted by Δ_0.

Then (cf. § 48) the area of $A_1B_1B_2A_2$ will be $\Delta_0 e^{-\frac{1}{k}}$;

that of $A_2B_2B_3A_3$ will be $\Delta_0 e^{-\frac{2}{k}}$, etc.

Thus the area of ABB_nA_n

$$=\Delta_0\left(1+e^{-\frac{1}{k}}+e^{-\frac{2}{k}}+\dots+e^{-\frac{n-1}{k}}\right)$$

$$=\Delta_0\left(\frac{1-e^{-\frac{n}{k}}}{1-e^{-\frac{1}{k}}}\right).$$

Therefore, as $n\to\infty$, this area approaches a limit, namely

$$\Delta=\frac{\Delta_0}{1-e^{-\frac{1}{k}}}.$$

This is the area of the region bounded by two axes of a Limiting-Curve and an arc such that the tangent at one end is parallel to the axis through the other end.

The unit of area has not yet been chosen in this discussion. We now fix it so that the area denoted above by Δ will be k^2 the unit of area.

With this measurement

$$\Delta_0=k^2\left(1-e^{-\frac{1}{k}}\right).$$

Also the area of ABA_nB_n will be $k^2\left(1-e^{-\frac{n}{k}}\right)$.

Next, let P be a point on AB, or AB produced, such that the arc $AP=s$.

Then area APP_1A_1 : area $ABB_1A_1=s:k$,

and area $APP_nA_n=ks\left(1-e^{-\frac{n}{k}}\right)$.

Taking x, first, a rational number, and then treating the irrational number x as the limit of a sequence of rational numbers, we find from the above that the area bounded by the arcs of two Concentric Limiting-Curves, distant x apart, the larger one being of length s, is equal to

$$ks\left(1 - e^{-\frac{x}{k}}\right).$$

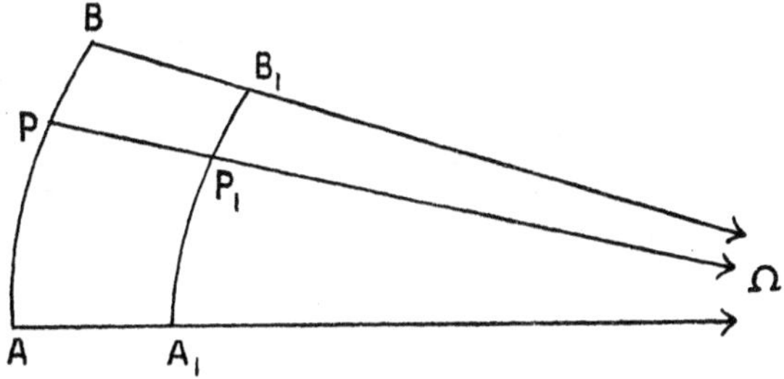

FIG. 82.

From this result the expression for the element of area in Limiting-Curve Coordinates will now be deduced.

Let P, Q, R and S be the points

(ξ, η), $(\xi + \delta\xi, \eta + \delta\eta)$, $(\xi + \delta\xi, \eta)$, and $(\xi, \eta + \delta\eta)$ [cf. Fig. 80].

Then $$\text{arc PS} = \delta\eta\, e^{-\frac{\xi}{k}}, \quad [\S\, 68]$$

and $$\text{PR} = \delta\xi.$$

Therefore the area PQRS is given by

$$k\,\delta\eta\, e^{-\frac{\xi}{k}}\left(1 - e^{-\frac{\delta\xi}{k}}\right).$$

When $\delta\xi$, $\delta\eta$ are small, this becomes, to the lowest order,

$$e^{-\frac{\xi}{k}}\,\delta\xi\,\delta\eta.$$

Therefore the element of area in Limiting-Curve Coordinates is

$$e^{-\frac{\xi}{k}}\,d\xi\,d\eta.$$

This is equal to the product of the two perpendicular chords PR and PS which bound the infinitesimal element, and with these units the expression for the element of area is the same as that in the Euclidean Plane.

§ 71. The Element of Area in Cartesian Coordinates.

This result can be obtained from the expression found in § 70, by using the methods of the Calculus.

We have

$$\left.\begin{aligned}\eta &= k \tanh \frac{y}{k} e^{\frac{x}{k}},\\ e^{\frac{x-\xi}{k}} &= \cosh \frac{y}{k}.\end{aligned}\right\} \quad \text{[Cf. § 57 and § 69 (3).]}$$

These are the equations connecting (x, y) and (ξ, η).

To find the element of area in Cartesian Coordinates (x, y), we need only replace

$$e^{-\frac{\xi}{k}} d\xi \, d\eta$$

by

$$e^{-\frac{x}{k}} \cosh \frac{y}{k} \frac{\partial(\xi, \eta)}{\partial(x, y)} dx \, dy.$$

After reduction, we obtain

$$\cosh \frac{y}{k} dx \, dy.$$

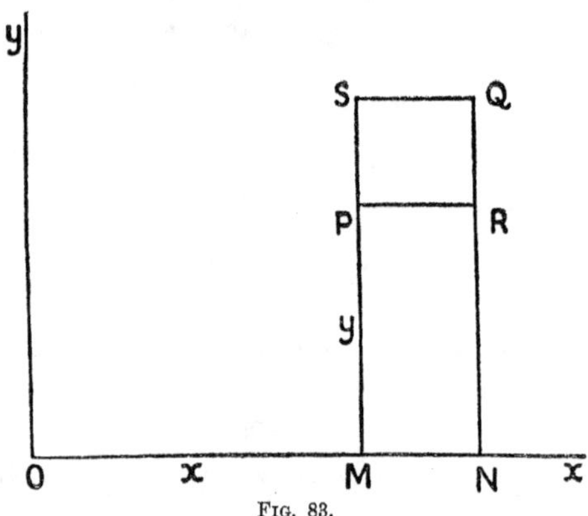

FIG. 83.

The result, however, can be found directly as follows:

Let P, Q be the points (x, y), $(x + \delta x, y + \delta y)$.

Let the Equidistant-Curves through P and Q with Ox as base-line meet the ordinates at R and S (Fig. 83).

The figure PRQS becomes a rectangle in the limit, and we can use the Euclidean expression for its area (cf. § 70).

Then $$\text{arc PR} = \cosh\frac{y}{k}\,\delta x \quad [\S\, 69\ (2)]$$

and $$\text{PS} = \delta y.$$

Hence the element of area in Cartesian Coordinates is

$$\cosh\frac{\mathbf{y}}{\mathbf{k}}\,\mathbf{dx}\,\mathbf{dy}.$$

§ 72. The Element of Area in Polar Coordinates.

As before, the result can be obtained by using the equations

$$\cosh\frac{r}{k} = \cosh\frac{x}{k}\cosh\frac{y}{k},$$

$$\tan\theta = \frac{\tanh\frac{y}{k}}{\sinh\frac{x}{k}},$$

which connect (r, θ) and (x, y).

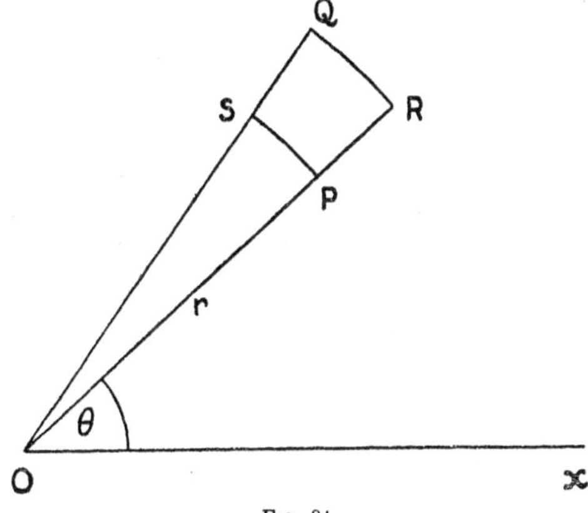

FIG. 84.

But it is simpler to obtain the element of area directly from the geometrical figure:

Let P, Q be the points (r, θ), $(r + \delta r, \theta + \delta\theta)$.

Let the circles through P and Q cut the radii at S and R, forming the element PRQS.

Then we have arc $PS = k \sinh \frac{r}{k} \delta\theta$, by § 69 (1),

$$PR = \delta r.$$

The figure PRQS becomes a rectangle in the limit.

Therefore *the element of area in Polar Coordinates is*

$$\mathbf{k \sinh \frac{r}{k} \, dr \, d\theta}.$$

The area of the circle of radius a is thus given by

$$\int_0^a \int_0^{2\pi} k \sinh \frac{r}{k} \, dr \, d\theta,$$

which becomes
$$2\pi k^2 \left(\cosh \frac{a}{k} - 1\right),$$

or
$$4\pi k^2 \sinh^2 \frac{a}{2k}.$$

§ 73. The Area of a Triangle and of a Quadrilateral with three Right Angles.

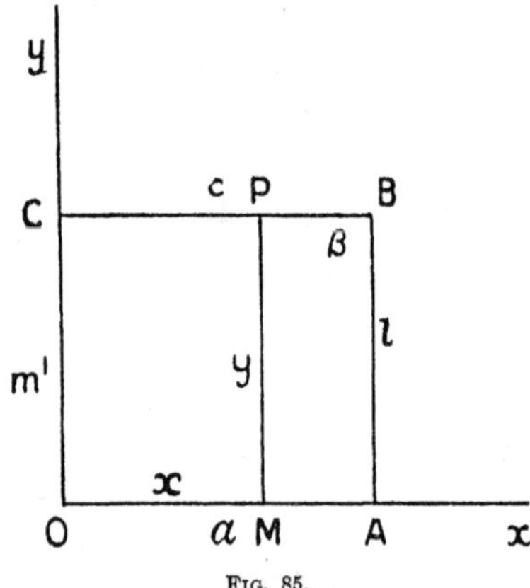

FIG. 85.

Let OABC be a quadrilateral with the sides a, m', c, l, as in Fig. 85, and the angles at O, A, C right angles; A lying on the axis of x and C on the axis of y.

Let P be any point on CB, and PM the perpendicular from P to OA.

Then, from the associated right-angled triangle for the quadrilateral OMPC, we have

$$\tanh\frac{y}{k}\cosh\frac{m}{k}=\cosh\frac{x}{k}. \quad (\S\,59,\ \text{V.})$$

But the area of the quadrilateral OABC is given by

$$\int_0^a\int_0^y \cosh\frac{y}{k}\,dx\,dy.$$

Denote this by S.

Integrating, we have

$$\begin{aligned} \text{S} &= k\int_0^a \sinh\frac{y}{k}\,dx \\ &= k\int_0^a \frac{\cosh\frac{x}{k}}{\sqrt{\sinh^2\frac{m}{k}-\sinh^2\frac{x}{k}}}\,dx \\ &= k^2\sin^{-1}\frac{\sinh\frac{a}{k}}{\sinh\frac{m}{k}}; \end{aligned}$$

$$\therefore\ \sin\frac{\text{S}}{k^2}=\frac{\sinh\frac{a}{k}}{\sinh\frac{m}{k}}.$$

But, from the associated right-angled triangle, we have

$$\tanh\frac{b}{k}=\frac{\sinh\frac{a}{k}}{\sinh\frac{m}{k}}. \quad (\S\,59,\ \text{III.})$$

And

$$\tanh\frac{b}{k}=\cos\beta. \quad (\S\,62.)$$

Therefore $$\sin\frac{S}{k^2} = \cos\beta.$$

Therefore $$S = k^2\left(\frac{\pi}{2} - \beta\right).$$

Thus the area of a quadrilateral with three right angles and an acute angle β is equal to

$$k^2\left(\frac{\pi}{2} - \beta\right)$$

on this scale.

But a triangle ABC (Fig. 86) is equal in area to Saccheri's Quadrilateral BCC′B′, in which the angles at B and C are each equal to half the sum of the angles of the triangle.

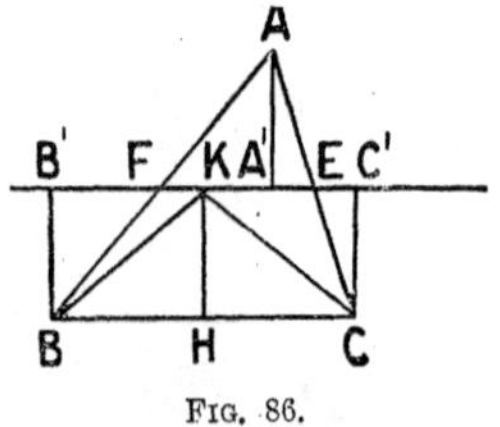

FIG. 86.

The triangle is thus equal in area to twice the quadrilateral with three right angles, and an acute angle equal to $\frac{1}{2}(A + B + C)$.

Using the result just found, the area of the triangle ABC on this scale of measurement is

$$k^2(\pi - 2\beta),$$

where $$2\beta = A + B + C.$$

In other words, the area of the triangle is the product of k^2 and its defect.

Comparing this with § 52, we see why the particular unit of area was chosen in § 70.

CHAPTER VI.

THE ELLIPTIC PLANE GEOMETRY.

§ 74. In Hilbert's Parallel Postulate, through any point A outside any line b, *two* parallels a_1 and a_2 can be drawn to the line, and these separate the lines in the plane of the parallels which cut b from the lines which do not cut it.

On the Euclidean Hypothesis, the two rays a_1 and a_2 together form one and the same line, and there is but *one* parallel to any line from a point outside it.

There is still another case to be examined, namely that in which all the rays through A cut the line b. In this case there is *no* parallel through a point outside a line to that line.

We shall see that this corresponds to the Hypothesis of the Obtuse Angle of Saccheri, in accordance with which the sum of the angles of a triangle exceeds two right angles. Saccheri and Legendre were able to rule this case out as untrue; but their argument depended upon the assumption that a straight line was infinite in length. Riemann was the first to recognise that a system of geometry compatible with the Hypothesis of the Obtuse Angle became possible when, for the hypothesis that the straight line is *infinite*, was substituted the more general one that it is *endless* or *unbounded*. (Cf. §§ 19, 20.)

The geometry built up on the assumption that a straight line is *unbounded*, but not *infinite*, and that *no* parallel can be drawn to a straight line from a point outside it will now be treated in the same manner in which the Hyperbolic Geometry was discussed.

§ 75. We proceed to the development of Plane Geometry when the assumptions

(i) *All straight lines intersect each other,*

(ii) *The straight line is not infinite,*

take the place of the Parallel Hypothesis of Euclid and his implicit assumption that the line is infinite.

Let A and B be any two points on a given line L.

The perpendiculars at A and B to the line must intersect, by assumption (i).

Let them meet at the point O.

Since ∠OAB = ∠OBA, we have OA = OB.

At O make ∠BOQ = ∠AOB (Fig. 87), and produce OQ to cut the line L at P.

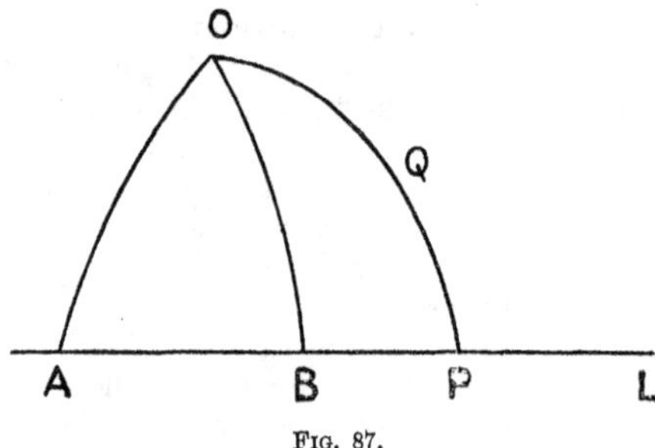

FIG. 87.

Then AB = BP and ∠OPA is a right angle.

By repeating this construction, we show that if P is a point on AB produced through B, such that AP = m. AB, the line OP is perpendicular to L and equal to OA and OB. The same holds for points on AB produced through A, such that BP = m. AB. In each case m is supposed to be a positive integer.

Now, let C be a point on AB, such that AB = m. AC, m being a positive integer. The perpendicular at C to L must pass through the point O, since if it met OA at O′ the above argument shows that O′B must be perpendicular to L and coincide with OB.

It follows that if P is any point on the line L, such that AP = $\frac{m}{n}$. AB, m and n being any two positive integers, OP is perpendicular to the line L and equal to OA and OB.

The case when the ratio AP : AB is incommensurable would be deduced from the above by proceeding to the limit.

Now, all points on the line are included in this argument, so that the perpendiculars at all points of the line L pass through the same point.

Now, let L′ be another line and A′, B′ two points upon it, such that the segment AB = A′B′.

The perpendiculars at A′, B′ meet in a point, which we shall call O′.

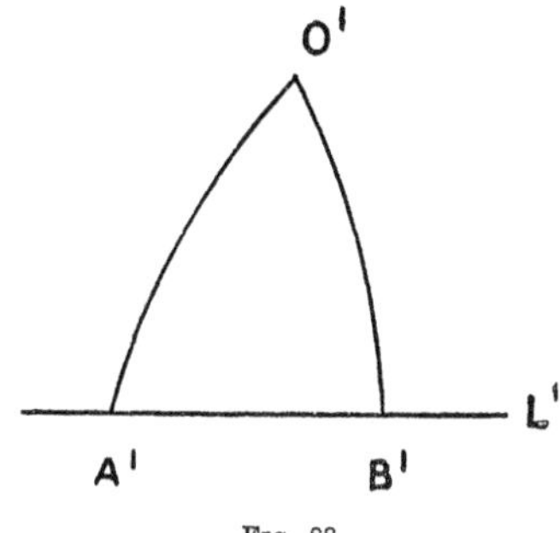

FIG. 88.

The triangles AOB and A′O′B′ have a side of the one equal to a side of the other, and the two angles adjacent to the sides are equal, each to each.

It follows that O′A′ = OA.

Thus we have shown that *the perpendiculars at all points on any line meet at a point which is at a constant distance from the line.*

The point will be called the Pole of the Line.

§ 76. Now, in Fig. 89, produce OA to O_1, where $O_1A = OA$. Join O_1B.

Then, from the triangles OAB and O_1AB, it follows that $\angle O_1BA = \angle OBA$ = a right angle.

Thus OB and O_1B are in a straight line.

Also, AO_1 produced must intersect AB at a point C, such that O_1C is perpendicular to AB, and OC will be also perpendicular to AB.

Thus OAO_1 produced returns to O, and the line is *endless* or *unbounded.*

Its length is four times the distance of the pole of the line from the given line.

We shall denote the constant distance OA by $\mathfrak{L}$, so that with this notation the length of the line is $4\mathfrak{L}$.

Thus two other assumptions of the ordinary geometry are contradicted in this geometry :

Two straight lines enclose a space ;

Two points do not always determine a straight line.

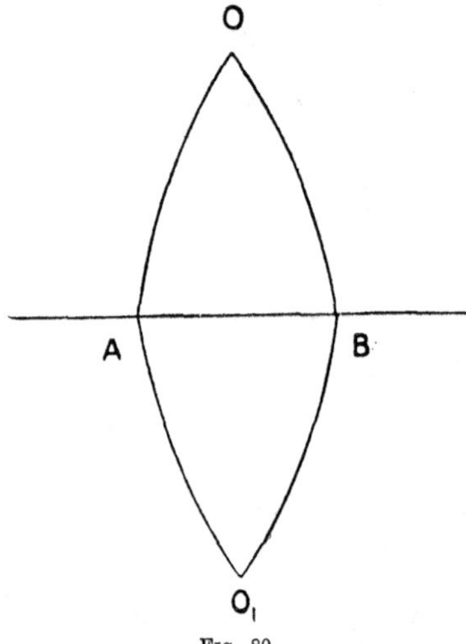

Fig. 89.

Through the two poles of a line an infinite number of lines can be drawn, just as through the two ends of a diameter of a sphere an infinite number of great circles can be drawn.

It is now clear that the argument which Euclid employs in I. 16 is not valid in this geometry. The exterior angle of a triangle is greater than either of the interior and opposite angles only when the corresponding median is inferior to $\mathfrak{L}$. If this median is equal to $\mathfrak{L}$, the exterior angle is equal to the interior angle considered ; if it is greater than $\mathfrak{L}$, the exterior angle is less than the interior angle considered.

Also, as I. 16 was essential to the proof of I. 27, it is now evident why in this geometry that theorem does not hold. Of course, if I. 16 did hold, there would have to be at least one parallel to a line through any point outside it. In a limited region of the plane, I. 16 does hold, and theorems dependent upon it are true in such a region.

The plane of this geometry has properties completely analogous to those possessed by the surface of a sphere. The great circles of the sphere correspond to the straight lines of the plane. Like the line, they are endless. Any two points on the surface of the sphere determine a great circle, provided the points are not the opposite ends of a diameter. The great circles through any point on the sphere intersect all other great circles.

We shall find that this analogy can be carried further. The sum of the angles of a spherical triangle is greater than two right angles. The sum of the angles of a triangle in this plane is greater than two right angles. The Sphèrical Excess measures the area of spherical triangles. With suitable units the area of plane triangles is equal to their excess. Indeed the formulae of this Plane Trigonometry, as we shall show later, are identical with the formulae of ordinary Spherical Trigonometry.*

§ 77. It must be remarked, however, that in the argument of § 76 it is assumed that the point O_1 is a different point from O. If the two points coincide, the plane of this geometry has a wholly different character. The length of a straight line is now $2\mathfrak{L}$ instead of $4\mathfrak{L}$. If two points P, Q are given on the plane, and any arbitrary straight line, we can pass from P to Q by a path which does not leave the plane, and does not cut the line. In other words, the plane is not divided by its lines into two parts.

The essential difference between the two planes is that in the one the plane has the character of a *two-sided* surface, and in the other it has the character of a *one-sided* surface.† The first plane—that which we have been examining—is usually called the spherical plane (or *double* elliptic plane); the second plane is usually called the elliptic (or *single* elliptic) plane.

The geometries which can be developed on both of these planes are referred to as Riemann's (Non-Euclidean) Geometries. It seems probable that the Spherical Plane was the only

* Spherical Geometry can be built up independently of the Parallel Postulate, so it is not necessary to say ordinary Spherical Trigonometry when referring to it.

† Cf. Bonola, *loc. cit.* § 75.

form in his mind. The Single Elliptic Plane and its importance in the higher treatment of the Non-Euclidean Geometries were first brought to light by Klein.

§ **78.** We shall now show that this geometry corresponds to Saccheri's Hypothesis of the Obtuse Angle, so that the sum of the angles of a triangle is always greater than two right angles.

The following theorem enables us to put the proof concisely :

1. *In any triangle* ABC *in which the angle* C *is a right angle, the angle* A *is less than, equal to, or greater than a right angle, according as the segment* BC *is less than, equal to, or greater than* 𝔏.

Let P be the pole of the side AC.

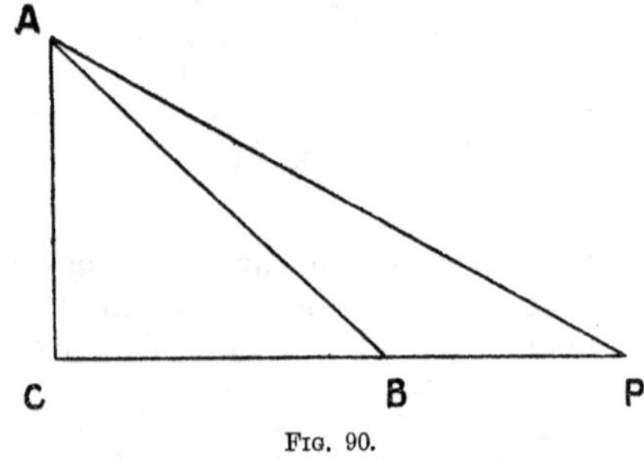

FIG. 90.

Then P lies upon BC, and PC = 𝔏.

Join AP.

Then ∠ PAC = a right angle.

If CB > CP, then ∠ BAC > ∠ PAC ; *i.e.* ∠ BAC > a right angle.

If CB = CP, then ∠ BAC = ∠ PAC ; *i.e.* ∠ BAC = a right angle.

If CB < CP, then ∠ BAC < ∠ PAC ; *i.e.* ∠ BAC < a right angle.

The converse also holds.

Now consider any right-angled triangle ABC in which C is the right angle.

If either of the sides AC or BC is greater than or equal to 𝔏, the sum of the angles is greater than two right angles by the above theorem.

If both sides are less than 𝔏, from D, the middle point of the hypothenuse, draw DE perpendicular to the side BC.

Let P be the pole of DE.

Produce ED to F, so that ED = DF.

Join AF and PF.

Then the triangles ADF and DEB are congruent, and AF, FB lie in one straight line.

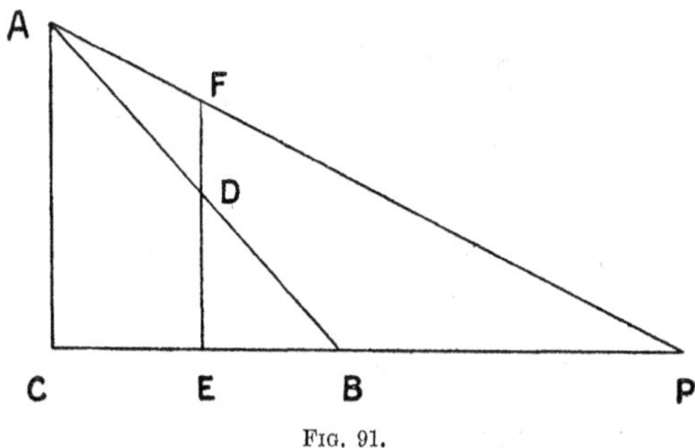

Fig. 91.

But we know that ∠PAC > a right angle, since CP is greater than 𝔏.

Therefore the sum of the angles at A and B in the right-angled triangle ACB is greater than a right angle in this case as well as in the others.

Thus we have proved that

2. *In any right-angled triangle the sum of the angles is greater than two right angles.*

Finally, let ABC be any triangle in which none of the angles are right angles.

We need only consider the case when two of the angles are acute.

Let ∠ABC and ∠ACB be acute.

From A draw AD perpendicular to BC; D must lie on the segment BC.

Then, from (2),

∠ABD + ∠BAD > a right angle

and ∠DAC + ∠ACD > a right angle.

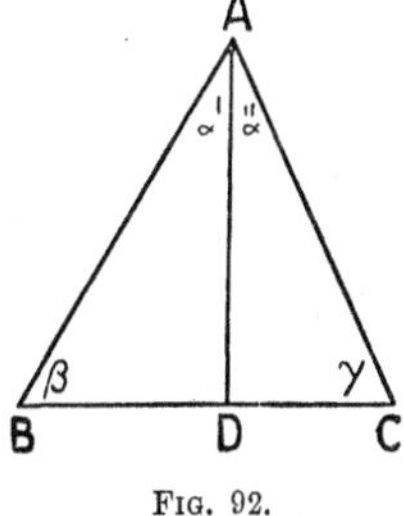

Fig. 92.

It follows that the sum of the angles of the triangle ABC is greater than two right angles.

Thus we have proved that

3. *The sum of the angles of any triangle is greater than two right angles.*

The amount by which the sum of the angles of a triangle exceeds two right angles is called its Excess.

§ 79. Saccheri's Quadrilateral, and the Quadrilateral with three Right Angles and one Obtuse Angle.

Let AC and BD be equal perpendiculars to the segment AB.

The quadrilateral ABDC we have called Saccheri's Quadrilateral.

Let E, F be the middle points of AB and CD.

We know that EF is perpendicular to both AB and CD; and that the angles ACD and BDC are equal.

But the sum of the angles of a quadrilateral must be greater than four right angles, since it is made up of two triangles.

It follows that the angles at C and D are obtuse.

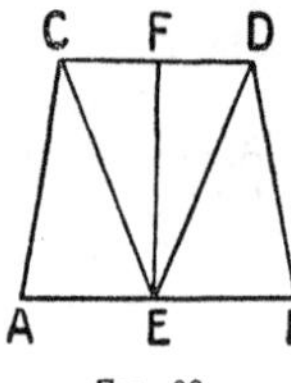

FIG. 93.

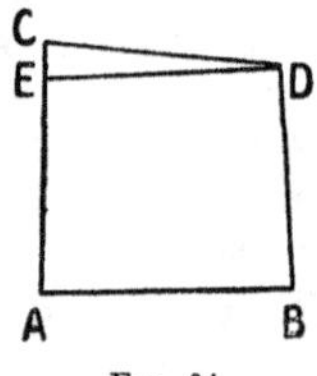

FIG. 94.

Thus the *Elliptic Geometry corresponds to Saccheri's Hypothesis of the Obtuse Angle.*

Now let ABDC (Fig. 94) be a quadrilateral in which the angles at A, B, and D are right angles.

The angle at C must be obtuse by § 78.

Each of the two sides containing the obtuse angle in a quadrilateral with three right angles is less than the side opposite to it.

To prove this, we proceed as follows:

If AC is not less than BD, it must be either greater than it or equal to it.

But we know that if AC = BD, ∠ ACD = ∠ BDC, which is impossible, as one is obtuse and the other a right angle.

If AC > BD, cut off AE = BD, and join ED.

Then we know that $\angle AED = \angle EDB$.

But $\angle EDB$ is acute, so that both must be acute, which is impossible.

Therefore AC must be less than BD.

Again, starting with AB and CD, which are both perpendicular to BD, we find that CD is less than AB, so our theorem is proved.

We shall not proceed further with the formal development of this geometry. There is no Theory of Parallels, for parallel lines do not exist in it. There is only one kind of circle, the locus of corresponding points upon a pencil of straight lines. The measurement of areas follows on the same lines as in the Hyperbolic Geometry.

Two triangles which have the same excess have equal areas, and conversely.

The area of a triangle is proportional to its excess.

CHAPTER VII.

THE ELLIPTIC PLANE TRIGONOMETRY.

§ 80. The following treatment of the Elliptic Trigonometry is due to Gérard and Mansion. Gérard discussed the Hyperbolic Trigonometry on these lines.* Mansion showed that the method discovered by Gérard was applicable also to the Elliptic case.†

The notation to be employed has first to be explained.

Let OA and OA′ be two lines meeting at O at right angles. Let OL be a third line making an acute angle with OA and OA′.

Let P be any point upon the line OL, such that OP < 𝕷.

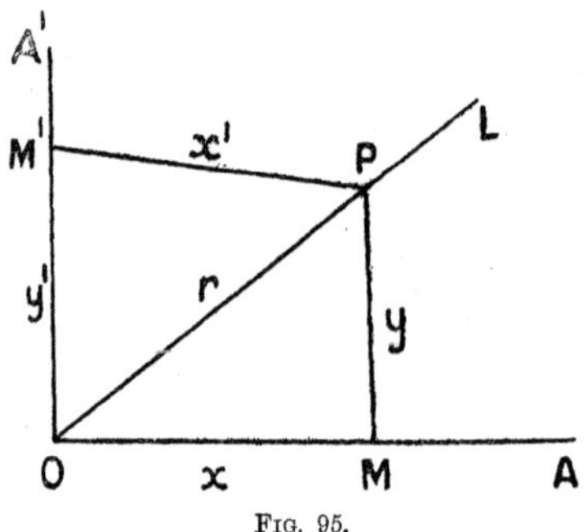

FIG. 95.

Let PM and PM′ be the perpendiculars to OA and OA′.

We denote OM, MP, and OP by x, y, and r; and OM′ and M′P by y' and x'.

* Gérard, *Sur la Géométrie non euclidienne* (Paris, 1892). Cf. also Young, "On the Analytical Basis of Non-Euclidian Geometry," *Amer. Journ. of Math.*, vol. xxxiii. p. 249 (1911); and Coolidge, *Non-Euclidean Geometry*, ch. iv. (Oxford, 1909).

† Mansion, *Principes Fondamentaux de la Géométrie non euclidienne de Riemann* (Paris, 1895).

§ 81. I. *If* P, Q *are any two points on* OL, *such that*

$$\mathrm{OP} < \mathrm{OQ} < \mathfrak{L},$$

and Pp, Qq *are perpendicular to* OA, *then* $\angle \mathrm{OP}p < \angle \mathrm{OQ}q$.

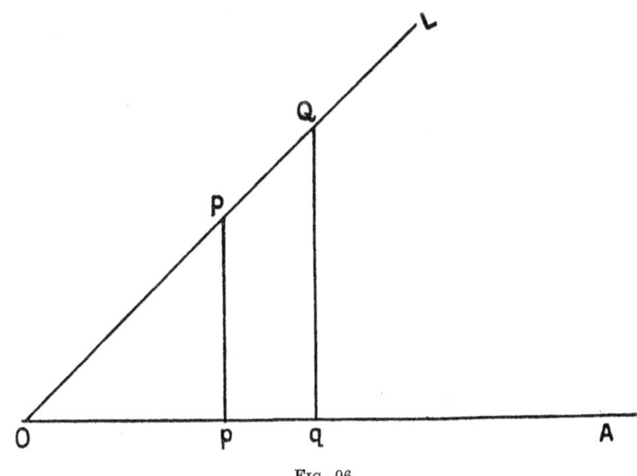

FIG. 96.

We know that $\angle p\mathrm{PQ} + \angle \mathrm{PQ}q > 2$ right angles.

Also $\angle \mathrm{OP}p + \angle p\mathrm{PQ} = 2$ right angles.

Therefore $\angle \mathrm{OP}p < \angle \mathrm{PQ}q$.

If S is the point on OL, such that $\mathrm{OS} = \mathfrak{L}$ and Ss is perpendicular to OA, we know that $\angle \mathrm{OS}s =$ a right angle.

It follows that $\angle \mathrm{OP}p < \angle \mathrm{OQ}q <$ a right angle.

II. *From* O *to* S, y *continually increases.*

Let P and Q be any two points upon OL, such that

$$\mathrm{OP} < \mathrm{OQ} < \mathfrak{L}.$$

Then we know that if $\mathrm{P}p = \mathrm{Q}q$, we must have $\angle p\mathrm{PQ} = \angle \mathrm{PQ}q$, which is impossible by (I.).

Again, if $\mathrm{P}p > \mathrm{Q}q$, cut off $p\mathrm{P}' = q\mathrm{Q}$, and join P′Q. (Fig. 97.)

Then $\angle p\mathrm{P}'\mathrm{Q} = \angle \mathrm{P}'\mathrm{Q}q$.

But $\angle \mathrm{PQ}q <$ a right angle.

Therefore $\angle pP'Q$ and $\angle P'Qq$ are equal acute angles, which is impossible.

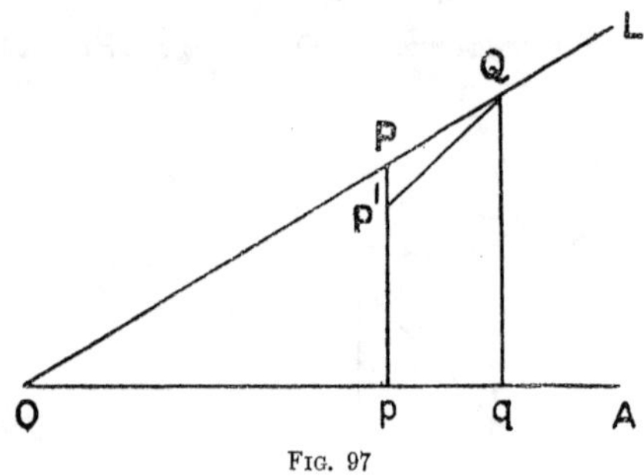

Fig. 97

Thus, as the point P moves along OL from O towards S, y continually increases.

III. *From* O *to* S, *the ratio* $\frac{x}{r}$ *continually increases.*

First, consider points upon OL corresponding to equal segments on OA.

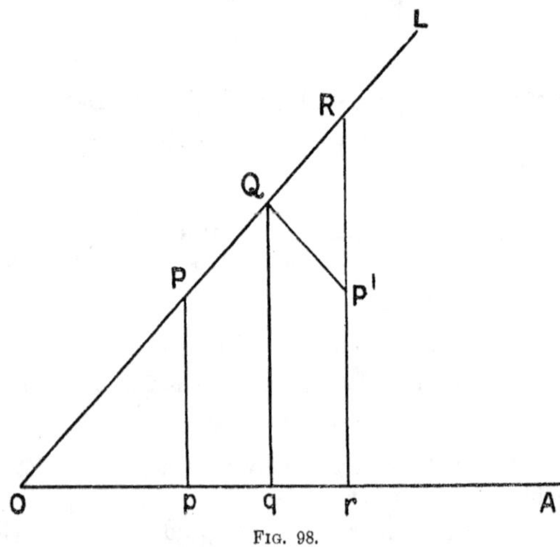

Fig. 98.

Let P, Q, R be three such points, so that

$$pq = qr.$$

Then we know that $p\mathsf{P} < q\mathsf{Q} < r\mathsf{R}$.
From $r\mathsf{R}$ cut off $r\mathsf{P}' = p\mathsf{P}$, and join QP'.
Then we have $\mathsf{PQ} = \mathsf{QP}'$ and $\angle \mathsf{QP}p = \angle \mathsf{QP}'r$.

Therefore $\angle \mathsf{QRP}' > \angle \mathsf{QP'R}$ and $\mathsf{QR} < \mathsf{QP}'$.

Thus, if $pq = qr$, $\mathsf{PQ} > \mathsf{QR}$.

Therefore, for equal increments of x, we have decreasing increments of r.

It follows from this that if P and Q are any two points upon OL, such that $\mathsf{OP} < \mathsf{OQ} < \mathfrak{L}$, and OM, ON are commensurable,

$$\frac{\mathsf{OM}}{\mathsf{OP}} < \frac{\mathsf{ON}}{\mathsf{OQ}}.$$

When OM and ON are incommensurable, we reach the same conclusion by proceeding to the limit.

Thus, from O to S, the ratio $\frac{x}{r}$ continually increases.

IV. *From* O *to* S, *the ratio* $\frac{y}{r}$ *decreases.*

First we consider points upon OL at equal distances along that line.

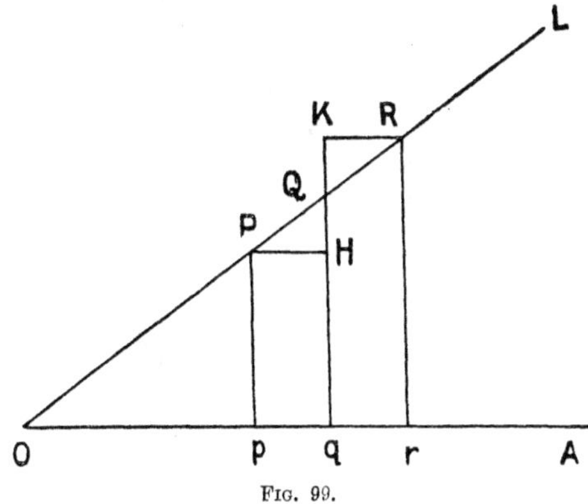

FIG. 99.

Let P, Q, and R be three such points, so that

$$\mathsf{PQ} = \mathsf{QR}.$$

From P and R draw PH and RK perpendicular to $\mathsf{Q}q$.

Then we know that $\mathsf{P}p < \mathsf{H}q$ and $\mathsf{R}r < \mathsf{K}q$ (§ 79).

But $\mathsf{QH} = \mathsf{QK}$. Therefore $\mathsf{Q}q - \mathsf{H}q = \mathsf{K}q - \mathsf{Q}q$.

It follows from the above that $\mathsf{Q}q - \mathsf{P}p > \mathsf{R}r - \mathsf{Q}q$.

Therefore, for equal increments of r we have diminishing increments of y.

It follows from this that if P and Q are any two points upon OL, such that $\mathsf{OP} < \mathsf{OQ} < \mathfrak{L}$, and OP, OQ are commensurable,

$$\frac{\mathsf{P}p}{\mathsf{OP}} > \frac{\mathsf{Q}q}{\mathsf{OQ}}.$$

When OP and OQ are incommensurable, we obtain the same result by proceeding to the limit.

Thus, as P moves along OL from O towards S, the ratio $\frac{y}{r}$ continually decreases.

V. *When* r *tends to zero, the ratio* x : r *tends towards a finite limit from above, and the ratio* y : r *tends towards a finite limit from below.*

From (III.) we know that $x : r$ continually decreases as r tends to zero, so that this ratio has a limit, finite or zero.

From (IV.) we know that $y : r$ continually increases as r tends to zero, so that this ratio either has a finite limit, not zero, or becomes infinite.

But from the quadrilateral whose sides are (x, y, x', y') we have $x > x'$. (Fig. 95.) Thus $x : r > x' : r$.

But, by (IV.), $x' : r$ either has a finite limit, not zero, or becomes infinite, as r tends to zero.

Therefore the limit of $x : r$ cannot be zero, and must be some finite number. Also $x : r$ approaches this limit from above.

But it follows from the preceding argument that $y' : r$ has a finite limit, not zero.

Also we know that $y < y'$, and thus $y : r < y' : r$.

It follows that $y : r$ has a finite limit, not zero, and it approaches this from below.

These two limits $\underset{r \to 0}{\mathrm{Lt}}\left(\frac{y}{r}\right)$, $\underset{r \to 0}{\mathrm{Lt}}\left(\frac{x}{r}\right)$ are chosen as the sine and cosine of the acute angle which OL makes with OA,* and the other ratios follow in the usual way.

* These limits are functions of the angle. It can be shown that they are continuous, and that with a proper unit of angle they are given by the usual exponential expressions. Cf. Coolidge, *loc. cit.* p. 53.

§ 82. We turn now to the quadrilateral with three right angles and one obtuse angle.

Let OABb be such a quadrilateral, the angles at O, B, and b being right angles.

Produce Ob, and cut off bc=Ob and $cd=bc$.

Draw the perpendiculars to Ob produced at the points c and d; and from A the perpendiculars to the lines just drawn.

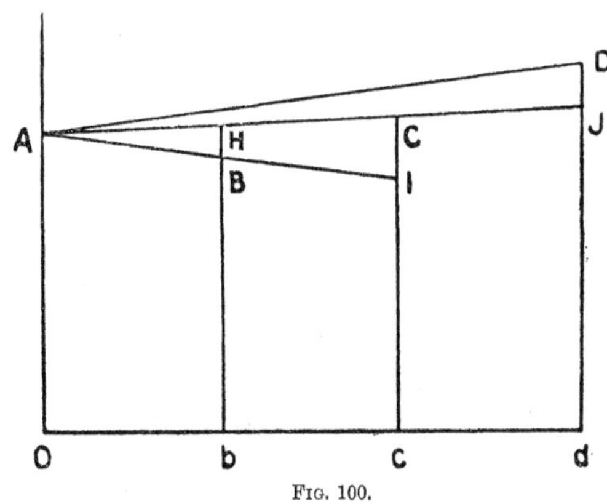

FIG. 100.

We thus obtain three quadrilaterals OABb, OACc, OADd, of this nature, standing on the bases Ob, Oc, and Od.

It is easy to show that the obtuse angles of these quadrilaterals increase as the bases increase.

Let bB produced meet AC at H, AB produced meet Cc at I, and AC produced meet Dd at J.

Then we have AB = BI, AB < AH, and AI > AC.

It follows that AB > AC − AB.

Also we have HC = CJ and AD < AJ.

Therefore AC − AH = AJ − AC, and finally AC − AB > AD − AC.

Thus AB > AC − AB > AD − AC.

§ 83. We return to the notation of § 80 and the figure OMPM′, in which the angles at O, M, and M′ are right angles, and the sides OM, MP, PM′, and OM′ are denoted by x, y, x', and y' respectively.

We shall now prove the following theorem:

In the quadrilateral with three right angles (x, y, x′, y′), *in which the sides* x′, y *include the obtuse angle, if* y′ *is kept fixed and* x *tends to zero, the ratio* x′ : x *tends to a finite limit* $\phi(y')$ *from above, and this ratio is less than* $\phi(y)$.

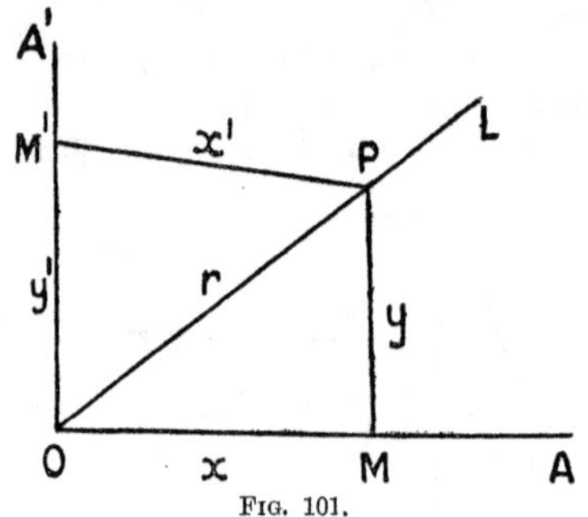

FIG. 101.

As in § 81 we find that $x' : x$ continually decreases as x tends to zero. It must have a limit, which may be zero or some number less than unity.

Produce MP, and draw M′Q perpendicular to MP.

From § 82 we know that as x decreases, the ratio $\frac{M'Q}{x}$ increases.

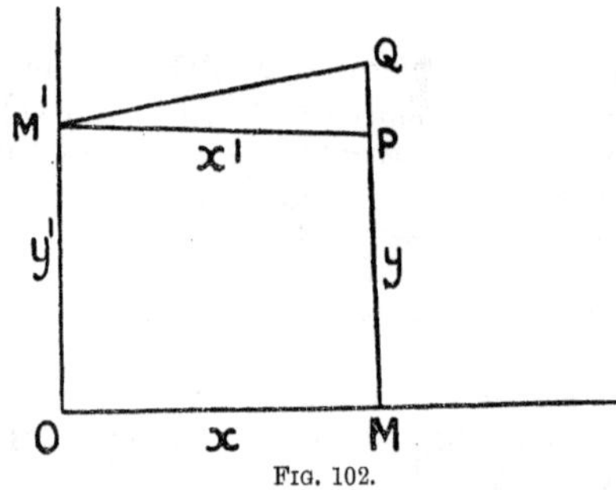

FIG. 102.

It must therefore have a finite limit, not zero, or become infinite.

But $\frac{M'Q}{x} < \frac{M'P}{x}$, since $M'Q < M'P$.

Thus $\underset{x \to 0}{\text{Lt}} \left(\frac{x'}{x}\right)$ cannot be zero.

This function is associated with the segment M′O, denoted by y', and will be written as $\phi(y')$.

Now we have seen that

$$\phi(y') > \text{M}'\text{Q} : x.$$

But in the quadrilateral OM′PM, the side PM plays the same part as OM′ in the quadrilateral OM′QM.

Thus $$\phi(y) > \text{M}'\text{P} : x.$$

Thus we have $$\phi(y') < \frac{x'}{x} < \phi(y).$$

Since $x' < x$, the function $\phi(y')$ is less than unity, except for $y' = 0$, when it becomes equal to unity.

§ 84. We shall now show that the function defined in the previous section is continuous.

Let OS and Os be two lines meeting at O, such that

$$\text{OS} = \text{O}s = \mathfrak{L} \text{ and } \angle \text{SO}s \text{ is acute.}$$

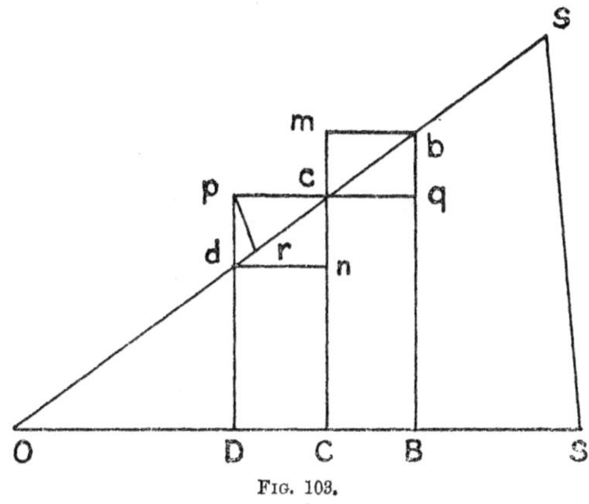

Fig. 103.

Then the angles at S and s are both right angles.

Let SB $= x - y$, SC $= x$, and SD $= x + y$.

Let the perpendiculars at B, C, and D to OS, meet Os at b, c, and d.

Through b and d draw bm and dn perpendicular to Cc.

From § 81 (III.), applied to the acute angles *dcn* and *bcm*, we have $cb < cd$, $cm : cb < c\mathsf{C} : c\mathsf{O}$, and $cn : cd < c\mathsf{C} : c\mathsf{O}$.

From the second of these relations we have

$$\frac{\mathsf{C}m}{\mathsf{S}s} - \frac{\mathsf{C}c}{\mathsf{S}s} < \frac{\mathsf{C}c}{\mathsf{S}s}\frac{cb}{c\mathsf{O}},$$

i.e.

$$\left(\frac{\mathsf{B}b}{\mathsf{S}s} : \frac{\mathsf{B}b}{\mathsf{C}m}\right) - \frac{\mathsf{C}c}{\mathsf{S}s} < \frac{\mathsf{C}c}{\mathsf{S}s}\frac{cb}{c\mathsf{O}}. \qquad \text{.................}(\alpha)$$

Then, by § 83, if $\mathsf{S}s$, and thus $\mathsf{B}b$ and $\mathsf{C}m$ tend to zero, we have

$$\text{Lt}\frac{\mathsf{B}b}{\mathsf{S}s} = \phi(x-y),$$

$$\text{Lt}\frac{\mathsf{B}b}{\mathsf{C}m} = \phi(y),$$

$$\text{Lt}\frac{\mathsf{C}c}{\mathsf{S}s} = \phi(x).$$

Further, $\text{Lt}\, cb = \mathsf{CB} = y$ and $\text{Lt}\, c\mathsf{O} = \mathsf{CO} = \mathfrak{L} - x$.

Therefore, from (α), we have

$$\frac{\phi(x-y)}{\phi(y)} - \phi(x) \overline{\overline{<}} \frac{y}{\mathfrak{L} - x}\phi(x),$$

i.e.

$$\phi(x-y) - \phi(x)\phi(y) \leqq \frac{y}{\mathfrak{L} - x}\phi(x)\phi(y). \qquad \text{..........}(\beta)$$

Again, from the inequality $\dfrac{cn}{cd} < \dfrac{c\mathsf{C}}{c\mathsf{O}}$, we have in the same way

$$\phi(x)\phi(y) - \phi(x+y) \leqq \frac{y}{\mathfrak{L} - x}\phi(x)\phi(y). \qquad \text{...........}(\gamma)$$

Adding (β) and (γ), we have

$$\phi(x-y) - \phi(x+y) \overline{\overline{<}} \frac{2y}{\mathfrak{L} - x}\phi(x)\phi(y) < \frac{2y}{\mathfrak{L} - x},$$

since $\phi(x)$, $\phi(y)$ are each less than unity. It follows that $\phi(x)$ is a continuous function of x.

§ **85.** We shall now show that

$$\phi(\mathbf{x}+\mathbf{y})+\phi(\mathbf{x}-\mathbf{y})=2\phi(\mathbf{x})\phi(\mathbf{y}).$$

With the figure of § 84, let the perpendicular at c to Cc meet Dd and Bb in p and q. From cd cut off $cr=cb$, and join pr.

Then we have $cp=cq$ and $pr=qb$.

We shall presently suppose Ss to become infinitesimal. In this case the angles at p and q differ infinitesimally from right angles, and $\angle dpr$ becomes infinitesimal.

It follows that dr is infinitesimal as compared with pd;* and that if Ss is an infinitesimal of the first order, dr is at least of the second order.

But $dp-qb=dp-pr<dr$.

And $dp-qb=(\mathsf{D}p-\mathsf{D}d)-(\mathsf{B}b-\mathsf{B}q)$.

Therefore we have

$$\text{Lt}\left(\frac{\mathsf{D}p}{\mathsf{C}c}\cdot\frac{\mathsf{C}c}{\mathsf{S}s}-\frac{\mathsf{D}d}{\mathsf{S}s}-\frac{\mathsf{B}b}{\mathsf{S}s}+\frac{\mathsf{B}q}{\mathsf{C}c}\cdot\frac{\mathsf{C}c}{\mathsf{S}s}\right)=0.$$

But $$\text{Lt}\left(\frac{\mathsf{D}p}{\mathsf{C}c}\right)=\phi(y)=\text{Lt}\left(\frac{\mathsf{B}q}{\mathsf{C}c}\right).$$

And $$\text{Lt}\left(\frac{\mathsf{C}c}{\mathsf{S}s}\right)=\phi(x),\qquad \text{Lt}\left(\frac{\mathsf{D}d}{\mathsf{S}s}\right)=\phi(x+y),$$

and $$\text{Lt}\left(\frac{\mathsf{B}b}{\mathsf{S}s}\right)=\phi(x-y).$$

Thus we have

$$\phi(x+y)+\phi(x-y)=2\phi(x)\phi(y).$$

§ **86.** We proceed to the equation

$$\phi(x+y)+\phi(x-y)=2\phi(x)\phi(y).$$

We are given that $\phi(x)$ is a continuous function, which is equal to unity when $x=0$, and when $x>0$, $\phi(x)<1$.

Let x_1 be a value of x in the interval to which the equation applies.

Then we can find k, so that $\phi(x_1)=\cos\frac{x_1}{k}$.

*Cf. Coolidge, *loc. cit.* p. 49.

The function $\cos x$ has here a purely analytical meaning, being defined by the equation

$$\cos x = 1 - \frac{x^2}{2\,!} + \frac{x^4}{4\,!} - \ldots .$$

It follows that
$$\phi(2x_1) = \cos \frac{2x_1}{k},$$
$$\phi(nx_1) = \cos \frac{nx_1}{k},$$
$$\phi\left(\frac{nx_1}{2^m}\right) = \cos\left(\frac{nx_1}{2^m k}\right).$$

Now let x be any other value of x in the interval. If it happens that this value is included in the set

$$nx_1 \text{ or } \frac{nx_1}{2^m},$$

we know that $\phi(x) = \cos\left(\frac{x}{k}\right)$, by the above.

But if it is not included in these forms, we can still find positive integers m, n by going on far enough in the scale, such that

$$\left(x - \frac{nx_1}{2^m}\right) < \epsilon,$$

where ϵ is any positive number as small as we please.

But $\phi(x)$ and $\cos \frac{x}{k}$ are continuous functions.

It follows that
$$\phi(x) = \cos \frac{x}{k}.$$

This value of k will be related to the measure of the line OS, denoted by $\mathfrak{L}$ in the previous sections.

§ **87.** We have now to deal with a rather complicated figure. From it we shall obtain the fundamental equation of this Trigonometry for the Right-Angled Triangle ABC, in which C is the right angle, viz.

$$\cos \frac{\mathbf{c}}{\mathbf{k}} = \cos \frac{\mathbf{a}}{\mathbf{k}} \cos \frac{\mathbf{b}}{\mathbf{k}}. \qquad \text{(1)}$$

Let ABC be a right-angled triangle, in which C is the right angle.

From a point b upon AB produced draw bc perpendicular to AC.

Move the triangle bcA along AC till it coincides with C and bc takes up the position b'C.

We thus have the triangle $b'a'$C congruent with bAc.

In the same way move the triangle bcA along BA until b coincides with B and the triangle takes up the position B$a''c''$.

Through the middle point I of a'A draw IL perpendicular to BA.

Then LI produced will be perpendicular to $b'a'$.

We thus obtain the common perpendicular to $b'a'$ and BA, the line KIL.

In the same way we obtain the common perpendicular MJN to AC and $a''c''$ through the middle point J of Aa''.

Finally, we draw b'Q perpendicular to AB and bb'' perpendicular to BC.

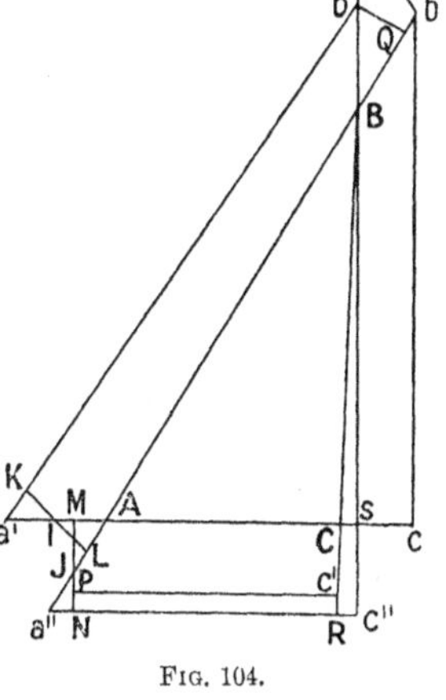

FIG. 104.

We have seen that as Bb tends to zero, we have

$$\text{Lt}\frac{bb''}{\text{B}b}=\text{Lt}\frac{b'\text{Q}}{b'\text{B}} \quad\text{.......................(i)}$$

In the same way $\quad \text{Lt}\frac{\text{MJ}}{\text{JA}}=\text{Lt}\frac{\text{IL}}{\text{IA}}.$

Thus $$\text{Lt}\frac{\text{MN}}{\text{A}a''}=\text{Lt}\frac{\text{KL}}{\text{A}a'}. \quad\text{.......................(ii)}$$

Dividing (i) by (ii) and remembering that Aa'' = Bb and Aa' = Cc, we have

$$\text{Lt}\frac{bb''}{\text{MN}}=\text{Lt}\frac{b'\text{Q}}{\text{KL}}\,.\,\text{Lt}\frac{\text{C}c}{\text{B}b'},$$

which may be written

$$\text{Lt}\frac{b'\text{Q}}{\text{KL}}=\text{Lt}\frac{bb''}{\text{C}c}\,.\,\text{Lt}\frac{\text{B}b'}{\text{MN}}. \quad\text{..............(iii)}$$

We shall now show that this equation is the same as

$$\phi(\text{AB})=\phi(\text{BC})\,\phi(\text{CA}).$$

From § 83, we have

$$\phi(\mathsf{LQ}) < \frac{b'\mathsf{Q}}{\mathsf{KL}} < \phi(\mathsf{K}b').$$

Now, when $\mathsf{B}b$ tends to zero, LQ and $\mathsf{K}b'$ tend to BA, and from § 84, $\phi(\mathsf{LQ})$ and $\phi(\mathsf{K}b')$ tend to $\phi(\mathsf{AB})$.

Thus, $$\text{Lt}\frac{b'\mathsf{Q}}{\mathsf{KL}} = \phi(\mathsf{AB}). \qquad \text{(iv)}$$

In the same way we have

$$\text{Lt}\left(\frac{bb''}{\mathsf{C}c}\right) = \phi(\mathsf{BC}). \qquad \text{(v)}$$

There remains the limit of $\dfrac{\mathsf{B}b'}{\mathsf{MN}}$.

Let s be the point at which $\mathsf{B}c''$ meets AC.

We know from § 81 (I.), that s lies between C and c, and we have $\mathsf{B}s > \mathsf{BC}$.

Then, since $\mathsf{C}b' = \mathsf{B}c''$, we have $\mathsf{B}b' > sc''$.

Therefore $$\frac{\mathsf{B}b'}{\mathsf{MN}} > \frac{sc''}{\mathsf{M}n} > \phi(\mathsf{N}c'').$$

Produce BC till it meets $a''c''$ in R.

We have $\mathsf{BR} > \mathsf{B}c''$, so that $\mathsf{BR} > \mathsf{C}b'$.

From BR cut off $\mathsf{B}c' = \mathsf{C}b'$.

Draw $c'\mathsf{P}$ perpendicular to MN.

Then we have

$$\frac{\mathsf{B}b'}{\mathsf{MN}} < \frac{\mathsf{B}b'}{\mathsf{MP}} = \frac{\mathsf{C}c'}{\mathsf{MP}} < \phi(\mathsf{P}c') < \phi(\mathsf{CM} - \mathsf{PM} - \mathsf{C}c').$$

Thus $$\phi(\mathsf{CM} - \mathsf{PM} - \mathsf{C}c') > \frac{\mathsf{B}b'}{\mathsf{MN}} > \phi(\mathsf{N}c'').$$

Proceeding to the limit,

$$\phi(\mathsf{AC}) = \text{Lt}\left(\frac{\mathsf{B}b'}{\mathsf{MN}}\right). \qquad \text{(vi)}$$

From (iii)-(vi), it follows that $\phi(\mathsf{AB}) = \phi(\mathsf{BC})\phi(\mathsf{CA})$, or with the usual notation from § 86,

$$\cos\frac{\mathbf{c}}{\mathbf{k}} = \cos\frac{\mathbf{a}}{\mathbf{k}}\cos\frac{\mathbf{b}}{\mathbf{k}}.$$

NOTE. At several points in this argument we have assumed that the segments concerned are less than $\mathfrak{L}$.

Once the fundamental theorem has been proved for triangles in which this condition is satisfied, it can be extended by analysis to all other cases.

§ 88. The remaining formulae are easily obtained:

To prove $$\tan \frac{b}{k} = \cos A \tan \frac{c}{k}. \qquad (2)$$

Let ABC be any right-angled triangle, with C a right angle.

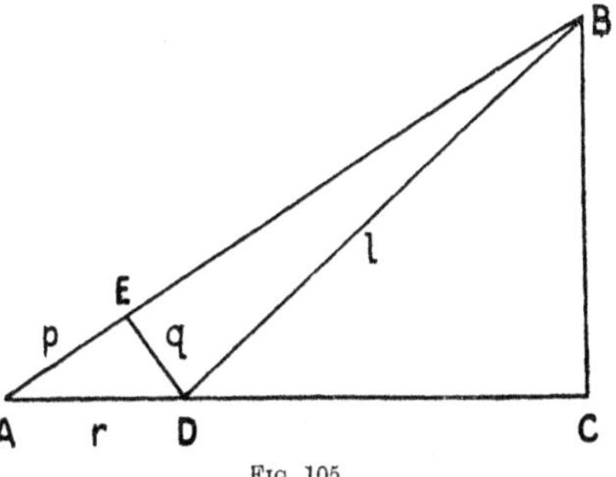

FIG. 105.

Take any point D on AC, and join BD.
Draw DE perpendicular to AB.
Let $AE = p$, $ED = q$, $AD = r$, and $BD = l$.
Then, from the triangle ABC, we have

$$\cos \frac{l}{k} = \cos \frac{a}{k} \cos \left(\frac{b-r}{k}\right)$$

$$= \cos \frac{a}{k} \cos \frac{b}{k} \cos \frac{r}{k} + \cos \frac{a}{k} \sin \frac{b}{k} \sin \frac{r}{k}$$

$$= \cos \frac{c}{k} \cos \frac{r}{k} + \cos \frac{a}{k} \sin \frac{b}{k} \sin \frac{r}{k}.$$

Also, from the triangle BDE, we have in the same way

$$\cos \frac{l}{k} = \cos \frac{c}{k} \cos \frac{r}{k} + \cos \frac{q}{k} \sin \frac{p}{k} \sin \frac{c}{k}.$$

Therefore $$\cos \frac{a}{k} \sin \frac{b}{k} \sin \frac{r}{k} = \cos \frac{q}{k} \sin \frac{p}{k} \sin \frac{c}{k}.$$

Using the equations $\cos\frac{c}{k} = \cos\frac{a}{k}\cos\frac{b}{k}$,

$$\cos\frac{r}{k} = \cos\frac{p}{k}\cos\frac{q}{k},$$

this gives

$$\frac{\tan\frac{b}{k}}{\tan\frac{c}{k}} = \frac{\tan\frac{p}{k}}{\tan\frac{r}{k}}.$$

This result holds however small r may be.

But we have seen that when $r \to 0$, $\frac{x}{r}$ has a definite limit other than zero, and that this limit is taken as the cosine of the angle. (§ 81.)

Therefore

$$\cos A = \operatorname*{Lt}_{r \to 0} \frac{\tan\frac{p}{k}}{\tan\frac{r}{k}}$$

$$= \frac{\tan\frac{b}{k}}{\tan\frac{c}{k}}.$$

§ 89. To prove that

$$\sin A = \frac{\sin\frac{a}{k}}{\sin\frac{c}{k}}. \qquad \ldots\ldots\ldots\ldots(3)$$

We have seen that as $r \to 0$, the ratio $\frac{y}{r}$ tends to a definite limit, other than zero, and that this limit is taken as the sine of the angle.

Now from the equation

$$\cos\frac{c}{k} = \cos\frac{a}{k}\cos\frac{b}{k},$$

we find that when a, b, and c are small,

$$c^2 = a^2 + b^2, \text{ to the lowest order.}$$

It follows that $\sin^2 A + \cos^2 A = 1$.

But, from § 88, we have

$$\cos A = \frac{\tan\frac{b}{k}}{\tan\frac{c}{k}}.$$

Therefore $$\sin^2 A = 1 - \frac{\tan^2\frac{b}{k}}{\tan^2\frac{c}{k}}$$

$$= \frac{\sin^2\frac{c}{k} - \tan^2\frac{b}{k}\cos^2\frac{c}{k}}{\sin^2\frac{c}{k}}$$

$$= \frac{1 - \sec^2\frac{b}{k}\cos^2\frac{c}{k}}{\sin^2\frac{c}{k}}$$

$$= \frac{1 - \cos^2\frac{a}{k}}{\sin^2\frac{c}{k}}$$

$$= \frac{\sin^2\frac{a}{k}}{\sin^2\frac{c}{k}}.$$

Therefore $$\sin A = \frac{\sin\frac{a}{k}}{\sin\frac{c}{k}}.$$

The remaining formulae,

$$\cos A = \cos\frac{a}{k}\sin B, \quad\text{(4)}$$

$$\sin\frac{b}{k} = \tan\frac{a}{k}\cot A, \quad\text{(5)}$$

$$\cos\frac{c}{k} = \cot A \cot B, \quad\text{(6)}$$

can be easily deduced from those already obtained.

The six equations (1)–(6) are the equations of ordinary Spherical Trigonometry, when $\frac{a}{k}$, $\frac{b}{k}$, and $\frac{c}{k}$ are substituted for a, b, c.

§ 90. The Trigonometry of the Oblique-Angled Triangle follows from that of the Right-Angled Triangle, the definitions of the sine and cosine being extended to obtuse angles. The formulae will be identical with those of ordinary Spherical Trigonometry, with the parameter k introduced.

The elements of arc and area can also be deduced as in Chapter V. In this case we shall have

$$ds^2 = \cos^2 \frac{y}{k} dx^2 + dy^2,$$

$$ds^2 = dr^2 + k^2 \sin^2 \frac{r}{k} d\theta^2,$$

$$d\mathsf{A} = \cos \frac{y}{k} dx\, dy,$$

$$d\mathsf{A} = k \sin \frac{r}{k} dr\, d\theta.$$

Also the Euclidean Formulae hold true in Infinitesimal Geometry on the Elliptic Plane.

CHAPTER VIII.

THE CONSISTENCY OF THE NON-EUCLIDEAN GEOMETRIES AND THE IMPOSSIBILITY OF PROVING THE PARALLEL POSTULATE.

§ 91. As we have already seen, the discovery of the Non-Euclidean Geometries arose from the attempts to prove Euclid's Parallel Postulate. Bolyai and Lobatschewsky did a double service to Geometry. They showed why these attempts had failed, and why they must always fail; for they succeeded in building up a geometry as logical and consistent as the Euclidean Geometry, upon the same foundations, except that for the Parallel Postulate of Euclid, another incompatible with it was substituted. They differed from almost all their predecessors in their belief that, proceeding on these lines, they would not meet any contradiction; and they held that the system of geometry built upon their Parallel Postulate was a fit subject of study for its own sake.

The question naturally arises: How can one be certain that these Non-Euclidean Geometries are logical and consistent systems? How can we be sure that continued study would not after all reveal some contradiction, some inconsistency? Saccheri thought he had found such in the Hyperbolic Geometry; but he was mistaken. Even Bolyai, many years after the publication of the *Appendix*, was for a time of the opinion that he had come upon a contradiction, and that the sought-for proof of the Euclidean Hypothesis was in his hands. He, too, was mistaken.

Of course, it is not sufficient simply to point to the fact that these geometries—developed into a large body of doctrine as they have been—do not offer in any of their propositions the contradiction which the earlier workers in those fields were convinced they must contain. We must be sure that, proceeding further on these lines, such contradiction could never be discovered. If we can prove this to be the case, then we know that Euclid's Parallel Postulate cannot be demonstrated.

§ **92.** There are several ways by which it is possible to establish the fact that the Hyperbolic and Elliptic Geometries are as logical and consistent as the Euclidean Geometry.*

Lobatschewsky, and to some extent Bolyai, relied upon the formulae of the Hyperbolic Plane Trigonometry. These are identical with the formulae of Spherical Trigonometry, if the radius of the sphere is imaginary. If the ordinary Spherical Trigonometry offers no contradiction, their geometry could not do so. However, this proof is not complete in itself, for it leaves aside the domain of Solid Geometry, and does not establish the impossibility of the difficulty appearing in that field. (Cf. Chapter II. §§ 15, 17.)

The most important of all the proofs of the consistency of the Non-Euclidean Geometries is that due to Cayley and Klein. In it one passes beyond the elementary regions within the confines of which this book is meant to remain. Other proofs are analytical. The assumptions of geometry are translated into the domain of number. Any inconsistency would then appear in the arithmetical form of the assumptions or in the deductions from them. This form of proof also seems to lie outside the province of this book.

Finally, there are a number of geometrical proofs, depending upon concrete interpretations of the Non-Euclidean Geometries in the Euclidean. The earliest of these—due to Beltrami, and dealing with the Hyperbolic Geometry—requires a knowledge of the Geometry of Surfaces. But an elementary representation of the Hyperbolic Plane and Space in the Euclidean was given by Poincaré.

" Let us consider," he says, " a certain plane, which I shall call the fundamental plane, and let us construct a kind of dictionary by making a double series of terms written in two columns, and corresponding each to each, just as in ordinary dictionaries the words in two languages which have the same signification correspond to one another :

Space. - - The portion of space situated above the fundamental plane.

---

* For a discussion on more advanced lines, cf. Sommerville's *Non-Euclidean Geometry*, ch. v. and vi. (London, 1914).

Plane. - -	Sphere cutting orthogonally the fundamental plane.
Line. - - -	Circle cutting orthogonally the fundamental plane.
Sphere. - -	Sphere.
Circle. - -	Circle.
Angle. - -	Angle.
Distance between two points.	The logarithm of the anharmonic ratio of these two points and of the intersections of the fundamental plane with the circle passing through these points and cutting it orthogonally.
Etc.	Etc.

"Let us take Lobatschewsky's theorems and translate them by the aid of this dictionary, as we would translate a German text with the aid of a German-French dictionary. *We shall then obtain the theorems of ordinary geometry.* For instance, Lobatschewsky's theorem: 'The sum of the angles of a triangle is less than two right angles' may be translated thus: 'If a curvilinear triangle has for its sides arcs of circles which cut orthogonally the fundamental plane, the sum of the angles of this curvilinear triangle will be less than two right angles.' Thus, however far the consequences of Lobatschewsky's hypotheses are carried, they will never lead to a contradiction; in fact, if two of Lobatschewsky's theorems were contradictory, the translation of these two theorems made by the aid of our dictionary would be contradictory also. But these translations are theorems of ordinary geometry, and no one doubts that ordinary geometry is exempt from contradiction." *

§ 93. To Poincaré is also due another representation of the Hyperbolic Geometry, which includes that given in the preceding section as a special case. We shall discuss this representation at some length, as also a corresponding one for the Elliptic Geometry, since from these we can obtain in a simple and elementary manner the proof of the impossibility of

* Poincaré, *La Science et l'Hypothèse.* English translation by Greenstreet, p. 41 *et seq.*

proving the Parallel Postulate and of the logical consistency both of the Hyperbolic and Elliptic Geometries. In this discussion the "dictionary method" of § 29 will be more fully explained.

We shall consider three families of circles in a plane—extending the argument to spheres later. These are the family of circles passing through a fixed point; the family of circles cutting a fixed circle orthogonally; and the family of circles cutting a fixed circle diametrally (*i.e.* the common chord of the fixed circle and any of the variable circles is to be a diameter of the fixed circle). Denoting the fixed point by O, and taking the fixed circle as a circle with centre O and radius k, the first family of circles has *power* zero with regard to O; the second, *power* k^2; and the third, *power* $-k^2$. We shall see that the geometries of these three families of circles agree with the Euclidean, Hyperbolic, and Elliptic Geometries, respectively.

§ 94. The System of Circles through a Fixed Point.

If we invert from a point O the lines lying in a plane through O we obtain a set of circles passing through that point. To every circle there corresponds a straight line, and to every straight line a circle. The circles intersect at the same angles as the corresponding lines. The properties of the family of circles could be deduced from the properties of the set of lines, and every proposition concerning points and lines in the one system could be interpreted as a proposition concerning points and circles in the other.

There is another method of dealing with the geometry of this family of circles. We shall describe it briefly, as it will make the argument in the case of the other families, which represent the Non-Euclidean Geometries, easier.

If two points A and B are given, these, with the point O, fully determine a circle passing through the point O. We shall call these circles *nominal lines*.* We shall refer to the points in the plane of the circles as *nominal points*, the point O being supposed excluded from the domain of the *nominal*

* In another place, cf. Bonola, *loc. cit.*, English translation, Appendix V., and *Proc. Edin. Math. Soc.*, Vol. 28, p. 95 (1910), I have used the terms *ideal points, ideal lines*, etc. For these I now substitute *nominal points, nominal lines*, etc., owing to possible confusion with the *ideal* points, *ideal* lines, etc., of §§ 37, 38.

points. We define the angle between two *nominal lines* as the angle between the circles with which the *nominal lines* coincide at their common point.

With these definitions, two different *nominal points* A, B in this Nominal Geometry always determine a *nominal line* AB, just as two different ordinary points always determine a straight line AB.

The *nominal points* and *lines* also satisfy the "axioms of order,"* which express the idea of between-ness, when the point O is excluded from the domain of the nominal points. If this point were not excluded, we could not say that of any three nominal points on a nominal line, there is always one, and only one, which lies between the other two.

Proceeding to the question of parallels, we define *parallel nominal lines* as follows:

The nominal line through a nominal point parallel to a given nominal line is the circle of the system which passes through the given point and touches at O *the circle coinciding with the given nominal line.*

Referring to Fig. 106 we see that in the pencil of nominal lines through A there is one nominal line which does not cut BC, namely, the circle of the system which touches OBC at O.

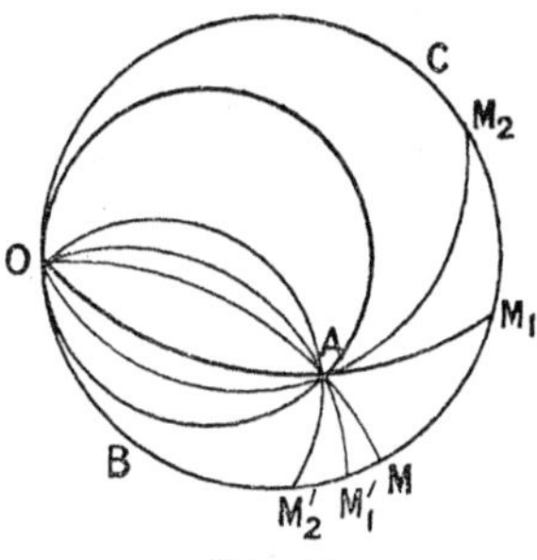

Fig. 106.

This nominal line does not cut the nominal line BC, for the point O is excluded from the domain of the nominal points. It is at right angles to AM, the nominal line through A perpendicular to the nominal line BC. Every nominal line through

* Cf. Hilbert, *loc. cit.* § 3.

A making with AM an angle less than a right angle will cut BC on the side of OAM in which the acute angle lies.

Therefore in the geometry of these nominal points and lines the Euclidean Parallel Postulate holds.

§ 95. Before we can deal with the metrical properties of this geometry, we require a measure of length. *We define the nominal length of a nominal segment as the length of the rectilinear segment to which it corresponds.*

From this definition it is not difficult to show that *the nominal length of a nominal segment is unaltered by inversion with regard to a circle of the system; and that inversion with regard to such a circle is equivalent to reflection of the nominal points and lines in the nominal line which coincides with the circle of inversion.*

Now, if we invert successively with regard to two circles of the system (*i.e.* if we reflect in two nominal lines one after the other), we obtain what corresponds to a displacement in two dimensions. A nominal triangle ABC takes up the position A′B′C′ after the first reflection; and from A′B′C′ it passes to the position A″B″C″ in the second. The sides and angles of A″B″C″ (in our nominal measurement) are the same as the sides and angles of the nominal triangle ABC, and the point C″ lies on the same side of A″B″ as the point C does of AB.

Further, we can always fix upon two inversions which will change a given nominal segment AB into a new position such that A comes to A′, and AB lies along a given nominal line through A′. We need only invert first with regard to the circle which "bisects" the nominal line AA′ at right angles. This brings AB into a position A′B″, say. Then, if we invert with regard to the circle of the system which bisects the angle between A′B″ and the given nominal line through A′, the segment AB is brought into the required position.

The method of superposition is thus available in the geometry of the nominal points and lines. Euclid's argument can be "translated" directly into the new geometry. We have only to use the words nominal points, nominal lines, nominal parallels, etc., instead of the ordinary points, lines, parallels, etc., and we obtain from the ordinary geometry the corresponding propositions in the geometry of this family of circles.

It should perhaps be pointed out that the nominal circle with centre A is an ordinary circle. For the orthogonal trajectories of the circles of the system through A (*i.e.* of the nominal lines through A) is the family of coaxal circles with O and A as Limiting Points. The nominal lengths of the nominal segments from A to the points where one of these circles cuts the pencil of lines will be the same.

§ 96. The argument sketched in the preceding sections can be extended to Solid Geometry. Instead of the system of circles lying in one plane and all passing through the point O, we have now to deal with the system of spheres all passing through the point O.

The *nominal point* is the same as the ordinary point, but the point O is excluded from the domain of the nominal points.

The nominal line through two nominal points is the circle passing through O *and these two points.*

The nominal plane through three nominal points is the sphere passing through O *and these three points.*

The nominal line through a point A *parallel to a nominal line* BC *is the circle through* A *which lies on the sphere through* O, A, B *and* C, *and touches the circle* OBC *at the point* O.

It is clear that a nominal line is determined by two different nominal points, just as a straight line is determined by two different ordinary points. The nominal plane is determined by three different nominal points, not on a nominal line, just as an ordinary plane is determined by three different ordinary points not on a straight line. If two points of a nominal line lie on a nominal plane, then all the points of that line lie on that plane. The intersection of two nominal planes is a nominal line, etc.

The measurement of angles in the new geometry is the same as that in the ordinary geometry; the angle between two nominal lines is defined as the angle between the circles with which these lines coincide at their intersection. The measurement of length is as before. Inversion in a sphere through O is equivalent to reflection in the nominal plane coinciding with that sphere. Displacements, being point-transformations according to which every point of the domain is transformed into a point of the domain, in such a way that nominal lines remain nominal lines, and nominal lengths and angles are unaltered, will be given by an even number of inversions in the spheres of the system.

Thus, the geometry of these nominal points, lines, and planes is identical with the ordinary Euclidean Geometry. Its elements satisfy the same laws; every proposition valid in the one is also valid in the other; and from the theorems of the Euclidean Geometry those of the Nominal Geometry can be inferred, and *vice versa*.

The plane geometry of the nominal points and lines described in the preceding sections is a special case of the more general plane geometry based upon the definitions of this section.

§ 97. The System of Circles orthogonal to a Fixed Circle.

We proceed to discuss the geometry of the system of circles orthogonal to a fixed circle, centre O and radius k. We shall call this circle the fundamental circle. Then the system of circles has *power* k^2 with respect to O.

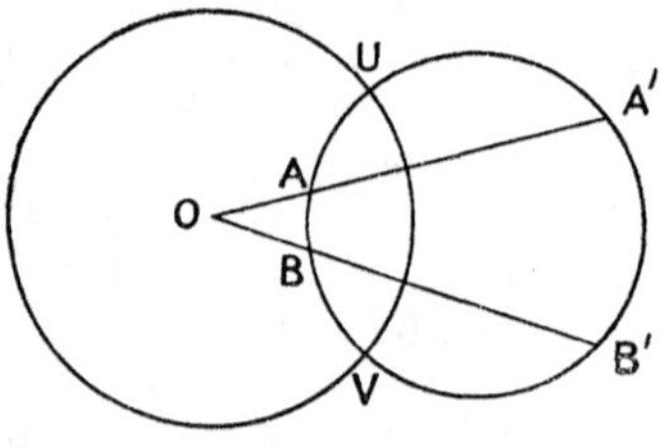

FIG. 107.

Let A and B be any two points within the fundamental circle and A′, B′ the inverse points with respect to that circle. Then A, A′, B, B′ are concyclic, and the circle which passes through them cuts the fundamental circle orthogonally. There is one and only one circle orthogonal to the fundamental circle which passes through two different points within that circle.

In discussing the properties of the family of circles orthogonal to the fundamental circle, we shall call the points *within* that circle *nominal points*. The points on the circumference of the fundamental circle are excluded from the domain of the *nominal points*.*

* In this discussion the *nominal points*, etc., are defined somewhat differently from the *ideal points*, etc., in the paper referred to on p. 156.

We define the nominal line through any two nominal points as the circle which passes through these two points and cuts the fundamental circle orthogonally.

Two different nominal points A, B always determine a nominal line AB, just as two different ordinary points A, B always determine a straight line AB. The nominal points and lines also obey the "axioms of order."

We define the angle between two intersecting nominal lines as the angle between the tangents at the common point, within the fundamental circle, of the circles with which the nominal lines coincide.

We have now to consider in what way it will be proper to define *parallel nominal lines.*

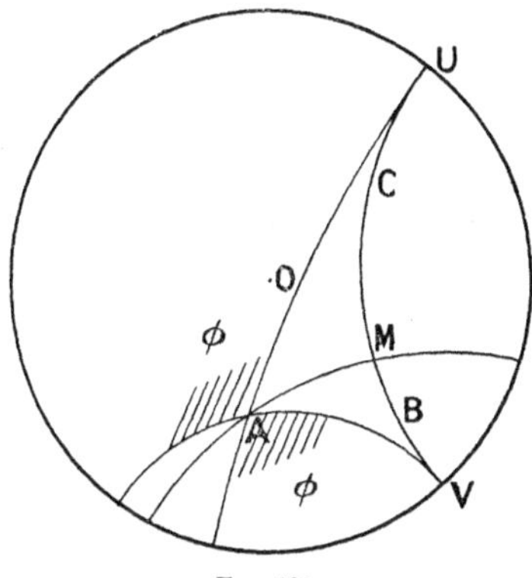

FIG. 108.

Let AM (Fig. 108) be the *nominal line* through A perpendicular to the *nominal line* BC ; in other words, the circle of the system which passes through A and cuts the circle of the system through BC orthogonally. Imagine AM to rotate about A so that these nominal lines through A cut the nominal line through BC at a gradually smaller angle. The circles through A which touch the circle through BC at the points U and V, where it meets the fundamental circle, are nominal lines. They separate the lines of the pencil of nominal lines through A, which cut BC from those which do not cut it. All the lines in the angle ϕ shaded in the figure do not cut the line BC ; all those in the angle ψ, unshaded, do cut this nominal line.

This property is what is assumed in the Parallel Postulate on which the Hyperbolic Geometry is based. We are therefore led to define parallel nominal lines in the plane geometry we are investigating as follows:

The nominal lines through a nominal point parallel to a nominal line are the two circles of the system passing through the given point which touch the circle with which the given nominal line coincides at the points where it cuts the fundamental circle.

Thus we have in this geometry two parallels—a right-handed parallel and a left-handed parallel—and these separate the lines of the pencil which intersect the given line from those which do not intersect it.

§ 98. At this stage we can say that any of the theorems of the Hyperbolic Geometry which involve only angle properties will hold in the geometry of the circles, and *vice versa*. Those involving metrical properties of lines we cannot discuss until the *nominal length* of a *nominal segment* has been defined.

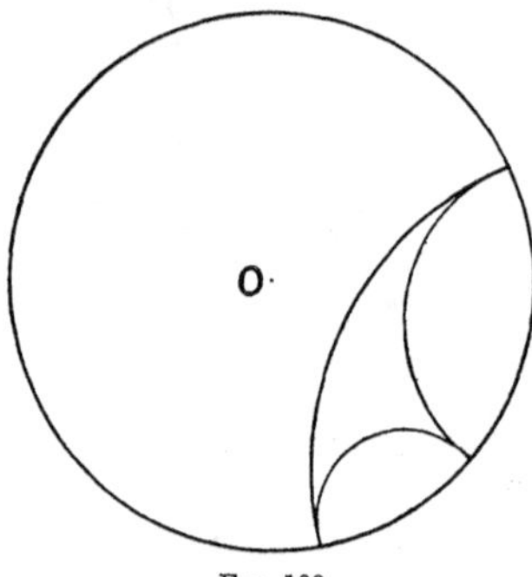

FIG. 109.

For example, it is obvious that *there are nominal triangles whose angles are all zero* (Fig. 109). The sides of these triangles are parallel in pairs, and we regard parallel lines as containing an angle zero.

Further, *we can prove that the sum of the angles in any nominal triangle is less than two right angles*, by inversion, as follows:

Let C_1, C_2, C_3, be three circles of the system—*i.e.* three nominal lines forming a nominal triangle, say PQR. We suppose these circles completed, and we deal with the whole circumference of each. Invert the circles from the point of intersection R′ of C_1 and C_2, which lies outside the fundamental circle. Then the nominal lines C_1 and C_2 become two straight lines C_1' and C_2', through the inverse of R. Also the fundamental circle C inverts into a circle C′, cutting C_1' and C_2' at right angles, so that its centre is at the point of intersection of these two lines. Again the circle C_3 inverts into a circle C_3', cutting C′ orthogonally. Hence its centre lies outside C′.

We thus obtain a curvilinear triangle in which the sum of the angles is less than two right angles; and since the angles in this triangle are equal to those in the nominal triangle, our result is proved.

Finally, *it can be shown that there is always one and only one circle of the system which will cut two not-intersecting circles of the system orthogonally.* In other words, *two not-intersecting nominal lines have a common perpendicular.*

All these results we have established in the Hyperbolic Geometry. They could be accepted in the geometry of the circles for that reason.

§ **99.** As to the measurement of length, we define the *nominal length* of a *nominal segment* as follows:

The nominal length of any nominal segment AB *is equal to*

$$\log\left(\frac{AV}{AU}\Big/\frac{BV}{BU}\right),$$

where U *and* V *are the points where the circle which coincides with the nominal line* AB *cuts the fundamental circle.* (Cf. Fig. 107.)

With this definition the nominal length of AB is the same as that of BA. Also the nominal length of the complete line is infinite. If C is any point on the nominal segment AB between A and B, the nominal length of AB is the same as the sum of the nominal lengths of AC and CB.

Let us consider what effect inversion with regard to a circle of the system has upon the nominal points and lines.

Let A be a nominal point and A′ the inverse of this point in the fundamental circle.

Let the circle of inversion meet the fundamental circle in C, and let its centre be D (Fig. 110).

Suppose A and A′ invert into B and B′.

Since the circle AA′C touches the circle of inversion at C, its inverse also touches that circle at C. But the points A, A′, B, B′ are concyclic, and the radical axes of the three circles AA′C, BB′C and AA′B′B are concurrent.

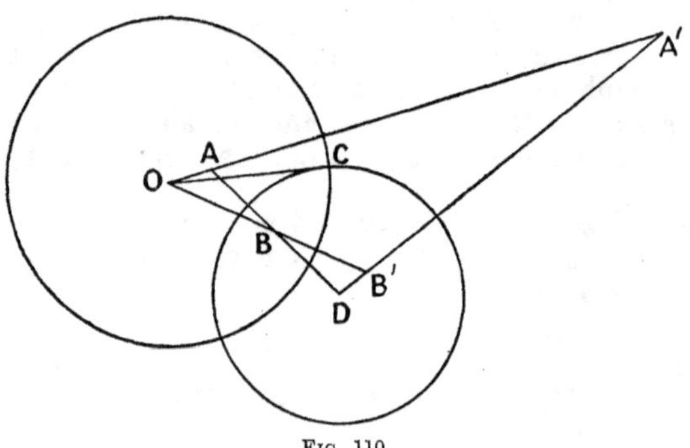

FIG. 110.

Therefore BB′ passes through O and $OB \cdot OB' = OC^2$. Thus the circle AA′B′B is orthogonal to the fundamental circle and also to the circle of inversion.

It follows that *if any nominal point* A *is changed by inversion with regard to a circle of the system into the point* B, *the nominal line* AB *is perpendicular to the nominal line with which the circle of inversion coincides.*

We shall now prove that it is " bisected " by that nominal line. Let the circle through A, A′, B and B′ meet the circle of inversion at M and the fundamental circle at U and V (Fig. 111). It is clear that U and V are inverse points with regard to the circle of inversion.

Then we have $\dfrac{BV}{AU} = \dfrac{CV}{CA}, \quad \dfrac{AV}{BU} = \dfrac{CV}{CB}.$

$$\therefore \frac{AV}{AU} \cdot \frac{BV}{BU} = \frac{CV^2}{CA \cdot CB} = \frac{CV^2}{CM^2} = \left(\frac{MV}{MU}\right)^2.$$

$$\therefore \frac{AV}{AU} \bigg/ \frac{MV}{MU} = \frac{MV}{MU} \bigg/ \frac{BV}{BU}.$$

Thus the nominal length of AM is equal to the nominal length of BM,

Therefore we have the following result:

Inversion with regard to any circle of the system changes any point A *into a point* B, *such that the nominal line* AB *is perpendicular to and "bisected" by the nominal line with which the circle of inversion coincides.*

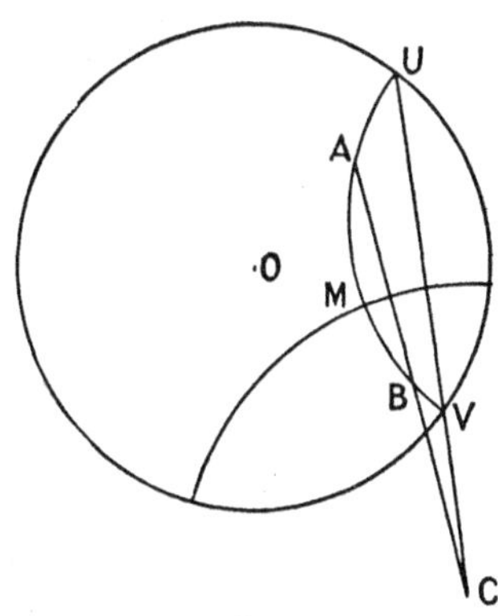

Fig. 111.

In other words,

Any nominal point takes up the position of its image in the nominal line coinciding with the circle of inversion.

We shall now examine what effect such an inversion has upon a nominal line.

Since a circle orthogonal to the fundamental circle inverts into a circle also orthogonal to the fundamental circle, any nominal line AB inverts into a nominal line *ab*, and the points U and V for AB invert into the points *u* and *v* for *ab* (Fig. 112).

When the circle of inversion and the nominal line AB intersect, the lines AB and *ab* meet on the circle of inversion. Denoting this point by M, it is easy to show that the nominal lengths of AM and BM are respectively equal to the nominal lengths of *a*M and *b*M. It follows that the nominal length of the segment AB is unaltered by inversion with regard to any circle of the system.

The same result can be obtained immediately from the corresponding figure when the nominal line AB does not cut the circle of inversion.

The preceding results may be summed up as follows :

Inversion with regard to any circle of the system has the same effect upon the nominal points and lines as reflection in the nominal line with which the circle of inversion coincides.

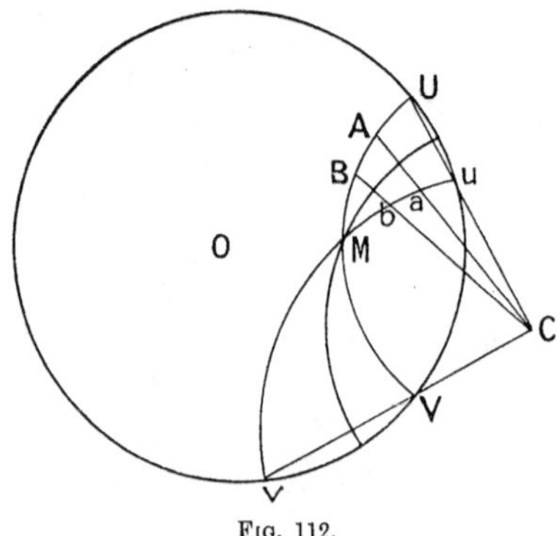

FIG. 112.

The argument of § 95 can now be applied to the geometry of this family of circles. Successive inversion with regard to two circles of the system corresponds to a displacement in two dimensions. We can always fix upon two circles of the system which will change a nominal segment AB into a new position, such that A coincides with P and AB lies along a given nominal line through P. The method of superposition is thus available in this geometry, and any theorems in the Hyperbolic Geometry involving congruence of linear segments can be at once "translated" into it.

§ 100. We notice that the definition of the nominal length of a segment fixes the *nominal unit of length.* We may take this unit segment on one of the diameters of the fundamental circle, since these lines are also nominal lines of the system. Let it be the segment OP (Fig. 113).

Then we must have

$$\log\left(\frac{OV}{OU}\Big/\frac{PV}{PU}\right)=1;$$

that is, $\log\left(\frac{PU}{PV}\right)=1$; that is, $\frac{PU}{PV}=e.$

Thus the point P divides the diameter in the ratio $e:1$.

The unit segment is thus fixed for any position in the domain of the nominal points, since the segment OP can be " moved "

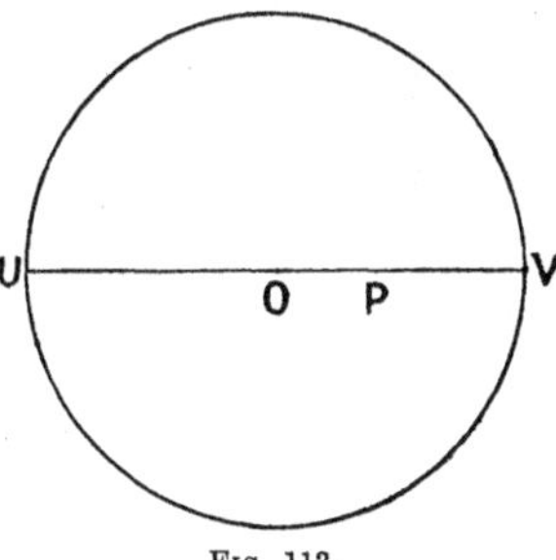

FIG. 113.

so that one of its ends coincides with any given nominal point.

A different expression for the nominal length, viz.,

$$k \log \left(\frac{AV}{AU} \Big/ \frac{BV}{BU}\right),$$

would simply mean an alteration in this unit, and taking logarithms to the base a instead of e would have the same effect.

§ 101. We are now able to establish some further theorems of Hyperbolic Geòmetry, using the metrical properties of this Nominal Geometry.

In the first place we can say that *Similar Triangles are impossible.* For if there were two nominal triangles with the same angles and not congruent, we could " move " the second so that its vertex would coincide with the corresponding angular point of the first, and its sides would lie along the same nominal lines as the sides of the first. We would thus obtain a "quadrilateral" whose angles would be together equal to four right angles; and this is impossible, since we have seen that the sum of the angles in these nominal triangles is always less than two right angles.

We also see that parallel lines are asymptotic; that is, they continually approach each other. This follows from the figure for nominal parallels and the definition of nominal length.

Further, it is obvious that as the point A moves away along the perpendicular MA to the line BC (Fig. 108), the angle of parallelism diminishes from $\frac{\pi}{2}$ to zero in the limit.

We shall now prove that the angle of parallelism, $\Pi(p)$, for the segment p, is given by

$$e^{-p} = \tan\left(\frac{\Pi(p)}{2}\right).$$

Consider a nominal line and a parallel to it through a point A.

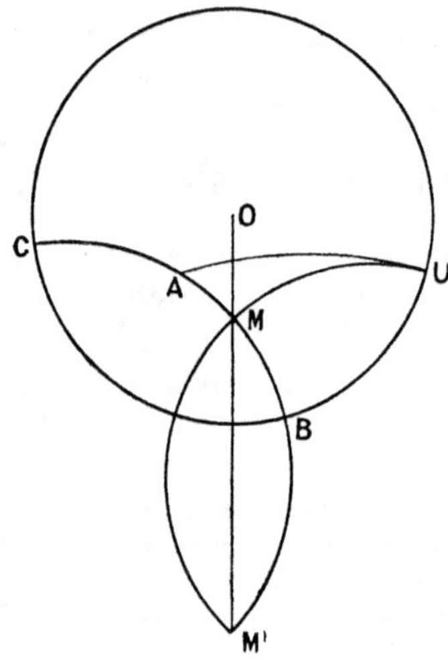

FIG. 114.

Let AM (Fig. 114) be the perpendicular to the given line MU and AU the parallel.

Let the figure be inverted from the point M′, the radius of inversion being the tangent from M′ to the fundamental circle.

Then we obtain a new figure (Fig. 115) in which the corresponding nominal lengths are the same, since the circle of inversion is a circle of the system. The lines AM and MU become straight lines through the centre of the fundamental circle, which is the inverse of the point M. Also, the circle AU becomes the circle au, touching the radius mu at u, and cutting ma at an angle $\Pi(p)$. These radii mu, mb are also nominal lines of the system.

Let the nominal length of AM be p.

Then we have
$$p = \log\left(\frac{\mathrm{AB}}{\mathrm{AC}} \Big/ \frac{\mathrm{MB}}{\mathrm{MC}}\right)$$
$$= \log\left(\frac{ab}{ac} \Big/ \frac{mb}{mc}\right) = \log\left(\frac{ab}{ac}\right).$$

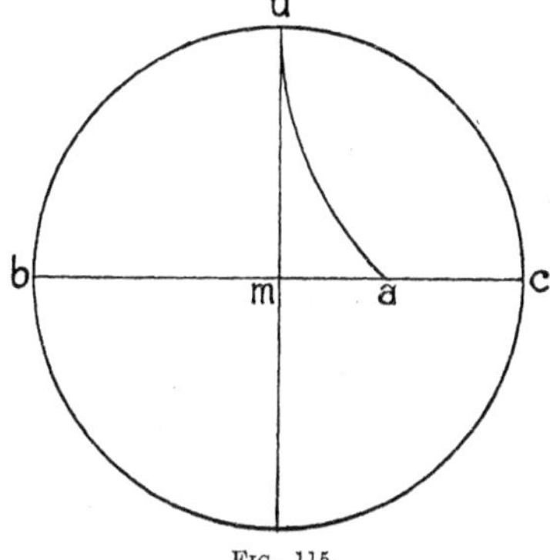

Fig. 115.

But from the geometry of Fig. 115, remembering that au cuts bc at the angle $\Pi(p)$, we have
$$ac = k\left\{1 - \tan\left(\frac{\pi}{4} - \frac{\Pi(p)}{2}\right)\right\},$$
$$ab = k\left\{1 + \tan\left(\frac{\pi}{4} - \frac{\Pi(p)}{2}\right)\right\},$$
where k is the radius of the fundamental circle.

Therefore
$$p = \log\cot\left(\frac{\Pi(p)}{2}\right)$$
and
$$e^{-p} = \tan\left(\frac{\Pi(p)}{2}\right).$$

Finally, in this geometry there will be three kinds of circles. There will be (i) the circle with its centre at a finite distance ;

(ii) the limiting-curve, with its centre at infinity, or at a point where two parallels meet; and (iii) the equidistant-curve, with its centre at the ideal * point of intersection of two lines which have a common perpendicular.

All these curves are ordinary circles, but they do not belong to the system of circles orthogonal to the fundamental circle.

As to the first, the nominal lines through a point A are all cut orthogonally by the circles of the coaxal system with A and its inverse point A′ as Limiting Points. Thus these circles are the circles of this nominal geometry with A as their centre. They would be traced out by the end of a nominal segment through A, when it is reflected in the nominal lines of the pencil.

As to the second, the circles which touch the fundamental circle at a point U cut all the circles of the system which pass through U orthogonally. They are orthogonal to the pencil of parallel nominal lines meeting at infinity in U.

Thus these circles are the circles of this nominal geometry with their centre at the point at infinity common to a pencil of parallel nominal lines. They would be obtained when the reflection takes place in the lines of this pencil.

As to the third, all circles through U, V cut all the nominal lines perpendicular to the line AB (cf. Fig. 111) orthogonally. Thus these circles are the circles of the nominal geometry with their centre at the *ideal* point common to this pencil of not-intersecting nominal lines. They would be obtained when the reflection takes place in the lines of this pencil.

These three circles correspond to the ordinary circle, the Limiting-Curve and the Equidistant-Curve of the Hyperbolic Geometry.

§ 102. The Impossibility of proving Euclid's Parallel Postulate.

We can now assert that it is impossible for any inconsistency to exist in this Hyperbolic Geometry. If such a contradiction entered into this plane geometry, it would also occur in the interpretation of the result in the nominal geometry. Thus a contradiction would also be found in the Euclidean Geometry. We can therefore state that it is impossible that any logical

* Cf. § 37.

inconsistency could arise in the Hyperbolic Plane Geometry, provided no logical inconsistency can arise in the Euclidean Plane Geometry. It could still be argued that such a contradiction might be found in the Hyperbolic Solid Geometry. An answer to such an objection is forthcoming at once. The geometry of the system of circles, all orthogonal to a fixed circle, can be readily extended into a three-dimensional system. The *nominal points* are the points inside a fixed sphere, excluding the points on the surface of the sphere from their domain. The *nominal lines* are the circles through two nominal points cutting the fixed sphere orthogonally. The *nominal planes* are the spheres through three nominal points cutting the fixed sphere orthogonally. The ordinary plane enters as a particular case of these nominal planes, and so the plane geometry just discussed is a special case of a plane geometry of this system. With suitable definitions of nominal lengths, nominal parallels, etc., we have a solid geometry exactly analogous to the Hyperbolic Solid Geometry. It follows that no logical inconsistency could arise in the Hyperbolic Solid Geometry, since, if such did occur, it would also be found in the interpretation of the result in this Nominal Geometry, and therefore it would enter into the Euclidean Geometry.

By this result our argument is complete. However far the Hyperbolic Geometry is developed, no contradictory results could be obtained. This system is thus logically possible, and the axioms upon which it is founded are not contradictory. Hence it is impossible to prove Euclid's Parallel Postulate, since its proof would involve the denial of the Parallel Postulate of Bolyai and Lobatschewsky.

§ 103. The System of Circles cutting a Fixed Circle diametrally.

We shall now discuss the geometry of the system of circles cutting a fixed circle centre, O and radius k, diametrally. The points in which any circle of the system cuts the fixed circle are to be at the extremities of some diameter. We shall call the fixed circle, as before, the fundamental circle. The system of circles with which we are to deal has power $-k^2$ with respect to O.

Let A and B be any two points within the fundamental circle, and A′, B′ the points on OA and OB, such that $OA . OA' = -k^2$ and $OB . OB' = -k^2$.

Then A, A′, B, B′ are concyclic, and the circle which passes through them cuts the fundamental circle diametrally (Fig. 116). There is one, and only one, circle cutting the fundamental circle diametrally, which passes through two different points within the fundamental circle.

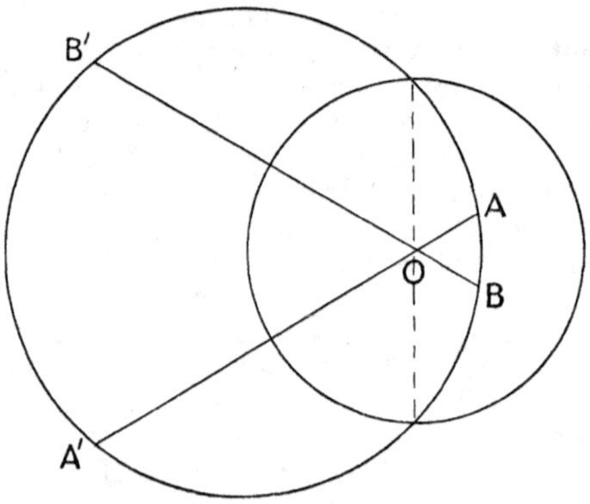

Fig. 116.

In discussing the properties of the family of circles cutting the fundamental circle diametrally, two methods can be followed. We can restrict the *nominal points* of the geometry to the points within and upon the fundamental circle. In this case we regard the points on the circumference at the extremities of a diameter as one and the same nominal point. In the other case, we extend the field of nominal points outside the circle to infinity, and the points on the circumference do not require special treatment.

These two alternatives, we shall see below, correspond to the two forms of the Elliptic Geometry, in one of which every straight line intersects every other straight line in one point, while in the other form, straight lines have always two points of intersection. *The nominal lines are the circles which cut the fundamental circle diametrally.*

When the field of nominal points is restricted to points within or upon the fundamental circle, *any two different nominal points* A, B *determine a nominal line* AB. Also *any two nominal lines must intersect at a single nominal point.*

When the domain of the nominal points is both within and without the fundamental circle, two nominal points do not always determine uniquely a nominal line. If the points A and B are upon the circumference of the circle at opposite ends of a diameter, a pencil of nominal lines passes through A and B. Again, if the points A and B lie on a line through O and OA . OB $= -k^2$, the same remark holds true.

Further, with the same choice of nominal points, every nominal line intersects every other nominal line in two nominal points.

The simplest way of discussing the properties of the system of circles with which we are dealing, is to make use of the fact that they can be obtained by projecting the great circles of a sphere stereographically from a point on the surface of the sphere on the tangent plane at the point diametrally opposite. If the centre of projection is a pole of the sphere, the equator projects into the fundamental circle, and one hemisphere projects into points outside this circle, the other into points within it. This projection is a conformal one, and the angle at which two great circles intersect is the same as the angle at which the corresponding circles in the plane cut each other.

We define the angle between two nominal lines as the angle between the circles with which they coincide.

We are now able to prove some of the theorems of this Nominal Geometry.

Since all the great circles perpendicular to a given great circle intersect at the poles of that circle, it follows that *all the nominal lines perpendicular to a given nominal line intersect at one point, in the case when the nominal points are within or upon the circumference of the fundamental circle; in two points, when this field is both within and without.* (Cf. §§ 75-77.)

The point of intersection is spoken of as *a pole*, or *the pole*, of the line.

Again, in a right-angled spherical triangle ABC, in which C is the right angle, the angle at A $\gtreqless$ a right angle, according as the pole of AC lies on CB produced, or coincides with B, or lies between C and B.

When translated into the language of the nominal geometry, we have the theorem which corresponds to § 78 (1).

Further, the sum of the angles of a spherical triangle is greater than two right angles. It follows, since the projection is conformal, that *the sum of the angles of a nominal triangle in this geometry is greater than two right angles.* (Cf. § 78 (3).)

However, the metrical properties of this geometry cannot be treated so easily as were the corresponding properties in the geometry of the system of circles cutting the fundamental circle orthogonally. The same argument to a certain extent applies, but in the definition of nominal lengths the intersections with an imaginary circle have to be taken. It should be added that in the extension to solid geometry the system of spheres cutting a fixed sphere diametrally has to be employed.

The fuller discussion of this nominal geometry will not be undertaken here. If it is desired to establish the fact that no contradiction could appear in the Elliptic Geometry, however far that geometry were developed, there are simpler methods available than this one. The case of the Hyperbolic Geometry was discussed in detail, because it offered so elementary a demonstration of the impossibility of proving the Parallel Postulate of Euclid.

§ 104. We have already quoted some remarks of Bolyai's on the question of whether the Euclidean or the Non-Euclidean Geometry is the true geometry.* We shall conclude this presentation of our subject with two quotations from modern geometers on the same topic:

"What then," says Poincaré, "are we to think of the question: Is Euclidean Geometry true? It has no meaning. We might as well ask if the metric system is true, and if the old weights and measures are false; if Cartesian coordinates are true and polar coordinates false. One geometry cannot be more true than another; it can only be more convenient. Now, Euclidean Geometry is, and will remain, the most convenient: first, because it is the simplest, and it is so not only because of our mental habits or because of the kind of intuition that we have of Euclidean space; it is the simplest in itself, just as a polynomial of the first degree is simpler than a polynomial of the second degree; secondly, because it sufficiently agrees with the properties of natural solids, those bodies which we compare and measure by means of our senses.†

---

* Cf. § 15.

† Poincaré, *La Science et l'Hypothèse.* English translation, p. 50.

And another French geometer writes:

"We are then entitled to say that the geometry which most closely resembles reality is the Euclidean Geometry, or at least one which differs very little from it; . . . the error is too small to be apparent in the domain of our observations and with the aid of the instruments at our disposal.

"In a word, not only have we theoretically to adopt the Euclidean Geometry, but in addition this geometry is physically true."*

The matter can be put in another way. The question whether the Euclidean Geometry is the true geometry has no place in Geometry—the Pure Science. It has a place in Geometry—the Applied Science. The answer to the question—if an answer can be given—lies with the experimenter. But his reply is inconclusive. All that he can tell us is that the sum of the angles of any triangle that he has observed—however great the triangle may have been—is equal to two right angles, subject to the possible errors of observation. To say that it is exactly two right angles is beyond his power.

One interesting point must be mentioned in conclusion. In the Theory of Relativity, it is the Non-Euclidean Geometry of Bolyai and Lobatschewsky which, in some ways at least, is the more convenient. Gauss's jesting remark that he would be rather glad if the Euclidean Geometry were not the true geometry, because then we would have an absolute measure of length, finds an echo in the writings of those who in these last years have developed this new theory.†

---

* Hadamard, *Leçons de Géométrie élementaire*, vol. i. p. 286 (Paris, 1898).

† Cf. the letter to Taurinus, quoted on p. 24. Also the letter to Gerling given in Gauss, *Werke*, vol. viii. p. 169.

A similar remark is to be found in Lambert's *Theorie der Parallel-Linien*, § 80; see Engel u. Stäckel, *loc. cit.* p. 200.

INDEX OF NAMES OF AUTHORS.

Numbers refer to pages.

SUBJECT INDEX.

Numbers refer to pages.

PRINTED BY ROBERT MACLEHOSE AND CO. LTD. AT THE UNIVERSITY PRESS, GLASGOW, GREAT BRITAIN.

www.ingramcontent.com/pod-product-compliance
Lightning Source LLC
LaVergne TN
LVHW010604110826
845149LV00003B/771

* 9 7 8 1 4 1 8 1 8 0 3 6 2 *